Cybercitizen

Cybercitizen

How to Use Your Computer to
Fight for ALL the Issues You Care About

Christopher Kush

St. Martin's Griffin ☙ New York

This book is dedicated to the many advocates I have trained over the years.

My work as a training consultant has put me at the forefront of some critical legislative battles, including the fights against heart disease, lung cancer, HIV, stroke, and workplace injuries. Enabling real people to put a face on their issues and directly educate our lawmakers about their lives, their challenges, and their experiences is more than an effective way to lobby government; it is an appropriate way to make public policy.

I, too, have been informed, and moved, and, I believe, improved by the stories of those who have had the courage, hope, and dignity to stand before our government to enlighten our representatives and, yes, to demand action. This is a rarely noted benefit of American Democracy—we not only have the opportunity to raise our voices, we also have the opportunity to listen, to learn, to have our compassion increased, and our perspective broadened by one another.

I hope this book will encourage those I have trained to continue their fight in ever new and creative ways and serve as a testament to the positive effect enlightened citizens can have on our government.

Contents

Acknowledgments ix

Prologue: American Democracy—the Relaunch 1

1 ★ Preambles and Declarations 10

2 ★ Campaigns and Elections 20

3 ★ The White House and Administration 57

4 ★ Congress 74

5 ★ The Supreme Court of the United States 102

6 ★ The News Media 110

7 ★ State and Local Government 130

8 ★ Issues, Associations, Groups, and Coalitions 168

9 ★ Your Own Private Idaho 237

Appendix: Internet Basics 250

Glossary 256

Index 263

Acknowledgments

I would like to thank the dozens of lawmakers, web masters, lobbyists, journalists, activists, campaign managers, and other experts who furnished me with information, insights, interviews, and editorial comments while I was writing this book. I am especially indebted to the time and talents of the following individuals:

Herbert Becker

Bob Biersack

Joan Blades

Alex Bloomingdale

Penelope Bonsall

Hon. Rick Boucher

Jean Michel Brevelle

Juan Cabanela

Greg Cohen

David Collins

Susan Cooper

Hon. Tom Davis

Hon. Vernon Ehlers

Zeki Erim

Zach Exley

Doug Feaver

Hon. Robert Goodlatte

Michael Grable

Marcy VL Hargan

Phil Kavits

Jim Key

Mark Kitchens

Peter Larson

Kevin Layton

Chris Long

Larry Makinson

Comm. David Mason

Howell Medley

Ian Mishalove

Nicco Mele

John Middletown

Ilona Nickels

Beth Parker

Larry Purpuro

Deron Robinson	Roger Alan Stone
Rose Ann Sharp	Bill Thorne
Linda Sinoway	Ryan Turner

A sincere thanks to those who helped me to initially propose and sell this book: Anya Richards and Barbara Feinman-Todd.

Thanks to my tenacious agent: Deborah Grosvenor.

Thanks for the thorough and insightful work by my editor at St. Martin's: Julia Pastore.

For support and encouragement: Kevin Schultze.

And a very special thanks to the friend and colleague who helped me to complete the book: Angela Taylor.

Cybercitizen

Prologue

American Democracy— the Relaunch

★

In Washington, D.C., along the stretch of Pennsylvania
Avenue that connects the White House with Capitol Hill, sits one of a number of immense white marble buildings—the National Archives and
Records Administration (NARA) of the United States of America. Seventy-
two Corinthian columns weighing ninety-five tons apiece provide a
moment of vertigo to those who trudge up the pebble-smooth steps on the
Constitution Avenue side of the building to pass between two forty-foot
bronze doors that, together with the columns, humble all who enter.
Inside this building, the Declaration of Independence, the Constitution of
the United States of America, and the beloved initial amendments to the
Constitution known as the Bill of Rights are kept. No, not kept—guarded
and protected like the priceless treasures they are.

Architect John Russell Pope designed the Archives to convey the
majesty of the documents housed within it, but at the top of the stairs, one
is struck as much by the technology used to guard the so-called "charters
of freedom" as the ancient metaphors in the architecture used to honor
them. Visitors must pass through metal detectors, X-ray machines, and
strategically placed video cameras. Glass encasements, filled with an inert
gas and emitting a greenish light, protect the documents from the forces of
nature, and security guards armed with handguns protect against the
forces of man. When night falls, the documents are lowered into an under-
ground vault for safekeeping. Like gold.

In different ways both the architecture and the technology convey that something precious resides within the cool, shadowy confines that is the temple, the vault, and the landmark called the National Archives—namely, the original documents that established the rules of the game called American democracy. Conceived by a disgruntled bunch of landed gentry, this system of government continues to inspire us, challenge us, and even divide us to the present day. The charters of freedom set a dynamic government into motion that would churn through the ages without ever being fully resolved. These documents established a system of checks and balances within the federal government to guard against tyranny, divided its power between the federal government and individual state governments to make things especially confusing, and, finally, mandated popular elections to ensure that the one constant in this new country would be change, and the one essential truth would be that there are two (or more) sides to every story. At the same time, they describe a set of principles so universally accepted by our citizens as to seem intuitive, assuming the power of natural law—that all men are created equal, that the lawmakers should be responsible to "the people," and that "the people" should elect the lawmakers.

It is a bit of a shock to remember, perhaps to discover, that these rules, these principles, were set down on parchment by the hand of mere mortals. It was parchment, and words, and ideas, anger and debate, dissents and compromise that gave birth to the ideals that so many depend on without reflection, no matter how much or how little we know about the actual day-to-day business of our government.

The light that illuminates the Declaration at the Archives does more than protect the parchment. Like stage lighting, it effuses our nation's founding document with a strange and powerful glow that seems to emanate from the magnificent ideas inscribed upon the parchment. Except for one thing . . .

You can't read it.

The document is that old, and by the time it was installed with the Constitution and the Bill of Rights in the pampering confines of the Archives, it had been improperly stored and carelessly mishandled to the point of disintegration. The handwritten ink is not, it seems, as enduring as the ideas it helped to describe.

Cut to the millennium—cut to you.

The eerie green light of your computer screen glows in the night long after the charters of freedom have been lowered deep into the vault within the Archives and the bronze doors have closed together with a resounding thud. With the aid of a computer and modem, you can scrutinize the Declaration from the comfort of your own home. And if you cannot physically come to within several thick panes of glass of where Thomas Jefferson boldly set our nation on the course of independence, at least you can read word-for-word how this country is organized and maybe, just maybe, discover the first inkling of what activists would call your *voice*—your ability to articulate the things that are important to you, your family, your community, your workplace, and the nation—in a way that helps inform the public debate.

Welcome to the relaunch of American democracy. Thanks to the Internet, in the relatively brief time period of the last decade, we have experienced unprecedented access to the information, the ideas, the ledgers, and the decision makers that constitute our government and affect our lives.

In an unexpected way, the Internet has become a partner in the preservation of the founding documents of our nation. For if imposing architecture, bronze doors, thick vaults, armed guards, surveillance cameras, metal detectors, inert gases, and special glass are the most effective ways we have of preserving physical documents, then the proliferation of the ideas contained therein, the understanding of their intentions, the appreciation of their function, and the regular, habitual exercise of allowable actions helps preserve and encourage the practice of a thing called American democracy. No longer are citizens solely relegated their vote, and the concept of political participation is assuming an increasingly broad definition.

Still it is important that we have the originals, that we can see them, know they are real, and be able to confirm, at will, that the ideas attributed to the founding documents are indeed the words inscribed upon the founding documents. For if it can be said in the new millennium that information is good, it must also be said that good information is better.

Myths About the Internet and American Democracy to Dispense with from the Start

But enough with praising the potential of the Internet. The incipient maturity of the World Wide Web has been accompanied by more than a few exaggerated hopes and fears. Chief among the promised potential, perhaps, is a supposed near-universal understanding of and direct experience with American democracy by its citizens. Certainly, the amount of information already available on the Internet has secured for Americans greater access to more . . . (More what? . . . words? . . . and pictures? . . . and sounds?)

I do think the Internet can have a profound effect on the relationship between everyday Americans and their government, their knowledge of and participation in the issues that affect or interest them. I am also sure that the Internet will not put American democracy on autopilot; it will not summarily resolve our differences; it will not preempt the need for everyday Americans to actively spur our government to get things done. Our Constitution was posted on the World Wide Web; it was not rewritten. The same rules that governed our public discourse before there was America Online still govern it today—word-for-word.

Part of realizing the Internet's potential is to be cognizant of its limitations. The Net does *not* provide comprehensive, verified information on every subject. And you know, it isn't really all that fast. (Now, isn't that heresy?) The Internet isn't always the shortest distance between two points, if you consider the amount of time you can lose by clicking around cyberspace trying to locate that web site you never knew existed. Sure, downloading information once you get there is a snap, but getting there can take hours, even days.

For the most part, the Internet is a happy land of snippets and short visits. It is a culture of clicking. The mouse finds an analogy in the remote control, and the World Wide Web can, in many ways, be likened to a television that you read. The supposed electronic repository of all the world's knowledge resembles a traditional library less than an extended cable package with almost unlimited channel selections—a wealth of knowledge to be sure but not to be confused with the robustness of information presented on the bound and printed page. As the World Wide Web begins to incorporate more streaming video and audio and animation, the relationship between television and the Internet will become more apparent, like reuinted twins separated at birth.

Oh, I am sure somebody has already put *War and Peace* online, but who would spend the time to click through it, or worse yet, print it out and read it? And even if you would click through it, they have not yet designed a computer that is comfortable resting on your stomach on the couch or that can be left in the sand at the beach. And yet, what printed index has ever matched the speed and ease with which a keyword search can rip through that huge text to find a vaguely recalled passage?

If the Internet does not quite resemble the dusty stacks and weighty tomes of accumulated knowledge in a traditional library, it might resemble a twenty-four reference section, with a highly caffinated reference librarian whose patience is never exhausted and whose brain is on steroids. In addition to its ability to index and retrieve, the Internet offers connection, communication.

It is unprecedented, but it is not boundless. It is not a panacea for all that plagues us privately and publicly as Americans. In and of itself, the Internet does not offer the solutions to our problems. It only offers to help. The advantages it offers are unprecedented, but they can be discovered, counted, and mastered. And once we have this new medium in perspective, we can begin to realize the Internet's true potential for American democracy and our potential as concerned and active citizens in our system of government.

Myth 1: The Internet Will Help Everyone Agree on Public Policy

Don't bet on it. Even as a long shot. Democracy is messy—and usually, the messier it is, the better job it's doing involving a broad cross section of interested parties with different backgrounds and interests (even if they all had to be made angry to participate). It is an unsettling fact that the concept of a healthy democracy to most Americans is gauged by how closely it resembles a totalitarian state. A government where every single person agrees on every issue, where there is only one compelling course of action for any given problem, and where dissent is nonexistent is called a "dictatorship." You may personally conflate the qualities of totalitarian regime with democratic nirvana, but do not expect such a situation to emerge in real life, no matter how much information and electronic interaction is suddenly available to "the people." So stop complaining that all politicians do is fight. That's part of the job description. Pick up some mud and join in the melee.

Myth 2: Public Policy Will Be Made Fast and Easy

Wrong again. Some Internet cheerleaders seem to be a little intoxicated with the implications of their first AOL account. Access to information does not make policy easier or less time consuming. The frustration most Americans feel as a result of their limited information about government has one big benefit—it does not require that you pore over any government reports or legislation. The last budget of the millennium passed by Congress ran to over two thousand pages. But if we now have access to such enormous documents, how is citizenship to be made faster and easier?

Over two hundred years' worth of elected officials in this country trying to address the issues of their day, make their mark on history, and stick it to the other party have created an extensive and complex body of law—and streams of funding that more closely resemble the Nile Delta than a peaceful-flowing river. Existing laws, even past failures, help define what may be done by us today to address the issues that face us. Contributing to this somewhat convoluted process requires effort on your part. The Internet makes it possible for you to accomplish much of the required research from the comfort of your own home, at any hour of the day or night, but our government remains large, complex, and, at times, contradictory. Try to enjoy the ride to enlightenment.

Myth 3: The Power of Your Opinion Can Be Increased by Carpet-Bombing American Legislators with E-mail

If you are the guy who E-mails everyone on the planet every time the synapses in your brain fire—please stop. It is still one person, one vote in America, and people who indiscriminately use E-mail to carpet bomb whole levels of government end up irritating their recipients more than compelling them to take a specific action. Only the legislators who were elected to represent you are responsible to answer your correspondence; and frankly, they are probably the only ones who care to see it, no matter how profound or moving you feel it is. Here is the good news: Heretofore, Americans have possessed a smattering of the information available to lobbyists and lawmakers. This limited the conversation that could occur between our elected officials and their constituents. Now your one voice can be far more informed than was before possible so that when you do communicate with your elected officials, your thoughts are relevant, helpful, and can actually contribute in a meaningful way to the public policy process in this country. Don't try to communicate *more* . . . communicate *better*.

Myth 4: With the Aid of Your Computer, You Will Win on Your Issues Once and for All

Grassroots organizers the country over are given to making this exaggeration—if you just make one phone call to Congress, or copy a prewritten letter, Congress will finally be enlightened and you can return to your normal, busy life. This wishful thinking has now extended to the Internet—usually in the form of E-mail action alerts and petitions. The churning juggernaut that is American democracy ensures that no single issue is ever truly won, ever.

No matter how noble, how seemingly necessary, or how responsible the issues you support seem to be, rest assured that there will always be an organized group of citizens who will claim that your positions on the issues will dissolve our fragile little union.

When you decide to be an advocate on an issue, go in for the long haul. Funding for federal, state, and local programs must be fought for every year, laws are tested in American courts, and new legislation is constantly being written. Programs need to be evaluated and updated to keep pace with the issues they address. Don't let this commitment dissuade you. Understand what your job is as an advocate, and it will become more manageable, and using the Internet can ensure that the time you invest as a cybercitizen is well spent.

Myth 5: One Day an Electronic System Will Allow Us to Decide All Matters of Public Policy by Majority Vote

This myth was ushered in by populist third-party candidate Ross Perot, our American every-millionaire, who, early in the days of the Internet promised electronic town voting centers where "the people" could determine what legislation passed and failed. This is a persistent and somewhat disturbing misconception. Many Americans believe that we are a nation where popular vote determines everything—that the majority always wins. This is not true now, nor was it ever true.

The majority wins when voting for elected office and when voting on the floors of the House or Senate, but our government is carefully constructed to make sure that the majority does not always get its way outside of these narrowly defined contests.

If the majority always won, we would have settled our policy disputes long ago by permanently installing the totalitarian regime that won our first election. In order to encourage a choice of candidates for elections, to think critically about proposed laws, and to dissuade the persecution of those who are not in the majority, it has long been recognized that the majority cannot always win and that matters of public policy should be forged through collaboration and compromise.

Our legislative system, often derided for its inefficiency, is one that attempts to accommodate as many viewpoints of various stakeholders on a given issue as possible. This makes the policies that emerge more convoluted. But it may also forestall this quarreling country from ever again approaching the brink of revolution. Though they may be few, or unpopular, a great cross section of voices can be heard in America. So forget that majority always rules, and do not hold your breath for the day when the legislative docket will appear on your computer every morning with your cup of coffee asking you to do the job of your elected officials in addition to your own.

Myth 6: America Will Go on Autopilot and the Issues Will Fade as Our Country Is Increasingly Run with Supercomputerized Efficiency

Hold on, Hal. Just because gigabytes of information are now available does not mean that people will become obsolete in the democratic process. All the computers, the statisticians, the Ph.D.s, and the lawyers in Washington have not yet been able to supplant the power of the simple, handwritten note from a constituent. Phone banks, broadcast fax machines, and even the Internet have not eroded the desire for politicians to hear from the folks back home.

Technology can complement the power of Americans to govern themselves, but it has not replaced it. Americans must now, and will forever have to, think, argue, compromise, and even protest at times. It is strange that many of these actions are generally held in low esteem. They have always been prime indicators that our democracy is functioning, however imperfectly, like a sweeping second hand on the face of the great American clock. It is unlikely that "the people" will ever become irrelevant in American politics or that the Constitution will be amended to read "of the computer, by the computer, and for the computer." American democracy resembles a demanding, fractious, irritating child more than a well-oiled machine. It needs to be baby-sat—by you, by me, by all of us.

What Are "My Issues" Anyway?

These are many reasons that Americans choose to become involved in a single piece, or a few select pieces, of legislation, rather than government business in general. Upon reflection you, too, may discover a burning desire to disagree with your Uncle Bob over the finer points of a bill in Congress. There are a multitude of urgent challenges facing each and every one of us as Americans: the economy, the environment, health care, racism, crime, education, taxes. Each of these policy areas is an immensely complex and important area of inquiry for us as citizens. The imperative need to find solutions for the challenges that face us may justify your attention to one of these areas. Here are some common reasons why you should consider becoming more involved in a specific issue:

An Issue Has Been in the News

Issues such as campaign finance reform, protecting social security, gun control, disaster relief, and the federal budget are covered extensively in print and electronic media; but the media, especially the electronic media, are not always adept at providing more than brief sound bites on a given issue. The World Wide Web allows you to see original documents, related information, and the actual text of any proposed legislation.

An Association You Belong to Has Sent Out an Action Alert

If you belong to a political organization or a trade association, you have probably received periodic action alerts stating that the world as we know it will come to an end if you don't call your member of Congress—right now! Frequently, action alerts provide a brief description of proposed legislation along with a message to deliver by phone, E-mail, or postal mail to your representatives. Time and space constraints tend to limit action alerts to short descriptions of pending legislation and analysis that sometimes verges on hysteria. Again, a more complete picture is usually available on the Internet.

You Care About a Problem in Your Community

Perhaps a friend of yours is suddenly diagnosed with a disease and desperately needs a research breakthrough; maybe a persistent problem is not getting addressed in your neighborhood, like crime or pollution; or maybe Congress is trying to cut funding to a program that you know has made a difference, like education. You have every right to know what your elected officials at every level of government are doing on the issues and the programs that you personally care about.

Election Promises

Your city council member may have made some promise during the campaign that you would like to see fulfilled—perhaps a new parking garage. You should expect your elected representatives to try their hardest to deliver on their campaign promises once in office. Finding out if the lawmaker's record matches his or her rhetoric takes some sleuthing, but it is possible, especially with the help of the World Wide Web.

However you become involved with a legislative issue, the Internet can help you research and understand the laws, regulations, and legislative proposals related to your interests. It can be time consuming, and despite the promises of the World Wide Web, remains a complex and compromising proposition to understand and interact with your government. American democracy is not easy, but it is possible. To help make your learning curve a little less steep, we have identified the most powerful actions that everyday Americans can take to influence their government and identified the best web sites for you to go to for information about the issues you care about and to be connected with the decision makers who ultimately must answer to your vote on Election Day.

Chapter One
Preambles and Declarations

★

Introduction

It seems every July Fourth, the network news needs to serve up a motley crew of teenagers outside some mall demonstrating how little they know about American history. "Was Alexander Hamilton a Founding Father of our country or a rock star?" And the inevitable answer, "Um, doesn't he have a cooking show?"

One recent news story focused on the fact that Americans did not know if the phrase "life, liberty, and the pursuit of happiness" came from the Constitution or the Declaration of Independence, but everyone seemed to know that "Just do it" came from Nike. I would wager that most Americans are as ignorant about the internal workings of most Fortune 500 companies as they are about their government. We know the slogans, but we have not reflected on their meaning or on the implications of these statements for our day-to-day lives. We know even less about the people behind the slogans—those who are in charge—and how to communicate with them.

It is primarily from observing and interacting with the people in government that we can develop a deep knowledge of how our government works, but it helps to know the rules that govern the game: how the people in charge got there in the first place and what they are allowed to do with their power. All of this is enumerated in the original documents that helped found our nation and that remain as relevant today as they did when they were originally committed to parchment.

But do not study the foundations of our democracy to find simple truths and easy answers. If setting a course of action for the government of the United States was as easy as reading a few pages, someone would have done it long ago. Our charters of freedom are better at providing insight as to why things seem so confusing and contentious—on the one hand establishing a majority vote to elect our representatives, while on the other hand protecting the right for the minority to organize against the majority. The founding documents also establish ideals that continue to challenge us to the present day, such as the phrase "all men are created equal," which did not, originally, include the right for women, or African Americans, or even nonlandholding white men to vote. And now does.

Speculation, confusion, and posturing about the true meaning of our founding documents still rages, and not just to settle questions on *Jeopardy*. Some of our most sticky public debates are centered around interpreting the Constitution, and the arguments considered by the highest court in the land help define the types of laws that can be enforced in the United States.

The current debate on gun control is a good example. The Second Amendment states: "A well regulated Militia, being necessary to the security of a free State, the right of the people to keep and bear Arms shall not be infringed." Does this mean that every American citizen has the right to own a gun, or does it, in fact, mean that only members of the National Guard are permitted to own guns? Both viewpoints have ardent defenders. And there are other positions besides, like those who say that every "able-bodied man" at the time the Bill of Rights was written was considered to be part of the militia, so that everyone has the right to bear arms. And those who say that whatever the particular historic context when the Bill of Rights was amended to the Constitution, our interpretation of that document must be predicated on our current problems and goals. Your position on gun control necessarily assumes a certain interpretation of the Second Amendment to the Constitution.

So surf the ancient texts. Marvel that words set down so long ago still remain instructive, even provocative, and subject to a certain amount of interpretation and change.

The Mayflower Compact

This was the first written constitution of North America, and perhaps the first time in what became the United States that somebody said, "Can't we all just get along?" Written by the Pilgrims in 1620, the Mayflower Compact established a system of government dependent on an impartial rule of law and subject to the king. Eventually, we got rid of the king part, but we retained the compact's tolerance of religious and other social differences among community members, so long as everyone obeyed the law.

The Declaration of Independence

The Declaration of Independence, drafted by Thomas Jefferson in 1776, asserted the principal beliefs of our nation—like that we were a nation, for one thing (no really, we mean it), and resulted in a revolution; but by the time the smoke cleared and all the points were added up, we really were a nation, really.

The Declaration did other things as well. This is the document that proclaimed certain truths to be self-evident—like that all men are created equal, even if the peculiar institution of slavery existed at the time, and would continue to exist until another bloody war, this time the Civil War, would establish once and for all that in America all men are really created equal. Unless it didn't.

There is also the bit about every citizen having the right to, "life, liberty, and the pursuit of happiness," which may or may not have been inserted as a joke after an all-night bender during the Continental Congress—one of the only times on the planet that a new government established a commitment to customer service.

The Federalist Papers

The Federalist Papers were perhaps the first action alerts issued in this country. They urged the citizens of the many states to support ratification of the fledgling Constitution. Written by Alexander Hamilton, James Madison, and John Jay, they are a collection of essays that appeared in New York State newspapers between 1787 and 1788 that attempted to assuage concerns about the proposed Constitution and support the need for a strong federal government. As such, the Federalist Papers form a cornerstone of democratic philosophy in this country. They are serious and wordy and continue to be studied for their thoughtful interpretation and defense of the Constitution.

The Constitution

Why did we have to memorize the preamble to the Constitution in school when it contains such an obvious example of questionable grammar—can anything be "more perfect"?

The Constitution still reads like a giant cheat sheet for high school civics class, which is basically what it is—a document concerned with such mundane matters as how our government is organized, how the president is elected, and how legislative districts are drawn.

In many ways the Constitution flies in the face of any number of popular business management seminars. What organization would ever assign the same areas of responsibility to three different bodies, promote open competition within the organization, and encourage the competition to challenge all decisions in their attempt to usurp your power? Behind the Constitution is an abiding philosophy that any power in the new country should be divided up into little bite-size pieces so that no government, or part of a government, or individual man could assert a tyrannical authority over the rest of the country.

The Bill of Rights

Many people were wary of the Constitution when it was first presented. Here was a government that was to be created by and of and for "the people," and a document that ignored their very existence by exclusively addressing the rights of "the government." To remedy this, a Bill of Rights was passed in 1791 as the first ten amendments to the Constitution. The Bill of Rights enumerates the specific rights of "the people" in a government of, by, and for them.

The Bill of Rights includes the right to free speech and to free assembly, freedom of religion, freedom of the press, and prohibitions

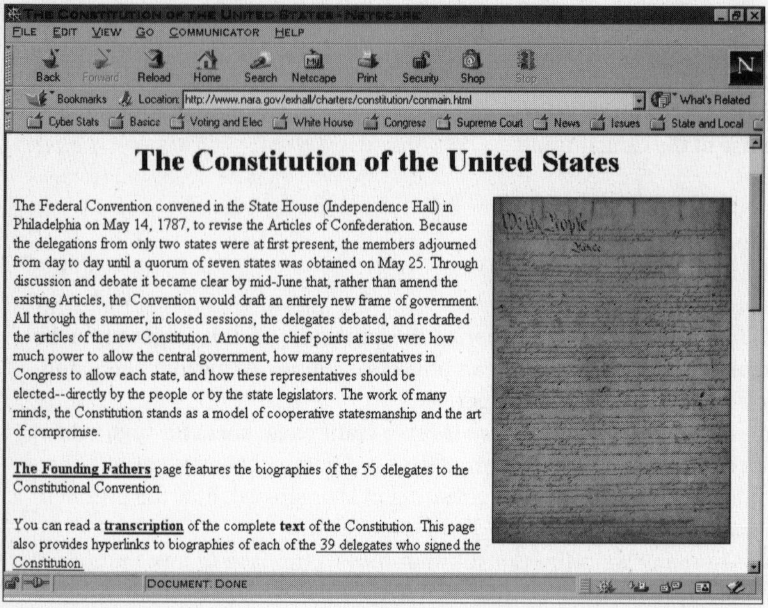
The Constitution of the United States - Netscape
File Edit View Go Communicator Help
Back Forward Reload Home Search Netscape Print Security Shop Stop
Bookmarks Location: http://www.nara.gov/exhall/charters/constitution/conmain.html
What's Related
Cyber Stats Basics Voting and Elec White House Congress Supreme Court News Issues State and Local
The Constitution of the United States
The Federal Convention convened in the State House (Independence Hall) in Philadelphia on May 14, 1787, to revise the Articles of Confederation. Because the delegations from only two states were at first present, the members adjourned from day to day until a quorum of seven states was obtained on May 25. Through discussion and debate it became clear by mid-June that, rather than amend the existing Articles, the Convention would draft an entirely new frame of government. All through the summer, in closed sessions, the delegates debated, and redrafted the articles of the new Constitution. Among the chief points at issue were how much power to allow the central government, how many representatives in Congress to allow each state, and how these representatives should be elected--directly by the people or by the state legislators. The work of many minds, the Constitution stands as a model of cooperative statesmanship and the art of compromise.
The Founding Fathers page features the biographies of the 55 delegates to the Constitutional Convention.
You can read a transcription of the complete text of the Constitution. This page also provides hyperlinks to biographies of each of the 39 delegates who signed the Constitution.
Document: Done

against unlawful search and seizure and against cruel and unusual punishments. Among all of these explicit rights is the implicit right to be unpopular in America—the inalienable right to march to our own respective drummer, to be free of any political party or religious doctrine we do not voluntarily submit to. The Bill of Rights protects individuals from undue restraint by the majority or any of the laws it might pass.

This is not to suggest that the Bill of Rights is itself above scrutiny. However inalienable our enumerated rights are, they do not fall beyond the reach of conflicting interpretation and debate. Sexual harassment, domestic terrorism, the death penalty, campaign finance reform, and gang violence are all issues from the day's headlines that have forced us to reexamine the dividing line between government intervention and individual liberties as established in the Bill of Rights.

The Emancipation Proclamation

This was Abraham Lincoln's bold declaration that "freed the slaves," except that it didn't really, and there had to be amendments to the Constitution to secure some basic liberties for African Americans, like the right to vote. And then there had to be more amendments to the Constitution to address other forms of discrimination. And even that did not make us all equal in each other's eyes really, because we continue to be a nation with differences that are based on the color of one's skin, and other things too, like one's gender, or one's race, or one's sexual orientation—even if we already fought one of our bloodiest wars to show that when we said everyone was created equal, sooner or later, we were going to have to act like we believed it.

President Lincoln's statement, however, shines with significance, if not in actuality, then on principle. It was a bold statement that the rights and ideals asserted by our Founding Fathers would continue to be adhered to and interpreted in a contemporary context, even if it was difficult or dangerous to do so. It was also an example that an action of immense moral importance can be politically expedient at the same time.

Democracy in America by Alexis de Tocqueville

If the Constitution is like an organizational chart that tells you how our federal government is organized, Tocqueville's classic, the first part originally published in 1835, explains how the system really works. If *Democracy in America* does not tell you where the bodies are actually buried, it does tell you how to get one of the grave diggers to lend you a shovel.

Leave it to a French aristocrat to avoid becoming intoxicated by the rhetoric of our Founding Fathers: "In their relations with strangers the Americans are impatient of the slightest criticism and insatiable for praise. . . . Even admirers are bored."[1]

To this day, there has not been a better description of how our government runs and the effect living in a democracy has on us as individuals. Indeed, some of the topics Tocqueville mused upon—why government bureaucracies are inefficient, why Americans are apathetic about voting, and the deep, unresolved problem of race in America—are still at the forefront of public debate.

At the heart of the work is the recognition of the power of grassroots organizing in America—how in a country where all men are created equal,

1. De Tocqueville, Alexis. *Democracy in America*. Eds. J.P. Mayer and Max Lerner, trans. George Lawrence. New York: Harper & Row, 1966.

those who can pool their voices and work together for common goals hold the balance of power. Fax machines, E-mail, long-distance phone service, and C-SPAN have done little to alter Tocqueville's observation that when a few people in America decide to speak with a common voice, lawmakers get nervous.

Cybercitizen Web Listings

Library of Congress
http://www.loc.gov

The **LIBRARY** *of* **CONGRESS**

The Library of Congress is the largest repository of recorded knowledge in the world and a living symbol that knowledge remains vital to democracy. The library's mission is to make its resources available and useful to the Congress and the American people and to sustain and to preserve a universal collection of knowledge and creativity for future generations.

SKILLS

http://lcweb.loc.gov/exhibits/declara/declara1.html ★ Skill 2: The Declaration
http://lcweb2.loc.gov/const/fed/fedpapers.html ★ Skill 3: The Federalist Papers
http://memory.loc.gov/ammem/bdsds/bdsdhome.html ★ Skill 4: The Constitution
http://lcweb.loc.gov/exhibits/treasures/troo.html ★ Skill 5: The Bill of Rights
http://lcweb.loc.gov/exhibits/treasures/treasures/troo.html ★ Skill 6: Emancipation Proclamation

UNIQUE FEATURES

http://memory.loc.gov/ammem/today/today.html ★ "Today in History" provides a daily journal of past events in our nation's history.

National Archives and Records Administration (NARA)
http://www.nara.gov

NARA

NARA is an independent federal agency that helps preserve our nation's history by overseeing the management of all federal records. NARA's mission is to ensure ready access to the essential evidence that documents the rights of American citizens, the actions of federal officials, and the national experience.

SKILLS

http://www.nara.gov/exhall/charters/declaration/decmain.html ★ Skill 2: The Declaration
http://www.nara.gov/exhall/charters/constitution/conmain.html ★ Skill 4: The Constitution

http://www.nara.gov/exhall/charters/billrights/billmain.html ★ Skill 5: The Bill of
  Rights
http://www.nara.gov/exhall/featured-documents/eman/emantrns.html ★ Skill 6:
  Emancipation Proclamation

UNIQUE FEATURES

http://www.nara.gov/exhall/charters/constitution/confath.html ★ "Founding Fathers"
  page provides short biographies of each of the delegates to the Constitutional
  Convention.
http://www.nara.gov/nara/president/address.html ★ Links of "Presidential Libraries"
  allows you to browse the papers and history of former presidents.

Annotated Constitution from Government Printing Office
http://www.access.gpo.gov/congress/senate/constitution/index.html
The Constitution of the United States "Analysis and Interpretation" provides an
annotated version of the Constitution detailing Supreme Court decisions related
to various sections of the document.

SKILLS

http://www.access.gpo./gov/congress/senate/constitution/in ★ Skill 4: The
  Constitution

ConstitutionFacts
http://www.constitutionfacts.com/
index.shtml
A well-organized site showcasing
the founding documents of our
nation, with state and foreign con-

Welcome to
ConstitutionFacts.com

stitutions as well. The information is presented in a variety of formats including games,
quotes, and time lines.

SKILLS

http://www.constitutionfacts.com/doi.shtml ★ Skill 2: The Declaration
http://www.constitutionfacts.com/cons.shtml ★ Skill 4: The Constitution
http://www.constitutionfacts.com/amendments.shtml ★ Skill 5: The Bill of Rights

UNIQUE FEATURES

http://www.constitutionfacts.com.amendments.shtml ★ List of proposed amendments to
  the Constitution that were never passed includes making marriage between races illegal,
  making divorce illegal, and the declaration of war subject to popular vote.
http://www.constitutionfacts.com/puzzles.shtml ★ Crossword puzzles from basic to
  expert can be printed out to test your knowledge of American history.
http://www.constitutionfacts.com/exam.shtml ★ Multiple-choice exams are provided to
  test your knowledge of the Constitution.

Democracy in America
http://xroads.virginia.edu/~HYPER/
DETOC/home.html
A project of the "American Studies Programs" at the University of Virginia, this site provides the complete text of *Democracy in America* with various maps, essays, and other documents, to provide a broad context of the time when de Tocqueville wrote this seminal work of American political thought.

FindLaw Constitutional Law Center
http://supreme.findlaw.com

A division of the FindLaw site, the Constitutional Law Center provides easy and interesting access to American primary documents, history, and interpretation.

SKILLS

http://supreme.findlaw.com/Documents/federalist.html ★ Skill 3: The Federalist Papers
http://supreme.findlaw.com/Documents/constitution.html ★ Skill 4: The Constitution
http://supreme.findlaw.com/Documents/constitution.html ★ Skill 5: The Bill of Rights

UNIQUE FEATURES

http://supreme.findlaw.com/Documents/consthist.html ★ History of the Constitution
  provides an illustrated, annotated history of the founding documents of our nation.

The Avalon Project
http://www.yale.edu/lawweb/avalonavalon.htm
The Avalon Project at the Yale Law School is dedicated to providing on-line access to the text of primary documents in the fields of law, history, economics, politics, diplomacy, and government. The site is extensively indexed and allows search by title, subject, author, and time of history.

SKILLS

http://www.yale.edu/lawweb/avalon/mayflowr.htm ★ Skill 1: Mayflower Compact
http://www.yale.edu/lawweb/avalon/declare.htm ★ Skill 2: The Declaration
http://www.yale.edu/lawweb/avalon/federal/fed.htm ★ Skill 3: The Federalist Papers
http://www.yale.edu/lawweb/avalon/usconst.htm ★ Skill 4: The Constitution
http://www.yale.edu/lawweb/avalon/rights1.htm ★ Skill 5: The Bill of Rights
http://www.yale.edu/lawweb/avalon/emancipa.htm ★ Skill 6: Emancipation Proclamation

TheHistoryNet
http://www.thehistorynet.com
Designed by America's largest publisher of history magazines, TheHistoryNet offers dynamic retellings of ordinary and extraordinary people in American history.

UNIQUE FEATURES

http://thehistorynet.com./AmericanHistory/articles/1296_cover.htm ★ George Washington's proposed retirement forced our first national elections to take place and set the stage for a resulting two-party system.

http://thehistorynet.com/THNarchives/HistoricTravel/ ★ "Historic Travel" articles provide descriptions of the places where important figures of American history lived, worked, and fought.

The History Place
http://historyplace.com
Dedicated to students, educators, and all who enjoy history, this site provides a detailed time line of American history, complete with information on historic figures, pictures, and multimedia files.

SKILLS

http://www.historyplace.com/unitedstates/revolution/mayflower.htm ★ Skill 1: Mayflower Compact

http://www.historyplace.com/unitedstates/revolution/decindep.htm ★ Skill 2: The Declaration

http://www.historyplace.com/unitedstates/revolution/constitution.html ★ Skill 4: The Constitution

http://www.historyplace.com/unitedstates/revolution/billrights.html ★ Skill 5: The Bill of Rights

UNIQUE FEATURES

http://www.historyplace.com/unitedstates/revolution/decindep.htm ★ RealAudio version of the Declaration of Independence is read by Peter Thomas.

Chapter Two

Campaigns and Elections

★

Introduction

Oh, how the more civic-minded among us fret over the fact that only
about half of the eligible Americans vote in our national elections. Meanwhile, surveys show that only 35 percent of Americans can identify their
representative in Congress. Perhaps we should spend less time lamenting
over those who don't care and don't vote and reserve some concern for
those who don't know who they are putting into public office.

The reality is that average Americans have a limited amount of time
to spend with their own children and even less time to gather election
information and go to the polls, no matter how important the offices in
question. Heretofore, the would-be voter who actually made an effort to at
least find out what the candidates for local office looked like would have
relied on a few rather limited sources of information—the media and campaign literature.

But the media like to focus on negatives and controversies, and
whatever issues are most likely to generate them. Media usefulness is further hampered by the fact that they usually focus on large national elections, applicable to their entire readership or viewership, e.g., the
presidency, leaving your city council and school board candidates, and
other offices that directly represent your district, control your schools,

your local police, and leave your utilities basically ignored, perhaps grant-ing as much as one short blurb per candidate on the eve of the election. The media are also grand purveyors of campaign advertising, which, as we all know, tackles the difficult issues with about as much subtlety as a sumo wrestler dressed for competition at a black tie wedding.

Campaign literature is worse. It is often insipid, biased, and it is sometimes nasty. One way to sidestep these frustrations is to join a politi-cal party and vote the party ticket in hopes that your political party has done all the work for you—that your party has fielded a list of capable can-didates who will represent you with skill and enthusiasm, who you are in complete agreement with your party on each and every issue that may arise, and whom the opposition has nothing to offer besides danger.

With the advent of the Internet, the amount and the specificity of election information available to Joe Voter has been both increased and conveniently indexed. It just might usher in an era of political free agency where voter dependence on the product recognition aspects of political parties is lessened.

You still cannot vote from the comfort of your own home (see "Why You Can't Vote Online . . . Yet"), but you can take a crucial first step in reg-istering to vote, and you can research candidate positions on the specific issues you care about, find out what corporations and organizations have donated money to local campaigns, amass voting records for incumbents, and question your local candidates for office directly via E-mail. In short, with a computer and some effort, you can change from Joe Voter into a cybercitizen.

And your political parties should not get off the hook, either, because if you are going to be partisan, now you can do it with the badger-ing persistence you'd expect to be tolerated in an organization that values your membership. Make your political party provide you with information about local campaigns and volunteer opportunities, and do not get left out of sharing your two cents on the state and federal party platforms. That way, you can be sure that local candidates for office and their positions on the issues do, in fact, represent the wishes of local party members. You can even request help in running for elected office, if you truly become inspired. Or enraged.

Why You Can't Vote Online . . . Yet

There seems to be no more popular expectation or common misconception about the Internet than that we should all be able to cast our votes from the comfort and privacy of our own homes. Let's face it, with the wonders of color and sounds and graphics streaming over the Net, it couldn't be that hard to create an on-line ballot.

Maybe one day, but not today. There are actually well-founded concerns about on-line voting. Most of them have to do with the integrity of an election system that cannot be closely monitored. One of the most important aspects of protecting our democracy is the confidence the public has that the system is fair and protected from manipulation. Accommodating new technology must be done very carefully, even if that new technology promises the convenience that so many of us claim to need on Election Day. Some of the considerations involved with on-line voting are the following:

* **Assurance that the votes can be tallied correctly**
* **Protection from external manipulation**
* **Protection from internal mischief**
* **Anonymity of the voter**
* **Eligibility of the voter**
* **Electronic signature—that is, a unique mark by the hand of the voter**
* **Assurance the transmission lines cannot be jammed or overloaded**

Although a limited amount of fraud can and does occur in traditional polling places and through absentee voting systems, using a system of phone lines and machines that cannot be inspected, raises serious concerns about protecting the integrity of our elections. Voting one day in the future may be as simple as clicking your mouse button. Getting there will not be.

There is an additional challenge to on-line voting that relates to equity. The Voting Rights Act stipulates that changes in practices or procedures with respect to voting must be approved by the attorney general who can oppose them if they have the purpose or effect of denying or abridging the right to vote on account of race, color, or membership in any minority group. The demographics of the Internet might possibly constitute such an abridgement by providing a convenient voting option that is not uniformly accessible. Nonetheless, both government and industry have begun to stick their toes into the deep pool of on-line voting and are testing the waters. A company called Vote Here has begun to test a commercial on-line voting system in the states of Washington and Arizona. Their software provides voting encryption and instantaneous election results for state and local elections. Should these demonstration projects meet expectations, they may offer on-line voting services in increasingly large venues. The secretary of state in California is talking about implementing a statewide on-line vote. Texas, New York, Iowa, Florida, and Minnesota are also debating using the new technology in elections. As for the federal government, the Department of Defense will allow millions of military personnel stationed overseas to vote electronically as part of the Federal Voting Assistance Program (FVAP). The votes will be transmitted and protected on the same lines that the Pentagon uses to send encrypted messages worldwide.

The Truth About the Internet: Demographics

The media are simply intoxicated with their ability to conduct polls at election time—and this populist tool is popping up like mushrooms on the World Wide Web. You can't search for a good supplier of shark cartilage without getting asked if you think the new university in Zaire should be built away from the flood plain. However interesting, on-line polls are limited in terms of speaking on behalf of all Americans.

It is estimated that some 150 million Americans will be online by the end of the year 2000. That means that nearly one in every two Americans will have access to the Internet, making it a formidable tool indeed for communicating with our fellow Americans and disseminating information. But what about those Americans who are not online? With all of our good intentions, and our intelligence, and our ability to communicate with people all over the world from our typewriters, don't we have the interests of everyone at heart?

The answer is that no, we probably do not. On-line Americans tend to be more educated than the national average and also more affluent. We are also younger, more employed, and more professional than your average American dreamer. That might seem to speak to a certain political bent but researchers have documented that the Internet does not harbor any single overriding political ideology. In other words, there are plenty of conservatives and liberals online, plenty of democrats and republicans, and plenty of independents and moderates as well. A broad cross section of the American public, to be sure, but not necessarily an accurate representation of the entire population.

Five Approaches to Campaign Fiance Reform: Getting the Money Out of the System

No one is more fired up about getting the money out of American politics than your member of Congress. They spend so much time debating it, putting proposals under a magnifying glass, and getting face time in the media discussing it that they never seem to get around to actually passing it.

As much hope is placed on the shoulders of campaign finance reform to "save democracy as we know it" as has been placed on the Internet. The fact is that campaigns are expensive. And even if every legislator could vote their conscience after taking money from special interests, it is just downright wasteful for someone to spend a couple of million bucks to get a job with the United States government.

Oh, something will get passed eventually—some small step in the right direction—something that can withstand a few good challenges, like being able to stand up in front of the Supreme Court—something that will be lauded as a major reform, but will actually be a minor reform. "The people" will have to just keep pushing the lawmakers to do the right thing until enough of these minor reforms are passed to add up to something significant.

> **Do Nothing—**The Supreme Court of the United States has found that individual donations to political campaigns and parties are inextricably expressions of free speech. It is the finding of the Supreme Court that it is unconstitutional to limit a citizen's ability to donate money for political party activities outside of specific campaigns for public office. That means no limits on what is commonly called "soft money." Supporters of this "do nothing" approach believe that donations are sufficiently regulated at present and that individuals should not be additionally burdened in terms of spending money

on politics. Recently, this school of thought went one step further, asking the Supreme Court to raise the limits of regulated campaign contributions (for specific candidates) to keep pace with inflation.

Regulate "Soft Money" Contributions—Individuals can contribute any amount of money to political parties for uses other than expressly advocating the victory or defeat of a candidate for federal office. This means unlimited donations can be used for rent, utilities, office supplies, salaries, and "issue advocacy." Regulating soft money would limit the size of donations to political parties for any use—including overhead.

Ban "Issue Advocacy" Campaigns—Special interest groups and political parties are currently allowed to spend unlimited funds on "issue advocacy" as long as they do not explicitly advocate the support or defeat of a specific candidate. This has prompted groups to spend millions of dollars to run ads that seem to transparently support their candidate, even if they do not explicitly say so. The federal election (backed by the Supreme Court) only recognizes "express advocacy" as being subject to contribution limitations, but any savvy candidate or party can get their message across without naming names.

Publicly Fund Campaigns for Public office—Removing the ability of any individual or group of individuals in a Political Action Committee (PAC) to contribute to the campaigns for political office would seemingly remove the ability for money to influence candidates for public office. Presently, candidates for president who are affiliated with a nationally recognized party can receive matching federal funds for their campaign. Some proposals recommend funding all campaigns for federal (or even state and local office). It is worth considering—but don't hold your breath. There are millions of lawyers, lobbyists, campaign organizers, candidates, and fundraisers who draw their daily bread from the current system, and government will be unlikely to change a system where the most likely consequence would be to put thousands of Americans out of work for the mere promise of electing more honest lawmakers.

Provide Free or Subsidized Advertising for Campaigns—Electronic media advertising (including television, radio, and production costs) is the most costly aspect of campaigns. Millions of dollars could be saved if the costs of advertising were provided either by the government or by the media themselves, either through free air time, advertising limits, or a subsidy. As you can imagine, there is no shortage of tax-payers who would rather not fund a possible alternative to campaign finance with their own hard-earned dollars—and the media, also, is likely to balk at sacrificing a huge and dependable revenue stream.

Skill 1: Register to vote.

It is an irritating detail of American democracy that we make people *register* to vote weeks before they actually vote. Other democracies on our planet do not require this obstacle and have higher voter turnouts for their elections. Indeed, in this country, registration laws at times have seemed ignominiously employed to deny people the right to vote rather than to facilitate the process (as with poll tests and taxes aimed at minimizing the vote of African Americans). And to make matters more complex, registration laws are established by individual states, which means that registration forms and deadlines tend to be different.

The so-called "Motor Voter" Act (also known as the National Voter Registration Act, NVRA) attempted to make voting registration easier and more uniform across the country. A single form, with minor alterations, is now accepted in states that require registration. The sad part is that although millions more Americans are now registered to vote as a result of

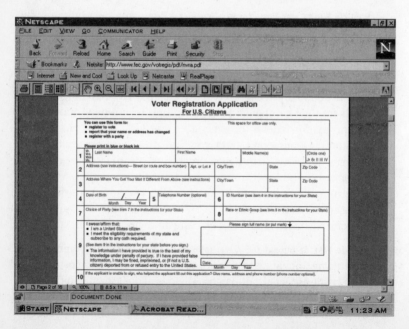

"Motor Voter," the amount who choose to do so has continued to dwindle in recent years.

But enough complaining—just register and be done with it. No seasoned politician will give you the time of day if you cannot say the following words: "I am a registered voter." Unless, of course, you can say the words, "Daddy left me a trust fund, and I have no idea what to spend the money on." Remember, you need to reregister if your primary address has changed since the last election (the same "Motor Voter" form can be used to notify your local registrar of voters of an address change).

The Internet has made registering to vote as simple as it is probably going to get. Because voting registration requires your written signature and the physical storage of the record to protect against fraud, you cannot truly register to vote online. You can, however, log on to any number of web sites, provide your name and address, and have a registration form sent to you. You then need to fill out the form, decide if you would like to join a political party (such as Democrat, or Republican, or the Reform Party), sign the form, and drop it in the mail. Even the postage is free.

Access to Primary Elections in the United States

OPEN (Anyone Can Vote in the Primaries)		CLOSED (You Must Be Registered with a Political Party to Vote in the Primary)	
Alabama	New Hampshire	Alaska	Michigan
Arkansas	New Jersey	Arizona	Nebraska
Georgia	North Dakota	California	Nevada
Hawaii	Ohio	Colorado	New Mexico
Idaho	South Carolina	Connecticut	New York
Illinois	Tennessee	Delaware	North Carolina
Indiana	Texas	District of Col.	Oklahoma
Iowa	Vermont	Florida	Oregon
Minnesota	Virginia	Kansas	Pennsylvania
Mississippi	Washington	Kentucky	Rhode Island
Missouri	Wisconsin	Louisiana	South Dakota
Montana	Wyoming	Maine	Utah
		Maryland	West Virginia
		Massachusetts	

Skill 2: Find out what's on the ballot.

U.S. Senate offices are held for six years, House offices are held for two, the president can serve two four-year terms, and your state and local lawmakers may be in office for any of the above-mentioned lengths of time. In addition to voting for candidates, voters are often asked to address bond issues authorizing local governments to finance programs, and are sometimes presented with ballot initiatives, proposed legislation that becomes law with a majority vote from the electorate.

The first step in being an informed voter is to know what you will be voting on come Election Day. Your state and local governments increasingly provide this information online, although a phone call to your local registrar of voters will secure the same information. In some states, ballot information is mailed to registered voters before the election, whether they request a sample ballot or not. Key pieces of information to obtain from your local registrar of voters include the following:

* **Voter registration form (if you have not requested one elsewhere—or confirmation that you are, indeed, registered to vote).**

* **Your list of federal, state, and local district numbers (the registrar will provide these with an address). Write these district numbers down for future use—you never know when you will need to contact your elected officials.**

* **The address of your local polling place (no, you probably cannot vote online, but your polling place should be close to where you live).**

* **The date of the next election (along with hours that the polls will be open—usually well before and well after work).**

* **The type of election it will be. (A primary election is usually held to narrow candidates down to one candidate per party, although sometimes primary elections are held to narrow the field of candidates without respect to party. In many states, you cannot vote in a party primary unless you are a registered member of that party. A general election determines who wins the office for the next term.)**

* **The ballot for the next election. (This should include a list of offices that are up for grabs, the candidates that are running for them, and any additional issues that must be voted on, such as ballot initiatives.)**

(See chapter 7: "State and Local Government," to see if your state has an on-line registrar of voters.)

The Role of a "Supersite"

One thing you begin to notice as you surf the Web is that, while there may be lots of web sites and lots of links, there is far less original material being generated behind all of that connectedness. Indeed some web sites are little more than collections of links that promise one-stop shopping, but that really provide a switch box that you can travel through to numerous destinations. I call these sites "supersites" and you can think of them as the warehouse information stores of the Internet.

Although supersites tend to be short on original information, in the American election arena where every single campaign, no matter how small, will soon be posting information, and where information can be gathered from numerous sources, an organized, easily navigable supersite with a memorable address or Universal Resource Locater (URL) is worthy of recognition. Well-organized web sites with extensive links are sometimes identified under "links" in the web listings at the end of each chapter.

Skill 3: Get a list of campaign contributors.

Let's face it, money does make a difference. Why does running for public office always seem to require money? *Because campaigns tend to be expensive.* Do candidates like the folks who give them money to run for public office? *Yes, a lot—as much as family—maybe more.* And what in the world do they talk about while eating cheese cubes at yet another rubber-chicken fund-raiser? *The topics that mutually interest them, like what the state legislature should do about their issues.* If the candidates ends up getting elected, do they tend to meet with these same groups when they come to visit the state capitol? *It would be downright inhospitable to do otherwise.* Is all this legal? *Yes, of course.* As long as the candidates don't directly sell their votes on specific pieces of legislation, which, of course, they would never dream of doing.

One of the truly exciting aspects of the Internet is that for the first time in history, information about who is funding your local campaigns for public office is available. Although campaigns for public office have long been required to keep meticulous records of all money going into and out of a campaign, obtaining and reviewing those records has not been a very easy task for you. Only individuals with a lot of time on their hands and little else on their minds would bother trekking to Washington,

D.C., to review these records directly at the Federal Election Commission (FEC). Since the birth of the Internet, several public interest groups have begun to process and present FEC information quickly and accurately online.

The information may now be available, but it still requires judicious use. Simply because you discover that a local candidate is receiving contributions from groups you abhor does not mean that they are running an illegal campaign, or selling their vote, or are involved in an international black helicopter conspiracy. A single campaign donation from an offensive group does not necessarily mean that your candidate is in bed with them but may indicate that they like their perfume—the candidate's past voting record might very well be in concert with the objectives of that particular group. Groups and candidates tend to gravitate to one another ideologically. Usually a voting record can be used to confirm or deny your suspicions.

Keep in mind that in the grand scheme of things, even the maximum allowable contribution from a Political Action Committee (PAC) is not all that much—probably not enough to sacrifice a reputation or endure public shame for the selling of votes—or worth the risk of jail time,

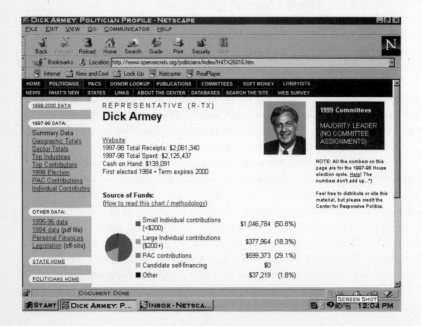

for that matter. With the rising cost of running an election campaign, most candidates are only too happy to accept money from whatever group offers it. In other words, sometimes PACs and candidates support each other for unfathomable reasons.

Skill 4: Review voting records and issue positions.

No, they are not the same thing. Voting records tell you what the legislator has done in the past. And if you have not recently been involved in elections, you might want to come in with the mind-set of an executive and find out what the person who is already there has been up to before you decide if you need to replace him or her.

Any national political association that is serious about making an impact will produce "report cards" based on the votes of elected officials over the course of an entire legislative session. Report cards are an effective way for special interest groups to hold lawmakers accountable for their votes and a wonderful way for you, the voter, to find out where your incumbent official stands on the specific issues you care about. Report cards have the added advantage of being able to cut through the procedural complexity of lawmaking to isolate the most relevant votes on a given issue, whether it took the form of a bill, an amendment, or a piece of omnibus legislation.

Issue positions include the vision, the plans, and the promises that the candidate offers to implement if elected or reelected to office. Whereas voting records are usually the province of associations, issue positions tend to be found in the media in response to the questions of reporters or on the web sites of the candidates themselves. An incumbent who has a voting record that clearly does not match his current issue positions should be suspect, and you should demand that they demonstrate their sincerity if they have recently shifted their position.

(See chapter 6, "The News Media," for a list of news-related web sites that can provide issue positions and chapter 8, "Issues, Associations, Groups, and Coalitions," for lists of political groups that provide voting records and score cards.)

Skill 5: Communicate effectively with a campaign via E-mail.

Sending E-mail to candidates is a good way to directly ask a local candidate a question or two about the issues that interest you. Why wait for the candidate to come down your street and ring your doorbell? Find the E-mail address of the local campaign, identify yourself as a voter who lives in the district, and ask them to respond to a brief inquiry. E-mail is the cyberequivalent of putting a microphone in the aisle of a town meeting. Any candidate who is not computer savvy at this point, or claims to be too busy during the campaign to answer a sincere question or two, may be telling you something about how responsive they would be if elected to public office. Keep in mind, however, that it is only fair that you ask a question or two. You should not expect to enter into a debate with the local candidates so much as signal your interest in, or opinion on, a specific issue. Other rules that apply to sending E-mail to elected officials apply here—do not send any attachments unless they are specifically requested, and do not start your relationship off by being sarcastic or disrespectful.

A thank-you E-mail for a personal response from the candidate is acceptable, even charming. Denigrating them because they do not share your views on a given issue is not. Help campaign for the other guy instead.

Skill 6: Contribute to a campaign or Political Action Committee that supports your positions on the issues.

Now that you can buy cars online, campaign donations could not have been that far behind. If we are all so thoroughly convinced that money makes a major difference in the voting records of our elected officials, why not try to peddle some of that influence ourselves by making a donation to our favorite campaign? The fact is that any candidate without significant cash is not likely to win their bid for public office. And since every little bit counts, even a modest contribution to a local candidate can foster the appreciation of the candidate.

As with other forms of campaign communication, candidates will try to woo your contribution online with general and inoffensive policy statements that scream integrity and fetching pictures that espouse a love of small children. Know this—candidates spend millions of dollars every election cycle on fund-raising campaigns with the hopes that you will send in a faceless check with no further strings attached. Never make a donation to a campaign without sending a separate E-mail stating what your hopes are for the campaign, e.g., I just pledged fifty dollars to your campaign—thanks for your commitment to heart disease research! That way, your money speaks for you, and helps solidify a candidate's dedication to the issues that concern you.

Once you have given money to a good candidate, you might want to consider making extra contributions to a Political Action Committee (PAC) that works on your issues. If a PAC is doing its job, it is educating candidates about your issues and the legislation you would like to see passed and making donations to the most promising candidates in a number of key districts. (See Sidebar below to identify individual contribution limitations.)

Guidelines for Giving

Legal guidelines have been established to limit the amount of money any single American or any PAC can donate to a political party or campaign. Make sure you stay within these boundaries when you contribute to a political campaign. If you are maxed out, consider volunteering for a campaign or engaging in some other activity that is not considered a "cash contribution." The Federal Election Commission has issued an advisory opinion that an individual citizen putting up a web site in support of or opposed to a candidate and not coordinated with any existing campaign does not fall under their reporting requirements.

(See chapter 9 "Your Own Private Idaho," for more.)

	To Each Candidate (Per Election)	To National Party (For Candidates)	To Any Other Political Committee (Such as a PAC)	Total Per Calendar Year
Individual	$1,000	$20,000	$5,000	$25,000
Multi-candidate committee (such as a PAC)	$5,000	$15,000	$5,000	No limit

Skill 7: Volunteer.

Those who develop a genuine affinity for a candidate, who are related by blood, or who have already given the amount of money allowed by law to the campaign may want to consider volunteer opportunities. Computer-savvy candidates are increasingly using the Internet to inform supporters of public events, rallies, and debates, and to help recruit, manage, and motivate campaign volunteers. Campaigns even use web sites to attract volunteers to help design and maintain their web sites.

Check out your local candidate's web site to keep abreast of volunteer opportunities that may fit your schedule or that especially suit your skill set. As with writing a check for a campaign, never volunteer without explaining to the candidate or the campaign manager why it is that you feel the candidate deserves to be elected to public office. You will want to distinguish yourself early on from volunteers who are simply personal friends, groupies, or have nothing better to do with their time. But *do not* corner the candidate every single time he or she comes into the office or attempt to steer their attention away from other important issues—a nuisance in the campaign office is impossible—but do try to have one brief, substantive exchange with the candidate so that it is clear that your time is given for a more important reason than the candidate's good looks or the campaign office's lukewarm coffee.

Even if you do not volunteer for a campaign, you may want to seize the opportunity to meet the candidate at some local appearance and see for yourself what kind of impression the candidate makes in person. Remember that, at its best, the Internet is an elevator, not a destination. Your surfing of election-based web sites should not only lead you to the election booth, but help begin to develop a relationship with your elected officials. It does not matter if you have little more to say than, "Good luck," or, "I like what you stand for," shaking a candidate's hand is potentially as good for you as it is for them. If elected, they will fondly recall the exchange—especially if you point out how honored you were to shake their hand on the campaign trail.

Skill 8: Comb the media for pertinent information.

Some well-founded criticism is leveled at the media during election time. Remember when Bob Dole fell off the podium during a campaign stop in the 1996 presidential election? Of course you do. Why? Because you had to watch it about a thousand times on television. How did it help clarify Dole's positions on the issues? It didn't.

The media tend to be easily sidetracked by the salacious and often play flag football with the current issues rather than adequately tackling them head-on. Subtle differences on the humdrum issues of the day get buried or ignored altogether. The media will focus on issues that put the candidates in stark contrast—that is, unless it gets distracted by the slightest whiff of illicit sex.

Thanks to media search engines on the Internet, you can become your own investigative journalist and ferret out information on the issues you care about, even if they aren't being addressed in the headlines or on televised debates. News media allow you to comb through news stories, features, candidate profiles, columns, and news wires to see if any of your local candidates for public office have addressed your issues, even if those comments did not make the top of the evening news broadcast. And don't forget what the pundits have to say. Those opinionated gasbags may be able to grill and analyze your local candidates with a withering determination you could only dream of.

(See chapter 6, "The News Media," for a list of news-related web sites.)

Skill 9: Check in with your political party.

Political parties attempt to concentrate and deliver large blocks of money and votes for candidates who share a broad set of ideas and values—often referred to as the party platform. But compliance with a party platform is completely voluntary on the part of candidates and presents a difficult task when one party is trying to coordinate campaigns at different levels of government and across the full spectrum of issues.

Once in office, however, the name of the game is to have a majority of your party on your side. In the case of Congress, the majority party gets to assign offices, make committee assignments, and determine the flow of legislation. The majority party gets to work on much of their party platform. The minority party gets to complain, and stonewall, and fight for every little legislative crumb they can wrangle from the majority—until the next election.

Joining a political party must be done as part of registering to vote— there is a check-off box where you can simply indicate the party of your choice. Note: If your state holds closed primaries, e.g., primary elections where only party members can vote for candidates, you must register as a member of a specific party to vote in the primary elections.

We all know there are Democrats and Republicans, but increasingly in the United States, third-party candidates and independents have begun to win elections to high office, including the cybercharged campaign for governor of Minnesota launched by former wrestler Jesse Ventura. The Internet is helping boost third-party candidates as viable alternatives to the more established parties of the donkey and the elephant.

As with giving money to campaigns, you want to make sure that when you join a political party, you do not become a silent contributor who never expresses your opinion on the issues that are important to you. Political parties are huge and complex organizations, and your interaction with them will depend on how accessible local party officials are and what your time and interest allow. There are numerous ways that a vocal party member can interact with the local party to be heard:

★ **Send E-mail to party officials**

★ **Make a donation online to the party**

★ **Become a local organizer for the party**

★ **Try to become a delegate to the national party convention and actually participate in writing and passing the party platform—especially contributing to an on-line plank—online, if possible.**

★ **Try to become a state elector for the presidential election**

★ **Request that your party post links to your local candidates**

★ **Make sure any PACs that you are involved with are communicating your issues clearly with party officials and enticing local candidates with possible donations**

★ **Run for public office yourself, and request information on filing and receiving money from the party coffers**

Skill 10: Research ballot initiatives.

In addition to voting for actual living, breathing candidates, Americans are increasingly getting to experience the thrill of passing laws on Election Day through ballot initiatives, optimistically known as "direct democracy." Perhaps a more accurate nickname might be "instant democracy."

In certain states, activists can qualify proposed legislation for the general election by gathering signatures. In cases where the legislature is unable or unwilling to legislate, such as with campaign finance laws, this might be a good way of forcing the hand of public policy because it is the only way to pass laws on these issues. In terms of a thoughtful, consensus-building approach to the issues by knowledgeable lawmakers who strive to provide a thorough airing of all sides, instant democracy tends to throw out the baby with the bathwater—avoiding legislative red tape and compromise by reducing complex political issues to simple solutions that do little to deepen the public's understanding of a complex social issue. But without elected officials who instill confidence in the government, the people may opt to self-legislate. What can you do?

If you are going to use your computer to get the dirt on the people who are running for office, you might as well get the dirt on the laws that are running for office too. Ballot initiatives are almost always presented as panaceas, magical cures for what ails us. You are going to have to read more than the campaign literature to be convinced that a potential law is a good idea. Try to ignore the animation and dazzling rhetoric on web sites put up by the initiative backers and focus on the substance of their proposals.

Questions to Ask About Ballot Initiatives

Who Wrote the Ballot Initiative and
Paid to Qualify It for the Ballot?

Don't rely on the grassroots name that is provided like, Really Nice Everyday Americans Who Love Children for Sound Policy. No concerned American spends a million dollars to collect signatures, especially the really nice ones. You can bet there are some seriously vested interests and corporate deep pockets behind every ballot initiative—the question is, are they groups you agree with and trust, or is someone yanking your chain?

How Much Will It Cost?

Legislation at any level of government usually gets evaluated in terms of what it will cost to implement, and sometimes good ideas can be extraordinarily expensive. By avoiding usual legislative channels, such analysis is often absent with ballot initiatives, making it seem like a proposed law will be free and easy to implement. Don't you believe it. Everything costs money. Can you find an accurate, outside estimate as to how much it will cost?

Is It Constitutional?

Another benefit of usual legislative channels is that lawyers who work for state and federal governments write bills so that they conform with the state and federal constitutions and any existing laws that are already in effect. Again, ballot initiatives are often found wanting in this respect. Many ballot initiatives have been passed only to get immediately challenged in court and were ultimately nullified because of conflicts with the Constitution. And you might as well forget any notion that direct democracy, by majority vote, is a legal way to deny any group of Americans their inalienable rights. No law, no matter how much overwhelming support it receives from the general populace, supersedes the Bill of Rights.

Will Supporting the Ballot Initiative Get Your
Elected Officials Off Their Butts?

One of the benefits of instant democracy is that it lets your elected officials know your dissatisfaction with their job performance in a given area. Oftentimes, when people begin circulating petitions for a ballot initiative, legislators will suddenly attempt to pass a similar measure through the usual channels—the advantage being that their legislation will be written to conform with existing law and include financial estimates. For this reason alone, you may want to support a ballot initiative, even if you agree that it is not the healthiest way for a democracy to make law.

Skill 11: Track election returns.

The lawmakers we elect may be disappointing, but at least the elections are exciting. All night long, you can watch a nonstop parade of winners and losers, and the agony of those caught in between. Ecstatic images of victory are tempered by the stoic countenances of defeat while the media attempts to blather itself into clairvoyance. This continues into the wee hours of the morning, when a few of the races around the country are sure to end in a thrilling photo finish. If you tire of watching the talking heads on television, or want to check out some of the local campaigns that don't warrant television coverage, there are several web sites that post election returns so you can follow along as the votes are tallied and posted.

How We Elect the President, or, The Electoral College Made Easy

Your members of city council, state representatives, and members of Congress are all elected by majority, as seems fitting in a system of government that labels itself a democracy. However, the president of the United States gets elected in a slightly different way that is not purely democratic.

- ★ Each state gets a number of electoral votes that equals the total number of the state's representatives in Congress. (DC gets three votes.)

- ★ State political parties prepare for victory by selecting individual "electors" at their nominating conventions.

- ★ The party of the presidential candidate that gets the most popular vote in the state sends all of its electors to Washington following the election. These electors vote for president—usually giving all votes to the candidate of the winning party.

- ★ Three times in American history (1824, 1876, and 1888), the candidate who was elected president by the Electoral College did not win the overall popular vote.

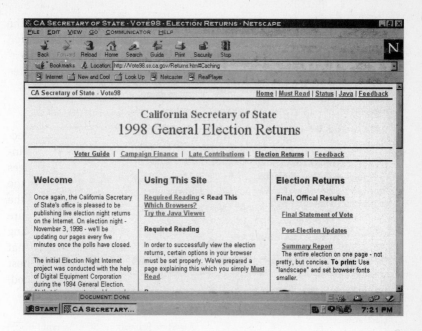

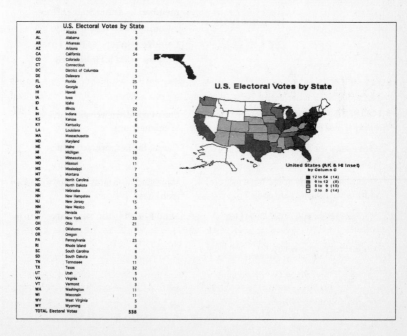

	U.S. Electoral Votes by State	
AK	Alaska	3
AL	Alabama	9
AR	Arkansas	6
AZ	Arizona	8
CA	California	54
CO	Colorado	8
CT	Connecticut	8
DC	District of Columbia	3
DE	Delaware	3
FL	Florida	25
GA	Georgia	13
HI	Hawaii	4
IA	Iowa	7
ID	Idaho	4
IL	Illinois	22
IN	Indiana	12
KS	Kansas	6
KY	Kentucky	8
LA	Louisiana	9
MA	Massachusetts	12
MD	Maryland	10
ME	Maine	4
MI	Michigan	18
MN	Minnesota	10
MO	Missouri	11
MS	Mississippi	7
MT	Montana	3
NC	North Carolina	14
ND	North Dakota	3
NE	Nebraska	5
NH	New Hampshire	4
NJ	New Jersey	15
NM	New Mexico	5
NV	Nevada	4
NY	New York	33
OH	Ohio	21
OK	Oklahoma	8
OR	Oregon	7
PA	Pennsylvania	23
RI	Rhode Island	4
SC	South Carolina	8
SD	South Dakota	3
TN	Tennessee	11
TX	Texas	32
UT	Utah	5
VA	Virginia	13
VT	Vermont	3
WA	Washington	11
WI	Wisconsin	11
WV	West Virginia	5
WY	Wyoming	3
TOTAL Electoral Votes		**538**

And the Winner Is . . . A Candidate Worksheet

Election Stuff

Am I registered to vote?
Do I know where my polling place is?

Do I know the date of the next election?

If I am not going to be in town, or cannot make it to the polls for some other reason, have I requested an absentee ballot?

Secretary of State or State Board of Elections.

Districts and candidates

Do I know what federal, state, and local districts I live in?

Do I know the names of the candidates who are running in the upcoming election?

Secretary of State or State Board of Elections.

★ President   ★ U.S. Senator
★ U.S. Representative   ★ Governor
★ State Senator   ★ State Assembly-member   ★ Other State Offices
★ County Superviser   ★ City Councilmember   ★ Other Local Officers   ★ Ballot Initiatives

Candidate Questions

How has the current officeholder voted on my issues in the past?

Where does the candidate get his or her money from?

What plans does he or she have to address the issues I care about?

How accessible and organized is he or she?

Will he or she get my vote?

State legislative web sites or VoteSmart.org

Center for Responsive Politics

Candidate web sites and News media web sites

Send E-mail to the candidate

Campaigns and Elections Web Sites

Federal Election Commission (FEC)
http://www.fec.gov

Congress created the FEC in 1975 to enforce the statute that governs the financing of federal elections. The commission's six members are appointed by the president and confirmed by the Senate. No more than three commissioners can be members of the same political party. FEC issues advisory opinions in response to petitioned requests for clarification of the federal campaign finance law to a specific, factual situations.

SKILLS

http://www.fec.gov/pages/Voteinst.htm ★ Skill 1: Voter Registration
http://www.fec.gov/1996/sdrindex.htm ★ Skill 3: Campaign Finance
http://www.fec.gov ★ Skill 11: Election Returns

UNIQUE FEATURES

http://herndon 3.sdrdc.com/ao/ ★ "Advisory Opinions" are FEC decisions on specific election-related inquiries.

http://www.fec.gov/pages/citnlist.htm ★ "On-line Guide for Citizens" explains contribution limits and other election-related guidelines.

http://www.fec.gov/finance/finmenu.htm ★ "Campaign Finance Reports" provides the reports and statistics from presidential and congressional races.

Alliance for Better Campaigns
http://www.bettercampaigns.org

Alliance for Better Campaigns
Promoting political campaigns in which the most useful information reaches the the greatest number of citizens in the most engaging ways

Founded in 1998, the "Alliance for Better Campaigns" is dedicated to disseminating election information to the largest number of citizens possible. Their Campaign 2000 Project focuses on getting television networks to air nightly issue-based discussions with candidates before Election Day.

SKILLS

http://www.bettercampaigns.org/ ★ Skill 3: Campaign Finance
http://www.bettercampaigns.org/ ★ Skill 5: E-mail/Contact Info

UNIQUE FEATURES

http://www.bettercampaigns.org/resources.htm ★ "Resources" provides cogent issue briefings on some of the terms and challenges related to campaign finance reform.

Brookings Campaign Finance Pages
http://Brookings.org/gs/cf/cf_hp.htm

THE BROOKINGS INSTITUTION
Washington, D.C.

The Brookings Institution provides independent analysis and background materials on campaign finance reform issues in the United

States. Brookings strives to bring new knowledge to the attention of decision makers and afford scholars a better insight into public policy issues.

SKILLS

http://Brookings.org/gs/cf/cf_hp.htm ★ Skill 3: Campaign Finance

Center for Public Integrity
http://www.publicintegrity.org/main.html
The idea behind the Center for Public Integrity is to create a mechanism in which important, national issues can be investigated and analyzed by talented, responsible journalists and presented in full form reports without the normal time or space limitations of traditional news media.

SKILLS

http://www.publicintegrity.org/main_reports.html ★ Skill 3: Campaign Finance
http://www.publicintegrity.org/main.html ★ Skill 5: E-mail/Contact Info
http://www.publicintegrity.org/main join.html ★ Skill 6: On-line Contributions

UNIQUE FEATURES

http://www.publicintegrity.org/main_reports.html ★ "Investigative Reports" provide in-depth studies on various aspects of campaign finance and governing.

Center for Responsive Politics (CRP)
http://www.opensecrets.org/home/index.asp

opensecrets.org
THE ONLINE SOURCE FOR MONEY IN POLITICS DATA

CRP is a nonpartisan, nonprofit research group that tracks money in U.S. politics and its effect on elections and public policy. The center facilitates computer-based research on campaign finance issues aimed at creating a more educated voter and a more responsive government. This easy-to-navigate site tracks PAC donations to your Congress members and presents them in a user-friendly format packed with information.

SKILLS

http://www.opensecrets.org/home/index.asp ★ Skill 3: Campaign Finance
http://www.opensecrets.org/diykit/index.htm ★ Skill 4: Voting Records/Issue
http://www.opensecrets.org/resources.htm ★ Skill 12: Links

UNIQUE FEATURES

http://www.opensecrets.org/pacs/index.htm ★ PACs section breaks party contributions down by industry. State money maps provide party breakdowns by county in your state (http://www.opensecrets.org/states/index.htm).
http://www.opensecrets.org/2000elect/lookup/AllCands ★ "Donor Lookup" allows you to search FEC contribution data by name, employer, or zip code.
http://www.opensecrets.org/diykit/index.htm ★ "Do It Yourself Congressional Investigation Kit" shows the link between PAC contributions and votes in Congress by issue.

Common Cause
http://commoncause.org
Common Cause is a nonprofit, nonpartisan citizen's lobbying organization that promotes open, honest, and accountable government, and is supported by the dues and contributions of over 250,000 members. Their web site provides extensive information on state campaign finance issues.

SKILLS

http://www.commoncause.org ⋆ Skill 3: Campaign Finance
http://www.commoncause.org/congress/ ⋆ Skill 4: Voting Records/Issue
https://secure4.nmpinc.com/ccauselink/forms/join.htm ⋆ Skill 6: On-line Contributions

UNIQUE FEATURES

http://commoncause.org/laundromat/ ⋆ "Soft Money Laundromat" tabulates soft money donations to political parties by donor and industry.
http://www.commoncause.org/causenet/ ⋆ "CauseNet" provides regular action alerts and updates on campaign finance reform issues.
http://www.commoncause.org/congress/ ⋆ "Know Your Congress" feature provides a financial profile that gives you contact information, campaign finance information, and a voting record on campaign finance issues all on the same screen.

Destination Democracy
http://www.destinationdemocracy.org/intro.html
Benton Foundation web site provides a user-friendly introduction to the world of campaign finance, including an interactive road test designed to educate you about campaign finance and guide you to further study.

SKILLS

http://www.destinationdemocracy.org/intro.html ⋆ Skill 3: Campaign Finance
http://www.destinationdemocracy.org/frameset.html?roadtest.html ⋆ Skill 5: E-mail/ Contact Info

UNIQUE FEATURES

http://www.destinationdemocracy.org/frameset.html?roadtest.html ⋆ Take the "Road Test" to find out where you land on the map of possible campaign finance reforms.
http://www.destinationdemocracy.org/frameset.html?roadtest.html ⋆ "Scenarios and Questions" provide thoughtful frameworks for individuals to identify and explore campaign finance issues.

FECInfo
http://www.tray.com/fecinfo
Created and maintained by the former FEC web master, FECInfo provides much of the same information as the Center for Responsive Politics with fewer charts and graphs.

SKILLS

http://www.tray.com/fecinfo/ ★ Skill 3: Campaign Finance

UNIQUE FEATURES

http://www.tray.com/fecinfo/filing.htm ★ "Next Reports Due" notifies campaigns of upcoming deadlines for filing reports. Site can automatically notify you of filings when they are disclosed by FEC. (http://www.tray.com/fecinfo/ls.htm).

http://www.tray.com/fecinfo/_webl.htm ★ "U.S. Candidate Money Leaders" lists House, Senate, and presidential candidates who have raised the most money.

http://www.tray.com/cgi-win/_corppac.exe ★ "Recently Registered PACs" provides a list of corporations and other entities that have recently stepped into politics.

Public Campaign
http://www.publicampaign.org
Public Campaign is a nonprofit, nonpartisan organization dedicated to sweeping reform to dramatically reduce the role of special interest groups in America's elections and the influence of big contributors in American politics.

SKILLS

http://www.publicampaign.org/ ★ Skill 3: Campaign Finance
http://www.publicampaign.org/ ★ Skill 5: E-mail/Contact Info
http://www.publicampaign.org/regform.html ★ Skill 6: On-line Contributions

UNIQUE FEATURES

http://www.publicampaign.org/20things/20things.html ★ "20 Things You Can Do to Clean Up Elections" gives easy, practical actions that campaign finance reform advocates can take.

http://www.publicampaign.org/goldenleash.html ★ "Golden Leash Awards" are presented in recognition of outrageous favors, access, or trade-offs coinciding with special interest campaign contributions.

http://www.publicampaign.org/pubop.html ★ "The Power of Public Opinion" gathers polls on campaign finance reform.

Public Citizen Campaign Finance Reform Pages
http://www.publiccitizen.org
Founded by Ralph Nader in 1971, Public Citizen bills itself the consumer's eyes and ears in Washington. Public Citizen fights on a number of fronts including safer drugs and medical devices, cleaner and safer energy sources, a cleaner environment, fair trade, and a more open and democratic government. "Campaign Finance Reform" pages provide reports and fact sheets on campaign finance reform and action alerts.

Protecting Health, Safety and Democracy
Since 1971
President Joan Claybrook
Founded by Ralph Nader

SKILLS

http://www.citizen.org/congress/reform/refhome.html ★ Skill 3: Campaign Finance

ELECTION NEWS

C-SPAN Campaign 2000 Pages
http://www.c-span.org/campaign2000
The C-SPAN web site provides election news, commentary, and interaction for election 2000.

SKILLS

http://www.c-span.org/campaign2000/speeches.asp ★ Skill 2: Candidate and Ballot Info

http://www.c-span.org/campaign2000/speeches.asp ★ Skill 4: Voting Records/Issue

http://www.c-span.org/campaign2000/speeches.asp ★ Skill 11: Election Returns

UNIQUE FEATURES

http://www.c-span.org/campaign2000/advertising.asp ★ "Archival Campaign Ads" provides access to ads from the Political Communication Center at the University of Oklahoma, a repository of over 55,000 television and radio campaign ads from 1936 to present (http://www.ou.edu/pccenter/archives/archival.html).

http://www.c-span.org/campaign2000/search/ ★ "Campaign 2000 Video Search" uses groundbreaking technology to search video library by key words.

Political Humor on About.com
http://politicalhumor.about.com/entertainment/
politicalhumor/?REDIR_
Parodies aplenty and other mischievous fun reside in this collection of web links that connect users to political humor on the Internet.

UNIQUE FEATURES

http://politicalhumor.about com/entertainment/politicalhumor/mpchat.htm ★ Test your own one-liners in the "Political Humor Chat Room."

ROLL CALL Politics Page
http://www.rollcall.com/election/map.html
Capitol Hill's newspaper gives district-by-district analysis of each congressional race. An easy graphic interface using a point-and-click map of the United States gets you to the information you want.

The Hill Campaign 2000
http://www.hillnews.com/campaign.html
The Hill newspaper organizes its election-related coverage and provides links to state races, presidential contenders, open congressional seats, and Senate terms.

SKILLS

http://www.hillnews.com/campaign/trail.html#trail2 ★ Skill 2: Candidate and Ballot Info
http://www.hillnews.com/campaign/trail.html#trail2 ★ Skill 3: Campaign Finance
http://www.hillnews.com/campaign/trail.html#trail2 ★ Skill 5: E-mail/Contact Info
http://www.hillnews.com/campaign/trail.html#trail2 ★ Skill 9: Political Parties
http://www.hillnews.com/campaign/trail.html#trail2 ★ Skill 12: Links

UNIQUE FEATURES

http://www.hillnews.com/resources/openseats.html ★ "Open Seats" provides a list of retiring, deceased, or leaving House members. The schedule of Senate terms can be found at (http://www.hillnews.com/resources/senateterms.html).

POLITICAL PARTIES

Democratic National Committee (DNC)
http://www.democrats.org/hq/index.html
The DNC was established in 1848 and is now the oldest continuing party committee in the United States and the world. The DNC plans the party's presidential nominating convention, promotes the election of party candidates, and works with national, state, and local party organizations.

SKILLS

http://www.democrats.org/action/index.html ★ Skill 1: Voter Registration
http://www.democrats.org/contact.html ★ Skill 5: E-mail/Contact Info
http://www.democrats.org/support/ ★ Skill 6: On-line Contributions
http://www.democrats.org/hq/index.html ★ Skill 9: Political Parties

UNIQUE FEATURES

http://www.dems2000.com/ ★ Democratic convention and delegate information.
http://www.democrats.org/dweb/index.html ★ "The Democratic Web" provides links to state and local party affiliates and candidates.
http://www.democrats.org/action/training/index.html ★ Seminars are offered to would-be candidates and campaign managers.

Libertarian Party
http://www.lp.org

From its modest beginning twenty-four years ago in Colorado, the Libertarian Party now claims to be the third largest political party in the United States. Libertarians believe the answer to America's political problems is to rely on a free-market economy with little or no government intervention from taxes, to foreign policy, to business regulation, and personal freedoms.

SKILLS

http://www.lp.org/lp-contact.html ⋆ Skill 5: E-mail/Contact Info
http://www.lp.org/lp-membership.html ⋆ Skill 6: On-line Contributions
http://www.lp.org/lp-curr.html ⋆ Skill 7: Volunteer Information
http://www.lp.org/ ⋆ Skill 9: Political Parties

UNIQUE FEATURES

http://www.lp.org/lp-dirs.html ⋆ "Directories and Lists" provides links to state and local affiliates and candidates.

http://www.lp.org/conv/2000/ ⋆ "Year 2000 National Convention" provides links to the party's nominating convention.

http://www.self-gov.org/lp-quiz.shtml ⋆ "World's Smallest Political Quiz" tells where you reside on the political spectrum, left, right, or . . . libertarian.

Reform Party
http://www.reformparty.org

In 1992, a self-made Texas billionaire named Ross Perot spent over $60 million of his own money to run for president as an independent candidate. His organization, "United We Stand America," became the Reform Party, an increasingly viable third-party alternative in U.S. elections. The Reform Party is dedicated to reconnecting citizens with their government, term limits, and involving more people in the political process.

SKILLS

http://www.reformparty.org/support/vote.html ⋆ Skill 1: Voter Registration
http://www.reformparty.org/comments.html ⋆ Skill 5: E-mail/Contact Info
https://secure.com-us.net/reformparty/donate.html ⋆ Skill 6: On-line Contributions
http://www.reformparty.org/ ⋆ Skill 9: Political Parties

UNIQUE FEATURES

http://www.reformparty.org/convention2000/ ⋆ "2000 National Convention" provides information on the nominating convention.

http://www.reformparty.org/media/ircchat.html ⋆ "IRC Chat" room hosts nightly discussions for party members.

http://www.reformparty.org/candidates2000/ ⋆ "Candidates" provides links by state to Reform Party campaigns.

Republican National Committee (RNC)
http://www.rnc.org
Since its inception, the Republican Party has been at the forefront of the fight for individuals' rights in opposition to a large,
bloated government. Today, the RNC champions such issues as
reducing the size of government, streamlining the bureaucracy,
and returning power to the states.

SKILLS

http://www.rnc.org/StateInformation.asp?FormMode=Vote ★ Skill 1: Voter Registration
http://www.rnc.org/ContactUs.asp ★ Skill 5: E-mail/Contact Info
**http://www.rnc.org/Activist_Action.asp?FormMode=Activist&LinkType=Combo&ID=&Sec
tion=1** ★ Skill 6: On-line Contributions
http://www.rnc.org/volunteer.asp ★ Skill 7: Volunteer Information
http://www.rnc.org/NewsRoom_Action.asp?FormMode=Newsorgs ★ Skill 8: Media Links
http://www.rnc.org/ ★ Skill 9: Political Parties

UNIQUE FEATURES

**http://www.rnc.org/ConventionNews_Action.asp?FormMode=ConventionNews&LinkType
=Section&Section=0** ★ Convention news provides information and links on the
nominating convention.
http://www.rnc.org/directory.asp ★ "GOP Directory" provides links to state and local
affiliate parties and candidates.
http://www.rnc.org/NewsRoom_Action.asp?FormMode ★ "GOP University" provides
seminars and training to candidates and campaign managers.

POLLING

SelectSmart.com
http://www.selectsmart.com/PRESIDENT
Interactive on-line polling company matches your stands on the hottest
political issues with candidates for the White House.

SKILLS

CURTANDERSON@SelectSmart.com ★ Skill 5: E-mail/Contact Info

The Gallup Organization
**http://www.gallup.com/poll/pol_
elections.asp**
Premier polling organization provides results
of polls on various topics related to politics
and elections.

SKILLS

http://www.gallup.com/contact/pollcontact.asp ★ Skill 5: E-mail/Contact Info
http://www.gallup.com/poll/pol_elections.asp ★ Skill 10: Ballot Initiatives

UNIQUE FEATURES

http://www.gallup.com/poll/social_issues.asp ★ "Social Issues" and "Domestic Policy" provide polling information on social issues.

http://www.gallup.com/poll/business&economy.asp ★ "Business" and "The Economy" provide polling information on economic issues.

PRESIDENTIAL CANDIDATES

Al Gore
http://www.algore2000.com
Democratic presidential nominee's web site.

SKILLS

http://www.algore2000.com/vote/ ★ Skill 1: Voter Registration
http://www.algore2000.com/agenda/index.html ★ Skill 4: Voting Records/Issue
http://www.algore2000.com/townhall/ ★ Skill 5: E-mail/Contact Info
http://gore2000.org/secure/donate.html ★ Skill 6: On-line Contributions
http://algore2000.com/getinvolved/index.html ★ Skill 7: Volunteer Information

George W. Bush
http://georgewbush.com
Republican presidential nominee's web site.

SKILLS

http://www.georgewbush.com/issues/index.html
★ Skill 4: Voting Records/Issue
http://www.georgewbush.com/contact/index.html ★ Skill 5: E-mail/Contact Info
http://www.georgewbush.com/contribute/index.html ★ Skill 6: On-line Contributions
http://www.georgewbush.com/volunteer/index.html ★ Skill 7: Volunteer Information

The Great Internet Debate 2000
http://welcome.to/2000Debate
Americans for the Restoration of Constitutional Government developed this web site that posts views on the issues and links to the web sites of over twenty-two presidential hopefuls. This is a site where you can check out those enigmatic candidates who fall through the cracks of the major media.

SKILLS

http://welcome.to/2000Debate/ ★ Skill 4: Voting Records/Issue

Issues 2000
http://www.issues2000.org
Site provides White House candidate comments from news wires grouped according to issue topic. Icons used to provide candidate positions at a glance.

SKILLS

http://www.issues2000.org/ ★ Skill 4: Voting Records/Issue
http://www.issues2000.org/join.htm ★ Skill 5: E-mail/Contact Info
http://www.issues2000.org/join.htm ★ Skill 6: On-line Contributions

UNIQUE FEATURES

http://www.issues2000.org/Recent.htm#Top ★ "Most Recent Quotations" page can keep you up-to-date on all the most recent issues.

SUPERSITE

Latino Vote 2000
http://www.starmedia.com/latinovote2000
Spanish language election supersite provides electoral information and links to Latino, Latina, and other Spanish-speaking monolingual Americans.

Politics.com
http://politics.com
Electoral supersite provides background information on candidates, polling, humor, news, and financial information. This is a for-profit site that hopes to make its money through advertising to the politically interested.

SKILLS

http://politics.com/Candidates/Candidates.frame.htm ★ Skill 2: Candidate and Ballot Info
http://politics.com/money/money_frame.htm ★ Skill 3: Campaign Finance
http://politics.com/About/About_frame.htm ★ Skill 5: E-mail/Contact Info
http://politics.com/news/news_frame.htm ★ Skill 8: Media Links
http://politics.com/Directory/Directory_frame.htm ★ Skill 9: Political Parties
http://politics.com/Directory/Directory_frame.htm ★ Skill 12: Links

UNIQUE FEATURES

http://politics.com/ ★ "Watch the Pile Grow" money counter shows how much money is being raised by American candidates to spend on campaigns.
http://politics.com/money/money_frame.htm ★ Campaign Finance Primer provides definitions and other background information on campaign finance reform.

Votenet
http://www.votenet.com
Supersite offers political headlines and a special section for minority politics. Additional links provide campaign finance information.

SKILLS

http://votenet.com/ ★ Skill 3: Campaign Finance
http://votenet.com/ ★ Skill 8: Media Links
http://votenet.com/ ★ Skill 9: Political Parties
http://votenet.com/ ★ Skill 12: Links

UNIQUE FEATURES

http://www.votenet.com ★ "Minority News Daily" provides political information of interest to minorities.

4Politics
http://www.4politics.com
News and links can be found on the political page of this web engine.

SKILLS

http://www.4politics.com/ ★ Skill 8: Media Links
http://www.4politics.com/ ★ Skill 12: Links

America Online (AOL)
(members only)
While most Internet search engines provide an assortment of links and news clippings for their

users, America Online, favored by millions of Americans as their gateway to the Internet, provides a substantial amount of original content for its users, including chat rooms, E-mail interfaces, and special features.

UNIQUE FEATURES

(members only) ★ Write the White House provides Q & A with the Executive Branch.

Democracy Network
http://www.dnet.org
One of the best organized, most easily navigated, and interesting political web sites, the Democracy Network allows candidates and elected officials to post statements for public review. Ballot information, parties, candidates, issue positions, elected officials, and news media are organized by state or zip code.

http://www.dnet.org/index.shtml ★ Skill 1: Voter Registration
http://www.dnet.org/index.shtml ★ Skill 2: Candidate and Ballot Info
http://www.dnet.org/index.shtml ★ Skill 4: Voting Records/Issue
http://www.dnet.org/index.shtml ★ Skill 5: E-mail/Contact Info
http://www.dnet.org/index.shtml ★ Skill 8: Media Links
http://www.dnet.org/index.shtml ★ Skill 9: Political Parties
http://www.dnet.org/index.shtml ★ Skill 10: Ballot Initiatives
http://www.dnet.org/index.shtml ★ Skill 11: Election Returns

ELECnet

http://www.iupui.edu/
~epackard/eleclink.html

ELECnet
election administration resources on the internet

Elecnet provides election-related resources on the Internet and allows
users to locate election dates, times, and locations by state.

SKILLS

http://www.iupui.edu/~epackard/eleclink.html ★ Skill 1: Voter Registration
http://www.iupui.edu/~epackard/eleclink.html ★ Skill 2: Candidate and Ballot Info

Election Connection

http://www.gspm.org/electcon
George Washington University listing of campaign web sites
for the U.S. House of Representatives, U.S. Senate, and gover-
norships by state.

THE
ELECTION
CONNECTION

SKILLS

http://www.gspm.org/electcon/ ★ Skill 2: Candidate and Ballot Info

FREEDOMCHANNEL

http://www.freedomchannel.com

FREEDOMCHANNEL

FREEDOMCHANNEL is a free, nonpartisan site that
provides access to video-on-demand of gubernatorial candidates, federal candidates, and
issue groups. FREEDOM CHANNEL allows the would-be voter to compare the video statements of local candidates on the issues that they care about.

SKILLS

http://www.freedomchannel.com/votereg/index.html ★ Skill 1: Voter Registration
http://www.freedomchannel.com/vod/candidateissues/index.html
  ★ Skill 4: Voting Records/Issue
http://www.freedomchannel.com/forms/feedback.html ★ Skill 5: E-mail/Contact Info
http://www.freedomchannel.com/gateway/party_sites.html ★ Skill 9: Political Parties

UNIQUE FEATURES

http://www.freedomchannel.com/almanac_of_amer_pol.htm ⋆ "Almanac of American Politics" provides well-written biographies of incumbent elected officials and also provides demographic and voting trend information about your state and congressional district.

http://www.freedomchannel.com/vod/campaignspots/index.html ⋆ "Campaign Spots/Ads" allow you to peruse candidate commericals on your own time.

http://www.freedomchannel.com/todays/index.html ⋆ "Today's Interview" provides a brief Q & A with leading candidates and executives from issue groups.

GOVOTE.com
http://www.govote.com
Voting supersite provides links to voter registration, political information, and news.

SKILLS

http://www.govote.com/resources/voter_registration.asp ⋆ Skill 1: Voter Registration
http://www.govote.com/ ⋆ Skill 4: Voting Records/Issue
http://www.govote.com/about.htm ⋆ Skill 5: E-mail/Contact Info
http://www.govote.com/news/index.asp ⋆ Skill 8: Media Links
http://www.govote.com/resources/political_parties.asp ⋆ Skill 9: Political Parties
http://www.govote.com/resources/voter_registration.asp ⋆ Skill 12: Links

League of Women Voters
http://www.lwv.org
The League of Women Voters is a non-partisan, political organization that encourages the informed and active

participation of citizens in government, whatever their gender, and influences public policy through education and advocacy. The national site provides links to state chapters where detailed local election information is available.

SKILLS

http://lwv.org/electioncentral/registration.htm ⋆ Skill 1: Voter Registration
http://lwv.org/electioncentral/voters_online.htm ⋆ Skill 2: Candidate and Ballot Info
http://www.lwv.org/lwvwebs.html ⋆ Skill 5: E-mail/Contact Info
http://www.lwv.org/cntribu.html ⋆ Skill 6: On-line Contributions
http://www.lwv.org/lwvwebs.html ⋆ Skill 7: Volunteer Information

UNIQUE FEATURES

http://www.lwv.org/legpri.html ⋆ "Legislative Priorities" works to educate and activite citizens about election-related laws such as campaign finance reform.

http://lwv.org/electioncentral/publications.htm ⋆ "Publications" provides basic citizen information from how to pick a candidate and follow your issues to how to watch a debate.

POLITICAL RESOURCES ON-LINE
http://politicalresources.com
POLITICAL RESOURCE DIRECTORY

POLITICAL RESOURCES ON-LINE
Tools for Candidate, Issue and Corporate Campaigns

publisher maintains this site that provides links to political business and offers some useful links for the layperson as well. Voters can search for campaign links by state.

SKILLS

http://politicalresources.com/ ★ Skill 2: Candidate and Ballot Info
info@politicalresources.com ★ Skill 5: E-mail/Contact Info
http://politicalresources.com/ ★ Skill 9: Political Parties

UNIQUE FEATURES

http://politicalresources.com/ ★ "Calendar" provides a monthly list of up-coming state and national political events, including primary elections.

Politics1
http://www.politics1.com

Politics1 is published and edited by the former assistant attorney general of Florida, a confessed political junkie. This political supersite provides links to various campaigns and news sites as well as on on-line newsletter, the *Politics1 Report,* that provides updates on election news.

Politics1.com

SKILLS

publisher@politics1.com ★ Skill 5: E-mail/Contact Info
http://www.politics1.com/news.htm ★ Skill 8: Media Links
http://www.politics1.com/parties.htm ★ Skill 9: Political Parties

UNIQUE FEATURES

http://www.politics1.com/states.htm ★ "The States: Races & Links" provides links to local races, political parties, and media.
http://www.politics1.com/newsletter.htm ★ *Politics1 Report* newsletter delivers the timely election news blurbs to your on-line mailbox.
http://www.politics1.com/issues.htm ★ "Issues & Debates" provides links to ideological organizations categorized by both "left" and "right."

Project Vote Smart
http://www.vote-smart.org

Project Vote Smart

Project Vote Smart researches, tracks, and provides independent factual information on over thirteen thousand candidates and elected officials. Voting records, campaign issue positions, performance evaluations by special interests, campaign contributions, background information, and contact information are available on its web site.

SKILLS

http://www.vote-smart.org/index.phtml ★ Skill 1: Voter Registration

http://www.vote-smart.org/index.phtml ★ Skill 2: Candidate and Ballot Info.

http://www.vote-smart.org/ce/?titlehead=Candidates+@+Elected+Officials&checking=#finance ★ Skill 3: Campaign Finance

http://www.vote-smart.org/congresstrack/votes/?checking= ★ Skill 4: Voting Records/Issue

http://www.vote-smart.org/about/help/membership.phtml?checking= ★ Skill 6: On-line Contributions

http://www.vote-smart.org/about/help/vol_int.phtml?checking= ★ Skill 7: Volunteer Information

http://www.vote-smart.org/issues/news.phtml?checking= ★ Skill 8: Media Links

http://www.vote-smart.org/organizations/POLITICAL_PARTIES/?checking= ★ Skill 9: Political Parties

http://www.vote-smart.org/state/sindex.phtml?checking=&info_type=E ★ Skill 10: Ballot Initiatives

UNIQUE FEATURES

http://www.vote-smart.org/speeches/index.phtml?checking= ★ "Presidential Speech" search allows you to scan public statements for references to the issues that interest you.

http://www.vote-smart.org/about/data.phtml#NPAT?checking= ★ "National Political Aptitude Test" is a nonpartisan questionnaire soliciting candidate positions on current issues that attempts to accurately guage their positions.

http://www.vote-smart.org/ce/ratekeys.phtml?checking= ★ "Performance Evaluations" by special interest groups provide one-stop shopping for voting report cards on a wide variety of issues.

Rock the Vote
http://www.rockthevote.org
Founded by record executives in 1990, Rock the Vote encourages young people to register to vote at concert venues and through the use of public service announcements that feature rock and movie stars.

SKILLS

http://www.rockthevote.org/main_register.html ★ Skill 1: Voter Registration

http://www.rockthevote.org/main_inside.html ★ Skill 5: E-mail/Contact Info

http://www.rockthevote.org/main_volunteer.html ★ Skill 7: Volunteer Information

VoxCap campaign 2000 Subchannel
http://www.voxcap.com/
VoxCap's election 2000 update provides news, campaign links, and member-driven "clubs" to discuss the issues and candidates.

SKILLS

http://www.voxcap.com/anon/_scape/subchannels/subchannel110.dhtml
  ★ Skill 2: Candidate and Ballot Info

http://www.voxcap.com/anon/_scape/subchannels/subchannel110.dhtml
  ★ Skill 4: Voting Records/Issue

http://voxcap.com/contact.asp ★ Skill 5: E-mail/Contact Info

UNIQUE FEATURES

http://www.voxcap.com/clubs/ ★ "Make Your Own Club" feature allows you to attract like-minded people to your own web page, which can be customized with news articles, links, and chat features.

Web, White, & Blue
http://www.webwhiteblue.org
Web White & Blue was launched by the Markle Foundation and Harvard's Shorenstein Center to provide easy access to election information on the World Wide Web. It is a well-organized hyperlink supersite.

SKILLS

http://www.webwhiteblue.org/talkback.html ★ Skill 5: E-mail/Contact Info
http://www.webwhiteblue.org/electionnews.html ★ Skill 8: Media Links

Voter.com
http://www.voter.com
Voting supersite allows you to customize your political information according to electoral races, issues, and news. Official positions and other primary resources supplement the extensive on-line polls.

SKILLS

http://www.voter.com/voter/myelections/1,2258,1~22--,00.html ★ Skill 2: Candidate and Ballot Info

http://www.voter.com/voter/mygroups/1,2231,1~20--,00.html ★ Skill 4: Voting Records/Issue

http://www.voter.com/voter/info/contacts/1,2289,1~30--,00.html ★ Skill 5: E-mail/Contact Info

UNIQUE FEATURES

http://www.voter.com/mygroups/ ★ "My Groups" instantly connects you to advocacy organizations that you are interested in.

Chapter Three

The White House
and Administration

★

Introduction

Lancer. Searchlight. Dasher. Rawhide. These are the screen names of an earlier time—the monikers that the Secret Service has used to refer to the president of the United States of America.

The president is our fearless leader, incorrigible scoundrel, and occupant of one of the most famous addresses in the world. He (or she) gets the house, gets the title, gets the face time, but does not get to be king.

The president is our nation's father, who potentially gets disowned by his children every four years, a kingless king whose court openly ridicules him and thwarts his efforts, whose own judges can negate the bills he signs into law, but a man who is surrounded by enough pomp and circumstance, and limos, to make even the most self-assured movie stars envious of his ability to make an entrance.

Despite the president's clearly defined and limited formal powers—signing or vetoing legislation, appointing judges and ambassadors—the presidency can provide tremendous influence for the man or woman with vision and drive, and charisma enough to make an enormous staff do his bidding, keep Congress off his back, and generate favorable notices in the media. But he must have a thick skin. A very thick skin. The thicker, the better.

Millions of people who find themselves clicking around cyberspace seem to make their way to the White House web site as an initial, if not frequent, destination. The White House web site seems a comforting outpost in the virtual world of the future—the electronic equivalent of finding an American flag planted on the moon: There may not be water or oxygen, but if we find anybody living, at least we can talk about football.

For many Americans, the mansion at 1600 Pennsylvania Avenue represents the sum total of their knowledge of and interest in American government. This conception may be narrow, but it is not irrational. The president of the United States might really be the leader of the free world. It is also his job to communicate the goings-on in Washington and the rest of the world to us Americans. And besides that, the president is usually an interesting character (sometimes too interesting).

The White House web site makes it possible for any American to cut across the south lawn and enter the vaunted rooms of the presidential mansion where the business of the nation is carried out.

Since the White House web site was launched by President Bill Clinton and Vice President Al Gore on October 20, 1994, it has received over 120 million hits, and the president now regularly receives upward of 250,000 E-mail messages per year. In addition to serving as a link between the people and papers associated with the presidency, the White House web site also connects interested citizens with other on-line resources made available by the U.S. federal government.

The Presidential Job Description

Strong Arm of the Party

As the holder of the highest elected office in the land and Big Cheese of a vast federal bureaucracy, the White House is major political spoils for the political party that attains it. The president is often expected to reward the many interests that helped get him elected by staying true to the party platform and to use the media to help define the opposition party as bumbling, incompetent, and out-of-touch.

CEO

Upon entering the White House, the president becomes the manager of one of the largest organizations on the planet, maybe the universe. Managing this vast bureaucracy is a job that is dropped in his lap like a two-ton weight. It is undoubtedly too much for any one man to personally oversee all of the projects of the federal government. The president has extensive amounts of labor at his disposal and impressive amounts of information. His executive managers are referred to as his "cabinet" and consist of the men and women appointed to oversee the federal departments. The cabinet helps keep the president informed about the work of their various departments, and, in turn, transmits the overall vision and goals of the president back to their staff.

The Great Communicator/Mourner-in-Chief

The president is the mouthpiece for the nation and our national father figure. During any significant domestic or international crisis, the president is expected to give voice to what we, as Americans, feel—with dignity and sincerity.

Leader of the Free World

The president is the commander-in-chief of the American armed forces. He has one of the largest and most potentially destructive armies in the galaxy at his disposal. Never mind that only Congress can declare war—this prohibition has not stopped several presidents from engaging in police actions and other skirmishes with bombs. Aside from our armed forces, the president also has the power to nominate ambassadors to countries all over the globe, where he is looked to as a guardian of democracy, human rights, and, increasingly, the world economy. He is alternatively a feared leader and reassuring figure to people the world over. And then there is the CIA, too, which is secret.

Shameless Self-Promoter

Anybody who wants to run for president in the current political climate of tabloid-oriented media coverage and negative, destructive campaign rhetoric has got to have impressive drive to say the least—a thirst for immortality, a desire to make one's mark on history itself. These motives may sound a bit grand, but remember, presidents strive to be the employee-of-the-century. Take their aggressiveness with a grain of salt—that is, unless they start authorizing breaking into some other guy's campaign office.

Skill 1: Read presidential documents.

The President is the CEO of the largest financial entity in the nation (except, perhaps, for the Microsoft Corporation). The federal government employs over 3 Million people, owns more than five-hundred thousand buildings on over seven-hundred million acres of land, and manages a budget well in excess of 1 trillion dollars per year.

When major corporations change their workplace policies, it can land them on the front page of the business section. Such actions often act as bellwethers of things to come in the working world in general. Likewise, how the president runs "his business," exercises an enormous influence on how Americans relate to each other in the marketplace and at work. The president, through presidential orders, can, in effect, initiate large-scale workplace demonstration projects without having to brave the political maelstrom of passing legislation through Congress.

When the president makes a management decision, the working lives of millions of Americans can have their professional lives altered, or restructured, or reprioritized, often years before state and federal government seriously consider such changes. Take, for example, President Clinton's Executive Order regarding work accommodations for the mentally ill in 1999. In that single move, the, president sent an order that mental ill-

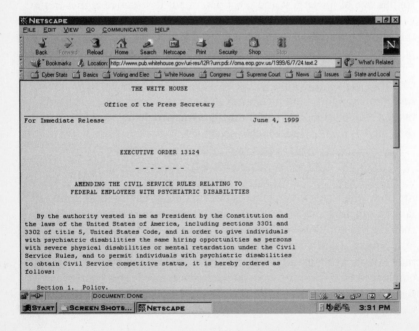

ness was not to be avoided or punished in the workplace, but acknowl-edged and accommodated, if possible—at a time when state government and the federal government were not remotely considering enacting such provisions. In short, executive orders are significant policy tools, even if they do not carry the weight of law.

In addition to issuing Executive Orders, the president is charged with communicating the day-to-day business of the federal government to the American people and to act as both figurehead and domestic com-municator on matters of international policy. This work is largely con-ducted by issuing press releases, speeches, and remarks, and by sharing similar documents from White House staff.

For the first time in history, the Executive Orders of the president and a wide range of other White House documents are available for your search and review at the White House web site. If you would like, you can even subscribe on line and automatically receive copies of all of the, presi-dent's Executive Orders as they are signed, or any of the multitude of White House communications that are produced (including speeches, press releases, presidential appointments, and other documents).

(See "Sidebar, On-line subscription tips," for information on how to manage automated E-mail, page 68.)

Executive Acts by the President

Appointments	Executive appointment to a federal position.
Convening	Calls for a government-sponsored meeting.
Declaration	Declares that some current state of affairs warrants government intervention.
Delegation	Give an official or an agency presidential authority in specific situations.
Directive	Directs officials and agencies to take some actions.
Executive Order	Orders procedural actions or organizational changes in federal departments.
Nomination	Nominates a person for a federal position.
Pardon	Pardons an individual for a crime.
Proclamation	Denotes a special occasion of observance.
Finding	Reports on the state of affairs, often in context of compliance with established law.

Skill 2: Send E-mail to the president.

The White House web site makes it easy for you to send E-mail to the president, the vice president, or the first lady. So easy it threatens to replace the most famous address in the world (1600 Pennsylvania Avenue) with "whitehouse.gov".

But what would the awesome experience of communicating your thoughts with the president of the United States be without some bureaucratic red tape? Sending an E-mail message to the, president involves using an extensive on-line form that helps identify who you are, where you live, and why you are writing. These forms are not a surveillance tool used to pry into your life, but a sophisticated routing system that makes sure your comments are sent along the proper channels for reading and responding. Many of the questions asked provide the White House with information you may forget to include in an E-mail—essential information for effective communication with the president.

Questions include whether you support or oppose specific pieces of legislation, or whether you are writing as a single, concerned citizen or are representing an organization. Do not be shy about admitting that you are "merely" a concerned citizen. Individuals who are not paid to work on an issue convey a sense of urgency and a credibility that paid professionals cannot.

Your street address is also requested so that the White House can send you a written response via regular mail—both as a formality and for security reasons. Online, you will receive an E-mail acknowledgment that your comments were received, but a substantive reply is sent through the United States postal system. The White House abides by a strict code of confidentiality (see below) that is available online, and insists that any information you provide about yourself will not be used for any reason other than to document your inquiry and to respond to it.

The White House Web Site Privacy Policy

Thank you for visiting the White House web site and reviewing our privacy policy. Our privacy policy is clear: We will collect no personal information about you when you visit our web site unless you choose to provide that information to us.

Here is how we handle information about your visit to our web site:

Information Collected and Stored Automatically

If you do nothing during your visit but browse through the web site, read pages, or download information, we will gather and store certain information about your visit automatically. This information does not identify you personally. We automatically collect and store only the following information about your visit:

> **1.** The Internet domain (for example, "xcomany.com," if you use a private Internet access account or, "yourschool.edu," if you connect from a university's domain) and IP address (an IP address is a number that is automatically assigned to your computer whenever you are surfing the Web) from which you access our web site;
>
> **2.** The type of browser and operating system used to access our site;
>
> **3.** The date and time you access our site;
>
> **4.** The pages you visit; and
>
> **5.** If you linked to the White House web site from another web site, the address of that web site.

We use this information to help us make our site more useful to visitors—to learn about the number of visitors to our site and the types of technology our visitors use. We do not track or record information about individuals and their visits.

If You Send Us Personal Information

If you choose to provide us with personal information—as in an E-mail to the president, vice president, or someone else, or by filling out a form with your personal information and submitting it to us through our web site—we use that information to respond to your message and to help us get you the information you have requested. We treat E-mails the same way we treat letters sent to the White House. We are required to maintain many documents under the Presidential Records Act for historical purposes, but we do not collect personal information for any purpose other than to respond to you. We only share the information you give us with another government agency if your inquiry relates to that agency or as otherwise required by law. Moreover, we do not create individual profiles with the information you provide or give it to any private organizations.

The White House does not collect information for commercial marketing.

Links to Other Sites

Our web site has links to many other federal agencies. In a few cases we link to private organizations, with their permission. Before leaving the White House web site, a page will appear informing you that you are leaving our server. Once you link to another site, you are subject to the privacy policy of the new site.

Kid's Page

We at the White House are especially concerned about protecting children's privacy. We hope parents and teachers are involved in children's Internet explorations. It is particularly important for parents to guide their children when children are asked to provide personal information online. The White house home page for kids encourages children to send E-mail messages to the White House. We ask children to type their name, E-mail address, and home mailing address as part of their message so that we can respond personally to them.

Providing this information is entirely optional. We specifically ask children to get their parents' permission before providing any information online—at our site or any other site—and hope parents will always be involved in those decisions. Most importantly, when children do provide information through the White House web site, it is only used to enable us to respond to the writer and not to create profiles of children.

Skill 3: Listen to the weekly radio address and other multimedia.

Ever since Pres. Franklin Delano Roosevelt harnessed the power of the airwaves to reassure a despairing nation that the federal government was in touch, working hard, and really cared about the daily struggles of its citizens, there has been enduring interest in regular communications from the president to "the people." Besides, the weekly radio address is a great opportunity to really stick it to the other party.

Radio is not without its limitations. Specific programs are often difficult to locate on the dial unless you are lucky enough to run into them between soccer practice and the grocery store. The White House web site makes it possible to listen to the president's weekly radio addresses at your convenience in just about any location. A transcript of the weekly radio address is also provided so that you don't have to suffer through any pregnant pauses.

(Note: Listening to the weekly radio address requires that you download and install the RealAudio Player. See Appendix for more details, or follow the instructions at the White House web site.)

What's in It for Me? Why You Might Want to Check Out the Weekly Radio Address of a President from the Other Party

The Presidency Is an Extremely Powerful and Influential Office No Matter What You Feel About the Person Who Occupies It

Quite aside from its potential as a bully pulpit, the president staffs and directs the federal departments that oversee everything from agriculture to education to defense to health to the IRS. The president's actions have a way of affecting your life, even if you did not vote for him.

It Is a Good Place to Begin Your Opposition Research

The White House has more statistics, more staff, and more lawyers at its disposal than the best-heeled political association in town, and they can all work together to generate the strongest possible defense of their policy initiatives. If you can knock a hole in the president's arguments, you just might have a case.

The President Has the Ability, Through Sheer Media Attention, to Push the Agenda in Congress

However much you disagree with the president's outlook on the issues you care about, it is often difficult to focus the attention of Congress on an issue until the president opens his big mouth about them, usually by taking a potshot at the inactivity of the opposition party in the media.

You Probably Don't Disagree with Everything the President Says

A sad phenomenon of a two-party political system is that members of one party will often sacrifice legitimate solutions on the altar of opposition polarization and demonization. To be sure, some politicians are so concerned with being at odds with the other party that they simply refuse to acknowledge good ideas when they come along. If you are interested in solutions rather than party-based mudslinging, it is important that you identify areas of agreement and compromise and demand that your own legislators put policy ahead of partisan politics. Checking out the weekly radio address is an essential tool to have if you are to effectively gauge the sincerity of your political organizations and your elected officials in finding solutions—rather than perpetuating skirmishes.

Skill 4: Download the federal budget from OMB.

The Office of Management and Budget (OMB) is one of the most powerful legislative tools at the president's disposal. OMB was established to help manage and coordinate the work of the myriad federal departments that make up our national government. OMB's central role also puts it in charge of supervising the federal budget—OMB controls the purse strings.

A projection of the federal budget is annually conducted by OMB and submitted with the president's State of the Union address to Congress. It is important to remember that OMB's budget recommendation is nothing more than an extremely detailed suggestion and does not carry

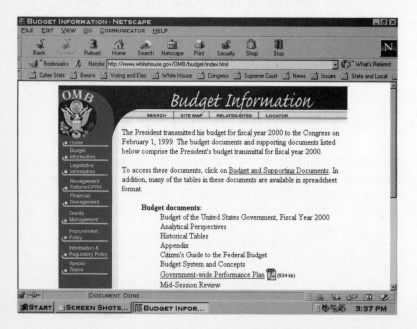

the force of law. It is, however, the president's best chance to justify increases in programs that he deems important.

The president's budget request is a massive document requiring reams of paper, usually taking the form of several bound volumes. Its sheer size has made it a difficult document to obtain and digest. Thanks to the World Wide Web, the federal budget is no longer difficult to obtain. Digestion remains difficult, but at least there are now alternatives. If you get frustrated downloading and printing out the several hundred pages of the federal budget, you can easily order a bound volume online from the Government Printing Office. It will arrive by regular mail.

Skill 5: Check out federal departments and independent agencies.

Much of the work of the federal government that affects your day-to-day life is implemented, managed, even conceived by the executive departments and independent agencies that comprise the bureaucracy of our federal government, everything from the IRS to the FBI, to the NIH, and a hundred other acronyms that stand for the bureaucracy of our national government. Congress and the president often sign general laws that federal departments must then apply to specific situations. Policies related to taxation, small business regulation, the environment, and health research might all originate within the framework of the federal bureaucracy.

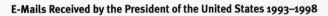

E-Mails Received by the President of the United States 1993–1998

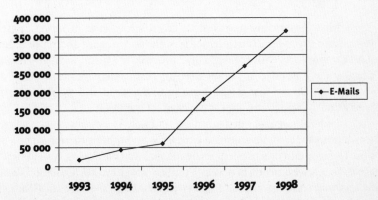

On-line Subscription Tips

The White House web site, congressional web sites, media outlets, and political associations increasingly offer to keep you informed by sending you automatic E-mail—forwarding any and all documents related to a specific area of interest directly to your on-line mailbox. This is sometimes referred to as being put on a "listserve" (literally a list of E-mail addresses) or "push mail." This sounds like getting your own personal clipping service for free, but such subscription services should be used carefully.

Like one thousand pounds of chocolate, an E-mail subscription service can quickly become too much of a good thing. No sooner do you subscribe to a few media outlets and political associations to stay informed on the issues you care about, then you get flooded with hundreds of E-mail messages demanding your attention. Your free clipping service becomes a really bad secretary. Think of the time it takes to sort through a hundred extra E-mails every day—there is such a thing as too much information. After a period of weeks or months, you may even begin to lose interest in the issues that once motivated you to search for more information on the World Wide Web.

Just because subscription services are a neat idea does not mean you have to use them. One of the advantages of the Internet is its flexibility—information is available many different ways. There is nothing wrong with avoiding a few of the bells and whistles your favorite web site has to offer. If you do decide to subscribe, here are some tips to keep "push mail" technology from getting out of control:

Don't Subscribe to More Than One or Two. You can mark other interesting web sites with the bookmark feature on your browser and search them by keyword as your time and interest allow.

Most Americans have only a scant knowledge of how Congress works, and the federal bureaucracy is even more distant and more diffuse than Congress. As with the legislative process, the business of any federal department is open to any interested American; and with the power of the Internet, slowly we just might begin to understand and weigh in on the regulation and programs that actually affect our lives.

Federal departments cannot pass laws. They can, however, pass regulations that can be enforced with fines and other sanctions if you are a business or that create needless headaches and confusing systems if you are a citizen who needs to access a federal program. All regulations must be announced in the *Federal Register,* published by NARA, before they are

Subscribe for a Time and Then Discontinue Your Subscription. There may be some breaking legislative issue that you want to follow closely, or you may be new to a political association and want to read everything they have to offer, or maybe you are between jobs and have all of the time in the world. When your interest or situation changes, unsubscribe to any automatic E-mail servers you cannot handle. Do not forget to write down your user name and password when you sign up. Put them in a place where you will be able to find them several months down the road, when your on-line mailbox is overflowing and you wish to devote more time elsewhere (one good way is to make a note at the bottom of your wall or desk calendar). Do not let yourself get lulled into deleting fifty E-mails every day. Send a cancel message to the web master if you cannot pull the plug yourself.

Take the Time to Narrow Your Subscriptions. Many list serves, including the White House web site, allow you to narrowly define the kinds of documents you receive and the issues they address. A brief on-line questionnaire is sometimes provided to help you zero in on the kinds of information you will find truly useful. It may take a few extra minutes to subscribe in this way, but it will save you many wasted hours by not clogging your mailbox with unwanted information.

Delete Any Message That You Have Not Read in Two Days. All information is not priceless. Some of it is downright extraneous. If you find yourself ignoring a subscription E-mail message for a few days, do not delay further—get rid of it. If it is timely material, it will be stale by the time you read it anyway; if it is not timely material, the only alternative you have is to catch up on E-mail during your vacation. Don't let the machine control you.

implemented. A period of public comment follows, usually through a public hearing in Washington but increasingly also soliciting comments from citizens via letters or the Internet. Final regulations are also published in the *Federal Register* with an accounting of public comments and concerns.

White House and Administration Web Sites

Executive Departments

Department or Agency	URL	Subdivisions of Interest
Department of Agriculture	http://www.usda.gov/	Forest Service
Department of Commerce	http://www.doc.gov/	Census Bureau, National Weather Service, U.S. Patent and Trademark Office
Department of Defense	http://www.dtic.dla.mil/defenselink/	U.S. Air Force, U.S. Army, U.S. Marine Corps, U.S. Navy
Department of Education	http://www.ed.gov/	ERIC (Educational Resources Information Center)
Department of Energy	http://www.doe.gov/	Superconducting Super Collider Project
Department of Health and Human Services	http://www.os.dhhs.gov/	Centers for Disease Control and Prevention, U.S. Food and Drug Administration, National Institutes of Health
Department of Housing and Urban Development	http://www.hud.gov/	
Department of the Interior	http://www.doi.gov/	Bureau of Indian Affairs, The National Park Service, Fish and Wildlife Service, U.S. Geological Survey
Department of Justice	http://www.usdoj.gov/	Drug Enforcement Administration (DEA), Federal Bureau of Investigation (FBI)
Department of Labor	http://www.dol.gov/	Bureau of Labor Statistics (BLS)
Occupational Safety and Health Administration (OSHA)	http://www.osha.gov/	

Department or Agency	URL	Subdivisions of Interest
State Department	http://www.state.gov/	Travel Information
Department of Transportation	http://www.dot.gov/	Federal Aviation Administration, National Highway Traffic Safety Administration, U.S. Coast Guard
Department of the Treasury	http://www.ustreas.gov/	Internal Revenue Service, U.S. Customs Service, U.S. Mint
Department of Veterans Affairs	http://www.va.gov/	

Select Independent Bureaus, Agencies, and Commissions

Central Intelligence Agency (CIA)	http://www.odci.gov/cia/
Environmental Protection Agency	http://www.epa.gov/
Federal Communications Commission	http://www.fcc.gov/
Federal Election Commission	http://www.fec.gov/
Federal Emergency Management Agency	http://www.fema.gov/
Federal Trade Commission	http://www.ftc.gov/
National Aeronautics and Space Administration	http://www.nasa.gov/
National Archives and Records Administration	http://www.nara.gov/
National Endowment for the Arts	http://arts.endow.gov/
Peace Corps	http://www.peacecorps.gov/
Securities and Exchange Commission	http://www.sec.gov/
Small Business Administration	http://www.sba.gov/
Social Security Administration	http://www.ssa.gov/
U.S. Postal Service	http://www.usps.gov/

Cybercitizen Web Listings

The White House
http://www.whitehouse.gov/WH/
Welcome.html
More than simply the mansion at 1600 Pennsylvania
Avenue, the White House is the supercybernexus of
power and information pertaining to the federal government.

SKILLS

http://www.pub.whitehouse.gov/WH/Publications/html/Publications.html
  ★ Skill 1: White House

http://www.whitehouse.gov/WH/EOP/html/principals.html   ★ Skill 2: Presidential E-mail
http://www.whitehouse.gov/WH/html/radio.html   ★ Skill 3: Weekly Radio

UNIQUE FEATURES

http://www.whitehouse.gov/WH/glimpse/tour/html/index.html   ★ Virtual tour of the
  White House allows you to view rooms and furnishings, past and present.

http://www.whitehouse.gov/WH/Services/   ★ "Commonly Requested Federal Services"
  provides links to the federal programs that most Americans are curious about or utilize.

http://www.whitehouse.gov/WH/glimpse/firstladies/html/firstladies.html   ★ "First
  Ladies of the United States" provides a portrait and biographical sketch of each first lady
  in our history.

HISTORY

The History Channel Speech Archive
http://www.historychannel.com/speeches/index.html
The History Channel has an on-line collection of historic speeches
from our presidents, vice presidents, and other political figures.
Through their own opinions, voices, and words these speeches
help reveal the people behind the office.

SKILLS

http://www.historychannel.com/speeches/index.html   ★ Skill 3: Weekly Radio

The History Place "Sounds of History"
http://www.historyplace.com/specials/sounds-
prez/index.html
Click on the thumbnail portraits to hear the words and
thoughts of former presidents.

SKILLS

http://www.historyplace.com/specials/sounds-prez/index.ht   ★ Skill 3: Weekly Radio

http://www.historyplace.com/unitedstates/revolution/decindep.htm ⋆ Link to a RealAudio version of the Declaration of Independence as read by Peter Thomas.

OMB

Office of Management and Budget (OMB)
http://www.whitehouse.gov/OMB

OMB assists the president in the development and execution of his policies and programs. OMB has a hand in the development and resolution of all budget, policy, legislative, regulatory, procurement, and management issues on behalf of the president.

Office of Management and Budget

SKILLS

http://www.whitehouse.gov/OMB/budget/index.html ⋆ Skill 4: Federal Budget (OMB)
http://www.whitehouse.gov/OMB/legislative/testimony/index.html ⋆ Skill 5: Federal Departments

SUPERSITE

Library of Congress Executive Branch Pages

The LIBRARY *of* CONGRESS

http://lcweb.loc.gov/global/executive/fed.html

Library of Congress' Judicial Branch pages provide links to available information about America's justice system.

SKILLS

http://lcweb.loc.gov/global/executive/fed.html ⋆ Skill 5: Federal Departments

Chapter Four

Congress

★

Introduction

So much alarm has been raised about American apathy at the voting
booth, it may be surprising to learn that the United States is one of the
most active and involved democracies in the world when you look at forms
of political participation other than voting, such as doing campaign work
or corresponding with elected officials.

It seems we are a country of nudges, if not a country of voters. In the
Information Age, voting, while important and necessary, may not be as
satisfying (or as powerful) as expressing your political views in other
ways—calling talk radio, sending an editorial to the local paper, or writing
a letter to your member of Congress. In the midst of a legislative session, a
vote cast last November may resonate like a fading echo, rivaled in futility
by the equally distant specter of next year's reelection. A vote cannot convey the voter's experiences, or priorities, feelings, or arguments on any of
the ten thousand pieces of legislation that will be introduced during a session of Congress.

In fact, there are many ways that a citizen of this country can participate in the political process besides voting. The fact that interested Americans can obtain more information about Congress more easily than ever
before increases these options. Americans now have the opportunity to

easily participate in the *legislative* process as well as the *electoral* process in this country.

How many people have ever seen a federal bill in the past? In the past, these documents were effectively limited to lobbyists and lawyers by the sheer difficulty of obtaining them. For the rest of us, information on pending legislation was limited to blurbs in the local newspaper. Seldom, if ever, could everyday Americans review matters before Congress for themselves. Even the all-powerful medium of television is not able to make the machinations in Congress transparent. Who can instantly make sense of the typical C-SPAN broadcast? What step of the legislative process are we watching? When will they vote? (Thanks to the C-SPAN web site, that information is now available online if you ever get lost.)

The challenge now is to be able to cut through the wealth of information on the Internet to focus on information that is truly empowering. The challenge is also to communicate effectively, for now you have the opportunity to interact with your elected representatives—to help or hinder their efforts on the legislative battlefield instead of simply in the polling booth. Information is power. Get some.

For its part, Congress sees itself as a stately institution, proudly sailing behind the technology curve. As one member of Congress explained, when he got to the House of Representatives, it was easier to send an E-mail to Russia than to the office next door. In the past few years, through internal cheerleading from fellow lawmakers and prodding of their constituents, the House of Representatives and the Senate have begun to offer both web sites and E-mail addresses for the lawmakers who work there. And the exigencies of keeping an up-to-date on-line presence have done more than a little tutoring for the landslide of legislative proposals in Congress related to the Internet—access, speed, E-commerce, and new definitions of privacy.

A Few Important Congressional Concepts

The Process Is Not Pretty

The federal legislative process is not always linear; in fact, it seldom is. Congress is often referred to as a "sausage factory," grinding out legislation. It is a place where 535 elected officials are vying with each other to put their personal stamp on each piece of legislation that hits the floor, trying to do what is right for the United States of America, laying the groundwork for their political reelection campaign, trying to curry favor with their political party faithful, trying to support the programs they believe in, and trying to get benefits for their home district. This means that no matter how important, timely, or justified you feel a piece of legislation is, there is bound to be opposition to it—*always*. And just when you've amassed a voting majority, someone will insist on changing something important or attempt to add something unrelated. The amazing thing about Congress is not the gridlock; the amazing thing is that legislation does, in fact, get passed—sometimes.

Congress Is Organized by Committee

To actually consider some ten thousand bills every session, Congress divides the work up among various committees made up of members who can closely scrutinize proposed pieces of legislation, lend the benefit of their expertise, and hopefully lay the groundwork for consensus that the full body can embrace. Generally, every bill passes through a subcommittee and then a full committee before it gets considered on the floor of the House or Senate. The committee hears expert testimony and makes any necessary changes to the bills before they proceed to the floor for a vote.

The advantage of the committee system is that bills can get a careful review or examination before the general body votes. There are several disadvantages. The process is almost always slow (although Congress can pass legislation quickly in an emergency) as each piece of legislation must necessarily survive numerous votes to become law. Further, the member you elected to Congress may not sit on the committee that has the most significant impact on the issues you care about.

Leadership

Having a majority is a big deal in Congress. It means that your party gets to dictate things like committee assignments, calendars, and schedules, and that your party, if unified, gets to pass, by majority vote, almost anything it really wants to (at least in the House). It means that in the end, your party is going to get a whole lot of what they want. If you have a majority in Congress, you also elect the *leadership*—members of your own party who handle the big-picture items during the legislative session like setting an agenda, brokering important compromises with the White House, and engineering legislative victories to sell in the next election. If a proposed piece of legislation runs counter to the beliefs or priorities of the majority's leadership, there is not much chance that it will survive to passage.

You Are Only Represented by Your Elected Officials

Although the majority leadership at times dictates the congressional agenda, and although the committee structure creates a system where some members are more powerful on certain issues than others, you are still represented by (and only by) your two senators and your member in the House. Every member of Congress does not care to hear your views or desires. Nor should they. A member of Congress usually has all he or she can deal with just responding to their own district or state, and the Constitution makes no promises that those who are not your representatives need to represent you or even listen to you.

Things You Can Expect from Your Member of Congress (or Any Other Elected Official Who Represents You):

- ★ Written response to your written inquiries
- ★ Effective representation of your local interests
- ★ Respectful and ethical conduct in public
- ★ Integrity (not to use the office for financial gain)
- ★ Explanation of his or her votes
- ★ Assistance in accessing local or federally funded programs
- ★ White House tour passes (Congress)
- ★ Recommendations for military academies (Congress)
- ★ Congressional gallery passes
- ★ Federal information from departments and angencies

And a Few Things That You Cannot Expect from Your Elected Officials:

- ★ To vote your way every single time
- ★ To devote attention to only one issue
- ★ To respond to threats or insults
- ★ To not run for reelection or not legally raise money to do so

* **To reveal details of their private lives, should they choose to keep them private**

Skill 1: Find out who represents you (districting).

Ask the next person who complains about Congress who their member in the House of Representatives is. Chances are they don't have the slightest idea.

Every American (except those who live in the District of Columbia or a U.S. territory) has two senators in the U.S. Senate (each serve six-year terms) and one member in the House of Representatives (each serve two-year terms). Congress is a geographic phenomenon. Your representatives are determined by where you live, not by political party, or the color of your skin, or any hobbies or other interests you might have, but simply by where you live. Districts for House members are based on population. Currently, each member of the House represents over 620,000 people.

Finding out the names of your senators is easy enough. The two senators who represent your state represent you. Your member in the House is a little more difficult to identify—but again, easier than ever before thanks to the Internet. There are numerous sites that provide what is called "zip districting"—they use your postal zip code to tell you who your representative in the House is. The one I like the best is called Zip To It! because it not only tells you who represents, you, but with the click of a button, provides an easy-to-read biography complete with contact information (see skill #2).

Note: postal zip codes are not determined by congressional district. If you do not know your zip + 4, these search engines might only be able to narrow your district down to a few possibilities. If you want to know for sure who represents you (and you do), get your zip + 4.

What Is My Zip + 4?

Most people are as aware of the extra four digits on their zip code as they are of their congressional representatives. Here are some easy ways to solve the mystery:

* **Check out the U.S. Postal Service web page: *www.usps.gov.***
* **Check your address label from a magazine subscription (their computers usually print your complete address on the label).**
* **Ask a neighbor.**
* **Call the U.S. Post Office toll free at (800) 275–8777 and ask them.**

Skill 2: Arm yourself with basic information.

Once you discover who represents you, you need to collect a few pieces of information about each of your three members of Congress (your representative and two senators)—contact information and background information.

In the age of age of fax machines and E-mail, there is a lot of contact information to gather on each of your elected officials, including the names and phone numbers of key staff. Also keep in mind that some of your representatives have multiple office locations—one in the national capitol (or state capitol for state legislators) and one (or more) at home in the district.

Getting a feel for the person who represents you is a more elusive task, but still important. If you want to effectively interact with your legislators, it helps to know something about them; it matters if they are a staunch conservative or a holdover from the hippie era in suit and tie. It matters if they are party faithfuls or independent-minded mavericks. It even matters what they did for a living before they got to Congress—were they a doctor? A preacher? A taxi driver? Congress recently had all three.

Here are some interesting pieces of information you may want to find out about your representatives in Congress.

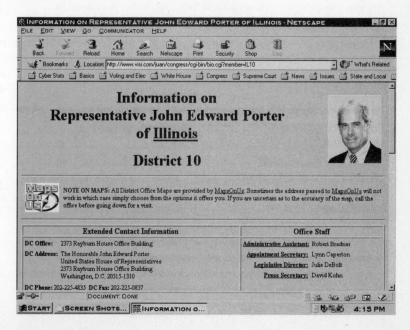

Information to Get	Why It's Useful	Recommended Site
Contact information, address, phone, E-mail, etc.	You need it to communicate with them and find their local office.	Zip To It!
Staff names and titles	Issues are divided up and assigned to various staff members. Staff tend to be more accessible and are knowledgeable about the issues they cover.	Zip To It!
Voting report cards	A glance at the voting report cards of extremely conservative or liberal groups can tell you a lot about where your member resides on the ideological spectrum. Report cards from associations that work on the issues you care about can provide even more specific information.	Project Vote Smart
Committee assignments	These can tell you if your member works directly with the issues you care about, or if he can only contribute a floor vote.	www.House.gov www.Senate.gov
Who paid for their campaign	Lets you know if they are especially beholden to any special interests, e.g., tobacco companies or trial lawyers.	Center for Responsive Politics
How they are presented in the media	A search for recent news stories on your representatives or your senators can tell you about their values and the issues that they feel are priorities.	News media web sites
Family, education, religion, former occupation, etc.	Reviewing this information can sometimes provide a nugget that can be used when corresponding with an elected official, e.g., "as a fellow Sundevil…" or "as dentists we both know . . . ," etc.	Zip To It!
Party	It matters—perhaps more than anything else. Your member's political party often represents a shared ideology in the U.S. Congress. Your member will be expected to vote along party lines on the floor and to further	Zip To It!

Information to Get	Why It's Useful	Recommended Site
	party goals in his or her committee work.	
What they think of themselves	Many members of Congress are only too happy to share their priorities and their opinions on the issues of the day. Check out their speeches, press releases, and web sites. Identifying bills they have cosponsored also provides a glimpse into their value system.	Congressional web sites including THOMAS (Library of Congress web site)
Check out their election results	You can tell a lot about your district and the type of legislator you are likely to have by how close the elections are. Districts that are evenly split between Democrats and Republicans tend to have more moderate legislators. So-called "safe" districts, with overwhelming party identification, can give rise to more partisan legislators.	Project Vote Smart

Skill 3. Download legislation.

Congress passes bills. Everything else is window dressing. Amid all of the partisan posturing, the gratuitous speech making, reelection positioning, moral grandstanding, and photo opportunities, Congress will affect your life and your pocketbook only insofar as it passes a bill to do so (a bill that the president signs).

There are four different types of measures that Congress passes. We will focus on proposed laws that must be passed by a majority vote in the House and Senate and signed by the president to become law, e.g., H.R.200 or S.112. Bills can be introduced in either the House or the Senate and are numbered sequentially during each two-year session of Congress. Only about six hundred bills of the ten thousand that are introduced survive to passage.[1]

The Library of Congress has created a powerful and relatively easy-

---

1. In addition to these bills, *joint resolutions* can be introduced and passed in the same manner but generally have a more limited scope. Joint resolutions usually address minor adjustments in existing laws or attend to emergencies. There are also *House resolutions* and *Senate resolutions* that merely express the opinions of Congress or tend to internal administrative needs. They are not considered law when passed and do not require the president's signature.

to-use web site called THOMAS that provides access to bills pending in Congress. Virtually overnight in 1995, as the result of a mandate by then-speaker Newt Gingrich, the legislative process and documents from the House of Representatives were made available online to the public. THOMAS was named after Thomas Jefferson, an early champion of public information, who proclaimed, "It is the responsibility of every American to be informed."

THOMAS provides information on major bills. These are bills that are likely to be scheduled for debate, hearing, floor action, and press conferences. Keep in mind that although THOMAS posts this information, there is a delay factor—fast-moving or newly amended legislation is hard to track using THOMAS, so you may want to check in with a political association if a bill you care about ends up on the front burner in Congress.

The first step in understanding pending legislation is to read the actual text of the bill—THOMAS will allow you to download and print major bills. This text is usually written in "legalese" to coincide with existing law and may be difficult for us mortals without law degrees to understand. For that very reason, a *bill digest* version of bills pending in Congress is also available. The bill digest version is the rewriting of a bill in plain English so that legal lay people (often members of Congress themselves) can understand the intentions of a proposed piece of legislation.

THOMAS's *"Bill Summary & Status"* feature provides some basic and useful information about bills, including:

Titles	Gives the official titles referring to the legislation—the bill "name."
Status	Tells you how far the bill has progressed in the legislative process and what votes have been taken on it.
Committees	Tells you the committee where the bill is being examined.
Amendments	Proposed changes to the bill since it was originally introduced.
Subjects	Provides an index of topics related to a bill—think "keywords."
Cosponsors	When legislators cosponsor a piece of legislation, they are favorably inclined to vote for it before the vote is actually taken. It means they are a strong supporters of the legislation.
Digest	Plain-English summary of the bill's intentions.
Bill text versions	The text of the bill at a specific stage in the legislative process.

Another prime source of information about federal legislation is available through the *Congressional Record*. The *Congressional Record* is the written record of the United States Congress. It is printed every day that Congress is in session and provides comprehensive documentation of floor sessions in both houses.

Bill Analysis Worksheet

Basic Information and Tracking

What level of government are you working with?

_____

What is the bill number?

_____

What is the title of the bill?

_____

Are there any keywords, phrases, or concepts associated with the bill?

_____

Where does the bill currently reside?

_____

Is the bill scheduled for any up-coming hearing or votes?

_____

Policy

What is the intent of the bill? (What problem does it hope to address? What are its goals?)

_____

What are the core provisions of the bill?

_____

Are there any estimated costs associated with the bill?

_____

Do you think you can support this bill?

_____

What are the three strongest reasons you have to support or oppose the bill?

1.

_____

2.

_____

3.

_____

Politics

Is there any group or legislators who oppose your position? Who are they?

_____

What are their strongest reasons for doing so?

1.

_____

2.

_____

3.

_____

Does the bill have the support of either political party or the leadership?

_____

Do the elected officials who represent you share your position on the issue?

_____

Have you educated them about your position?

_____

Do they sit on an especially important committee with regard to the legislation?

_____

Is there any way for you to use grassroots to support their position or pressure them to change their position?

_____

What would your message be?

What is the deadline for such action?

Skill 4: Track a bill.

To become a law, a bill must usually survive numerous votes in both the House and the Senate. The work of Congress is divided between numerous committees to make it more manageable and to develop areas of specialization among members of Congress. Committees scrutinize proposed legislation, hold hearings, build consensus, and generally give bills the attention they deserve. The drawback is that there are many opportunities to stall, alter, or kill a bill. That very reason makes it impor-tant for the citizen activist to know where a bill is in the legislative process—it might need your vocal support more than once if it is to become law, maybe even six or seven times, as it is heard in the various subcommittees and full committees in Congress.

Has the bill been assigned to a committee? Has it been heard in that committee? Has it been reported out of that committee? Is it scheduled to be voted on the floor? Have numerous members cosponsored the legislation?

All of this information is uniformly provided by THOMAS, which means that once you have done this a few times, you'll be able to locate and research bills with the most seasoned veterans in D.C.

Remember, if a bill is in a subcommittee that your own member of Congress does not sit on, you *cannot* simply assign yourself a new repre-sentative. In such a situation, your representative (or senators) can speak to, or testify in front of, the committee members who will decide the cur-rent fate of the legislation. If the bill is going to be voted on the floor, you can tell your representatives how you would like them to vote on the bill at that time.

Federal Legislative Process: How a Bill Becomes a Law

HOUSE
Bill Introduced
(referred to committee)

↓

Subcommittee Consideration
(report to full committee)
Full Committee Consideration
(report to floor)

↓

Floor Action
(sent to other chamber) ↗

SENATE
Bill Introduced
(referred to committee)

↓

Subcommittee Consideration
(report to full committee)
Full Committee Consideration
(report to floor)

↓

↖ **Floor Action**
(sent to other chamber)

↘ _____ ↙

**Conference
Committee**
(sent to the president)

↓

The President
(sign or veto)

What You Need to Know:

* Every piece of legislation must survive numerous votes before final passage.

* Committee members play a more powerful role in the fate of your legislation than noncommittee members.

* Many tactics exist to expedite, stall, or circumvent this process.

Skill 5: Send E-mail to Congress.

For all the disdain that surrounds campaign finance laws and the soiled reputation of lobbyists, you may be surprised at just how much power a sincere message from a constituent is able to wield on Capitol Hill, especially if that message is respectful and intelligent. Your representatives do not have the time or staff to study every single legislative issue out there in great detail, and they welcome thoughtful information from back home in the district.

E-mail offers constituents a method of communication with elected officials that is quicker and less expensive than anything else previously available but not without its limitations.

Each Congressional Office Is Unique

In the spirit of liberty that our country holds so dear, there is a great deal of latitude given to members of Congress as to how they run their offices. No two congressional offices are exactly the same—priorities differ, as does the experience of individuals who are assigned to different issues. Differences in legislative offices present a special challenge to E-mail. Great inconsistencies exist in terms of the speed with which offices read their E-mail and the importance they attach to it.

Some offices route every piece of E-mail to the correct staff and attempt to respond to it in writing. Some simply tally E-mail messages by issue as they do phone calls and then delete the message entirely. And some members read their E-mail infrequently, if at all.

Do a Little Research

Action alerts from special interest groups are notoriously shrill and often exaggerated. The complexity of the American legislative process, its many players, and the distance between you and Washington can make you sus-

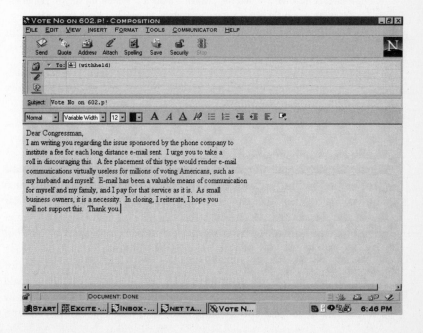

ceptible to misinformation, exaggerations, pranks, or just plain dated, inaccurate, and sloppy accountings of congressional business.

In 1999, Congress was deluged by one such hoax. A bill that never existed, "602.p." (not even an accurate bill number in Congress), supposedly was being considered that would tax long-distance phone use over the Internet. The amount of E-mails this hoax generated to Congress was ludicrous—and embarrassing for the constituents. Before you reply . . . verify.

What Is E-mail Good For?

E-mail is instant. If you learn of a vote that is taking place in Congress today, E-mail might be your only chance of communicating any substantive arguments in time.

Using E-mail helps train your legislators to accept computer technology as a legitimate method of communication from constituents. It will be years before the protocols for handling E-mail in different legislative offices are as standardized as they are for postal letters, but you can help speed that process along.

E-mail is inexpensive and fast, which makes it a wonderful way to communicate with computer-savvy offices, especially for making simple requests. E.g., "Could you let me know how Senator Jones voted on that bill," and for requesting things like American flags or White House tour passes.

E-mail is an especially good way to respond to issues that deal with communications technology or electronic freedom. It demonstrates the solidarity of the on-line community.

Write Your Rep

When sending E-mail to elected officials, the first and most important piece of information to include—as the very first line, if possible—is your address. There is no other way for a congressional office to verify that you live in the district, e.g., that you are someone they should listen to, as opposed to the hotheads who think they are making an impact by sending the same E-mail message to every member of Congress at once.

Many of the offices in the House of Representatives use the "Write Your Rep" interface for constituents who wish to send E-mail to their elected representatives. This interface essentially asks for you to input your name and address and the subject of your message before you type your on-line letter so that congressional offices can easily verify you are a constituent. Not every office uses this interface, but it should be viewed as a welcome idea for those who do.

Below is a sample E-mail message.

TO: *Stephen.jones@mail.house.gov*
RE: support H.R. 2498
CC: (none)
ATTACHMENTS: (none)

I am a constituent who lives at 142 W. Palm Street in Arbyville (zip, 25342). I urge you to cosponsor the Cardiac Arrest Survival Act (H.R. 2498), which promotes public access to defibrillation programs in federal buildings by helping place automated external defibrillators (AEDs) in these locations.

The legislation also provides Good Samaritan protection to AED users and acquirers in states that have not already provided such protection. AEDs are small, easy-to-use devices that can analyze heart rhythms to determine if a shock is necessary and, if warranted, deliver a life-saving shock to the heart.

Last year, my life was saved by an automatic external defibrillater when I suffered a heart attack at work. Fortunately for me, I was close to a hospital when I felt the first pains in my chest and called an ambulance. Lots of other people are not so lucky. We have the technology to save lives from cardiac arrest—what we need is to make this technology readily available so that people do not have to wait for an ambulance when precious minutes are ticking away. H.R. 2498 is a step in the right direction, and I hope you will become a cosponsor.

Please let me know of your actions regarding this matter. And thank you.

Skill 6: Obtain voting records.

Your senators can hem and haw all they want in an attempt to make you appreciate the difficulty of making any decision that affects our lives as Americans. Once your representative votes, there is no rhetoric and no excuse that speaks louder than their "yea" or "nay." Obtaining voting records is the final piece of the congressional puzzle. With voting records you can truly hold your representatives accountable and determine, once and for all, if they are helpful on the issues you care about, or unhelpful, or worse.

Tips for Sending E-mail to Elected Officials

Once E-mail was the cutting edge of technology, but Congress now receives millions of E-mail messages every session and is quickly learning to how to manage this new influx of information. Use these tips to communicate succinctly and effectively with any of your lawmakers, including your representatives in Congress. Staffers will appreciate E-mail that is sent with the following guidelines in mind and are more likely to take it seriously. Many of these tips for communicating with elected officials apply whether you send E-mail or postal mail.

Put Your Name and Address at the Top of the Message. Start your message with "I am a constituent who lives at..." The first thing your representative wants to determine is if you live in his or her district. If you don't . . . delete! Representatives do not have any obligation and little time to read messages from people who are not constituents.

Be Brief. Members of Congress and their staff are extremely busy. Respect their time and try to tell them only what they need to know. Two or three paragraphs should be sufficient, and the equivalent of two typed pages is an unofficial standard. Do not feel you have to make every single argument that relates to an issue—only the one or two strongest points you can make.

Be Clear About Your Position. Your request should be stated as a concrete, actionable item, e.g., "I would like you to support H.R.100" or "I hope you will oppose H.R.112." Being ambiguous opens the possibility of your legislator voting the wrong way or not doing anything at all.

Send Your Message as Soon as Possible. Do not wait around for the perfect time to send your message. Your message is worthless if it arrives after a critical vote.

Don't Flame. You are allowed to disagree with your member of Congress, but you will not be effective if you verbally abuse or threaten them—no matter what. Abusive letters seem more desperate than intimidating to the recipient, and they are seldom taken seriously. An air of mutual respect will encourage members to consider an alternative position and encourages a more flexible position on the issues where you disagree.

Don't Spam. Do not use attachments when sending a message to Congress. Congressional offices do not have time to read or print out extensive reports and clippings. Offer to provide supporting documents on request, but do not send Congress any files besides a brief message from you.

Don't Become Spam Yourself. Do not send Congress a message every single day about every single issue you read about or develop an opinion on. Spend your time running for public office instead. A congressional office that receives numerous messages from a single person on a variety of topics quickly loses sight of the urgency or expertise that the constituent can bring to a specific issue.

Establish Your Credibility. Explain if you are an expert in some area, e.g., if you are a banker or a mother. Also, do not shy away from saying that you are either a personal supporter or a party supporter, but never imply that because you voted for somebody or contributed money to their campaign that they owe you a vote. (If you are not a member of the same party, don't worry, just don't mention it; your representative still represents you.)

Don't Lie. Political professionals can spot a tall tale quicker than you can make one up. Any story that sounds a little too perfect or any statistic that is not substantiated will not help bolster your position but will instead weaken it and diminish the credibility of any future correspondence from you.

Don't cc Anybody. Resist those urges to send a copy of your message to every member of your state government, or Congress, or both. You will persuade no one and annoy everybody. As soon as a staffer has to scroll through a list of people who also received your E-mail, they will want to delete it. A legislative office wants to know that you have appealed to them for some specific action, not just sent them a copy of a memo that everyone else has received. Make each E-mail a personal request.

And the Most Important Tip: Humanize Your Massage. This suggestion is often left out of tip sheets on writing Congress, but it is the single most important piece of advice. In this technological age, sincerity is more refreshing than ever before. Most people are uncomfortable sharing their feelings, or talking about their own experiences, or are dissuaded from doing so because they somehow believe such information is inappropriate to the legislative process. Yet the one thing that can open another person's mind to new ideas, that can pique somebody's interest—the one thing that can turn an indifferent legislator into a supporter—is knowing that a piece of legislation will impact the real lives of their constituents in some meaningful way.

Proofread Your E-mail. Too often the speed and ease of sending E-mail is reflected in poor grammar and sloppy spelling. Even if a congressional staffer is able to figure out what you were trying to say, such errors reflect badly on the overall worth you attach to your correspondence with elected officials. Take a break before you press "send" and proof your message.

Try Not to Send Your E-mail in the Middle of the Night. Legislative staff will note the time stamp on E-mail messages sent to the office and—right or wrong—an E-mail sent at three o'clock in the morning creates speculation about your frame of mind when you sent it.

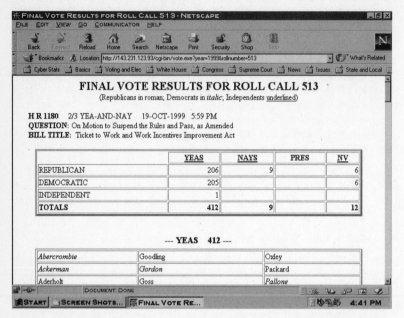

It is a telling fact that long after the House and Senate web sites were up and running and long after members began posting individual web sites, links to voting records were not available. Some members of Congress get squeamish when it comes to broad distribution of such public records, just as some were hesitant to broadcast gavel-to-gavel coverage on C-SPAN, but you have every right to see those voting records and to demand justification of why your member voted the way they did.

You do have to employ a certain amount of analysis when you scrutinize voting records. A vote "aye" (for a bill) or "no" (against a bill) is only part of the story. To fully understand why your members voted the way they did, you might need to look at their press releases, their floor speeches, and their own personal voting justifications. Sometimes legislators vote against bills they care about in favor of other bills that they believe address the problem better; sometimes there is a *poison pill* clause in a bill that outweighs any of the possible benefits in the legislation. Be sure to gather both accurate voting records and the context of the vote before you go on the attack against your member of Congress.

How to Constructively Vent

Okay, so you aren't allowed to flame members of Congress, but it would be disingenuous to pretend that expressing extreme dissatisfaction with Congress is not one of the true pleasures of democracy. The trick is to express dissatisfaction without being personally insulting, unfair, or denigrating. It is a distinction that can approach an art form. Here are some suggestions:

Flaming	Constructive Venting
You are so stupid!	I believe you may be misinformed on the issue.
I hate you for what you did!	I am disturbed by your recent vote.
I hope you get hit by a truck before the next election!	I could not, in good conscience, continue to support you at election time.
The blood of innocent victims is on your hands, murderer!	As one of this nation's leaders, I believe that you willingly accept a share in the responsibility for its actions.
You are so racist. I bet you are a Nazi!	Our forefathers recognized that catering to the wishes of the majority at the expense of the minority is as much a betrayal of our nation's ideals as it is a betrayal of our fellow Americans.
You are nothing but a sexist pig!	I find it hard to believe that you would hold your spouse in such low esteem.
All you care about is PAC money for your campaign!	I know you care about more than PAC (political action committee) money for your campaign.
And you're ugly, too.	(Don't go there.)

And if your legislator actually voted the way you wanted them to vote on a given bill, be sure to send an E-mail thanking them. Accolades are few and far between from constituents. A kind word will endear you to them and may, quite possibly, strengthen their resolve on an issue.

E-mail or Paper Mail—That Is the Question

Every time you consider communicating with a local campaign, your elected officials, or the media, you have a choice to make—do you send E-mail, which is quick, free, and convenient; or do you send printed mail, which is slower, costs more, but is more formal and easier to transfer among staff? The general thinking is that in the near future, E-mail will replace postal mail. We will all send our communications electronically and the trees will rejoice. As with most predictions about the Internet, this is a bit shortsighted and a bit premature.

There is a permanence, a formality to the printed letter that makes it seem more urgent than E-mail. Printed letters have unique paper sizes, colors, weights, fonts, margins, and spacing. In many ways, a printed letter underscores the fact that it contains the thoughts and feelings of an individual who took some effort to write the letter, and who takes themselves seriously enough to send a formal piece of communication.

By contrast, E-mail is so quick that it can seem effortless, as though the thoughts contained therein are not much of a priority to the writer. In addition, E-mails tend to share default font and spacing guidelines on the computers where they appear. This makes it more difficult to underscore the individuality of the writer. However, E-mail is fast, really fast, and people are learning to respect it. One advantage of E-mail over postal mail is that when writing to the print media, a letter to the editor or an editorial can simply be cut and pasted if an editor wishes to use it, whereas a printed letter must be retyped if a disk copy is not submitted with the letter.

Don't lament over the amount of money you paid for your computer if you choose to send a printed letter. Use your word processor and printer to send a handsome letter in a professionally addressed envelope. This will convey further respect for your thoughts and acknowledge the level of professionalism you expect from the office you are corresponding with.

Cybercitizen Web Listings

THOMAS
http://thomas.loc.gov
Named after Thomas Jefferson, outspoken supporter of a well-informed public, the Library of Congress maintains THOMAS, an indispensable web site that provides access to pending legislation in Congress. THOMAS allows you to download current legislation, track bills, identify sponsors, get schedules, and provides a myriad of other useful information.

In the Spirit of Thomas Jefferson, a service of The Library of Congress

SKILLS

http://thomas.loc.gov/ ★ Skill 3: Current Legislation
http://thomas.loc.gov/ ★ Skill 4: Bill Tracking
http://thomas.loc.gov/ ★ Skill 6: Votes

UNIQUE FEATURES

http://thomas.loc.gov/ ★ "Congressional Record" provides a written record of Congress, including transcripts of remarks by individual members. Use index to search by keyword, issue, member name, or date.

U.S. House of Representatives
http://www.house.gov
The official web site of the U.S. House of Representatives.

SKILLS

http://www.house.gov/writerep/ ★ Skill 1: Federal Districting
http://www.house.gov/house/MemberWWW.html ★ Skill 2: Bio and Contact
http://www.house.gov/writerep/ ★ Skill 5: Congressional E-mail
http//clerkweb.house.gov/evs/index.htm ★ Skill 6: Votes

UNIQUE FEATURES

http://www.house.gov/house/CommitteeWWW.html ★ "Committee Office Web Services" connects you to committee offices and schedules.

http://www.house.gov/house/1999_House_Calendar.htm ★ Legislative calendar tells you when the House will be in session and more specific schedules are available as well (from THOMAS).

http://clerkweb.house.gov/histrecs/history/history.htm ★ "Historical Information" gives you history on the buildings of Congress and the characters who have inhabited them.

U.S. Senate
http://www.senate.gov
The official web site of the U.S. Senate.

SKILLS

http://www.senate.gov/contacting/index_by_state.cfm
★ Skill 1: Federal Districting

http://www.senate.gov/senators/index.cfm ★ Skill 2: Bio and Contact
http://www.senate.gov/legislative/index.html ★ Skill 3: Current Legislation
http://www.senate.gov/legislative/index.html ★ Skill 4: Bill Tracking
http://www.senate.gov/contacting/index.cfm ★ Skill 5: Congressional E-mail

UNIQUE FEATURES

http://www.senate.gov/committees/index.cfm ★ "Committees" connect you to committee offices and schedules.

http://www.access.gpo.gov/congress/congoo4.html ★ "Senate Calendar of Business" tells you when the Senate will be in session and more specific schedules are available as well (http://www.senate.gov/legislative/legis_legis_committees.html).

http://www.senate.gov/learning/index.cfm ★ "Learning About The Senate" provides history, FAQ trivia, and a glossary of terms.

Zip To It!
http://www.visi.com/juan/congress/ziptoit.html

One of the first and still one of the best zip code–districting programs on the World Wide Web. Zip To It! was created by a frustrated citizen who couldn't find the address of his Congress member.

SKILLS

http://www.visi.com/juan/congress/ziptoit.html ★ Skill 1: Federal Districting
http://www.visi.com/juan/congress/ziptoit.html ★ Skill 2: Bio and Contact
http://www.visi.com/juan/congress/ziptoit.html ★ Skill 3: Congressional E-mail

UNIQUE FEATURES

http://www.visi.com/juan/congress/search.html ★ "Power Search" allows you to find representatives by state, party, and also provides lists of committee members (http://wqww.visi.com/juan/congress/committees.html).

C-Span
http://www.c-span.org

Created by America's cable television industry, C-SPAN provides gavel-to-gavel coverage of congressional proceedings. Their web site also provides schedule and educational information. C-SPAN is also on the cutting edge of video indexing technology—and you can now search their site for video clips based on keyword or member name.

SKILLS

http://www.c-span.org/watch/ ★ Skill 1: Federal Districting
http://www.c-span.org/watch/ ★ Skill 2: Bio and Contact
http://congress.nw.dc.us/cgi-bin/issue.pl?dir=c-span ★ Skill 3: Current Legislation
http://www.c-span.org/watch/ ★ Skill 5: Congressional E-mail
http://congress.nw.dc.us/c-span/subjvote.html ★ Skill 6: Votes

UNIQUE FEATURES

http://www.c-span.org/watch/ ★ "Video & Audio" provides streaming sound and video of C-SPAN television and radio broadcasts to your desktop.

http://www.c-span.org/guide/ ★ Schedule provides programming information for C-SPAN television and radio broadcasts.

http://www.c-span.org/questions/ ★ Expert Ilona Nickels provides interactive Q&As on Congress.

CapWeb

http://www.capweb.net/classic/index.morph

One of the very first World Wide Web sites designed to steer interested citizens to available on-line information related to the federal government, CapWeb has blossomed into a one-stop switch box connecting users to a vast array of political information on the Internet.

SKILLS

http://www.capweb.net/classic/index.morph ★ Skill 1: Federal Districting

http://www.capweb.net/classic/index.morph ★ Skill 2: Bio and Contact

http://www.capweb.net/classic/index.morph ★ Skill 5: Congressional E-mail

http://www.capweb.net/classic/jefferson/ ★ Skill 7: Links

UNIQUE FEATURES

http://www.capweb.net/perl-cgi/scripts/wwwboard/wwwboard.html
★ "Voicebox" allows you to compose and post your views on the issues for others to read and respond to.

Congressional Budget Office (CBO)

http://www.cbo.gov

CBO's mission is to provide Congress with objective, timely, nonpartisan analyses needed for economic and budget decisions and with the information and estimates required for the congressional budget process. CBO attempts to predict for Congress how much things will cost.

SKILLS

http://www.cbo.gov/ ★ Skill 3: Current Legislation

UNIQUE FEATURES

http://www.cbo.gov/cost.shtml ★ Cost estimates are provided by bill number.

General Accounting Office (GAO)

http://www.gao.gov

The only thing congress members love more than taking action on an issue is to study it to death. That job falls on GAO, which studies any government-related issue that a member of Congress requests interesting in writing. Because GAO often gathers original data, it is a treasure trove of reports and information.

UNIQUE FEATURES

http://www.gao.gov/reports.htm ★ "GAO Reports and Testimony" allows search for GAO reports by title or subject. Most can be downloaded in PDF format.

http://www.gao.gov/fraudnet/fraudnet.htm ⋆ "FraudNET" allows citizens to report suspected mismanagement, misuse, or waste of federal funding.

SUPERSITES

Grassroots.com
http://www.grassroots.com/

Grassroots.com
Your political action network.

Grassroots.com combines news media, election, and E-mail technology to help educate citizens about specific issues, connect them with the organizations that fight on their behalf, and put them in touch with their elected officials. Links to the web sites of groups and associations are helpfully organized by issue area for membership and donation information.

SKILLS

http://www.grassroots.com/scripts/community.dll?ep=0&ck=&ver=hb1.2.20
⋆ Skill 3: Current Legislation

http://www.grassroots.com/ ⋆ Skill 6: Votes

http://www1.grassroots.com/corporate/contact/index.html ⋆ Skill 7: Links

UNIQUE FEATURES

http://www.grassroots.com/scripts/community.dll?ep=2002&ck=&ver=hb1.2.20
⋆ Registered users are encouraged to form their own on-line groups to begin organizing for change.

Policy.com
http://www.policy.com

Policy.com The policy news & information service
Part of the VoxCap Network

Drawing its content from national special interest groups and political organizations, Policy.com provides issue briefings on a wide array of concerns, including a focus on the hot issues of the day.

SKILLS

http://www.policy.com/vcongress/ ⋆ Skill 1: Federal Districting
http://www.policy.com/vcongress/ ⋆ Skill 2: Bio and Contact
http://www.policy.com/vcongress/pending.html ⋆ Skill 3: Current Legislation
http://www.policy.com/vcongress/ ⋆ Skill 4: Congressional E-mail

UNIQUE FEATURES

http://www.policy.com/issuewk/1999/1004_95/index.html ⋆ "Issue of the Week" provides more extensive analysis of current issues thna you are likely to even find in the newspaper.

http://www.policy.com/ ⋆ Community links provide connections to influential think tanks, associations, universities, and businesses that contribute content to the site.

SpeakOut.com
http://speakout.com/speakout/simple/default.asp
Another low-impact grassroots site designed to get you to vote up or down on current issues and then sell the data to politicians and political organizations interested in polling data.

U.S. Government Printing Office (GPO)
http://www.access.gpo.gov
The mission of GPO is to inform the nation by producing, procuring, and disseminating printed and electronic publications of the Congress as well as the executive departments and establishments of the federal government.

SKILLS

http://www.access.gpo.gov/ ⋆ Skill 3: Current Legislation

UNIQUE FEATURES

http://www.access.gpo.gov/congress/senate/constitution/index.html ⋆ "Constitution, Analysis and Interpretation" provides an annotated version of the Constitution detailing Supreme Court decisions related to various sections of the document.

http://www.access.gpo.gov/congress/index.html ⋆ Congressional publications are available here.

VoxCap
http://www.voxcap.com/anon/_scape/channels/channel293.dhtml

VoxCap was created as a full-service, nonpartisan interface between American citizens, their government, and nonprofit organizations. More than simply providing content and links, VoxCap works to foster discussion and connection between like-minded users. "Create a Club" allows you to post news, links, and opinions on a variety of general issue areas from the environment to the economy, healthcare, and foreign relations.

SKILLS

http://congress.nw.dc.us/voxcap/ ⋆ Skill 1: Federal Districting
http://congress.nw.dc.us/voxcap/ ⋆ Skill 2: Bio and Contact
http://congress.nw.dc.us/voxcap/ ⋆ Skill 5: Congressional E-mail

E The People
http://www.e-thepeople.com/affiliates/national
This is a minimal impact, petition-style web site (see "The truth About On-Line Petitions"). Billing itself as an interactive town hall for Americans, E The People allows people to sign electronic petitions on a variety of issues, write to any of 170,000 elected officials, or start a petition of their own. News stories are also provided.

SKILLS

http://www.e-thepeople.com/affiliates/national/index.cfm?/PC=CONSELET
  ⋆ Skill 5: Congressional E-mail

UNIQUE FEATURES

http://www.e-thepeople.com/affiliates/national/index.cfm?pc=CONSELLET   ⋆ "Write a
  Letter" allows you to communicate with your federal, state, or local elected officials.

USA Democracy
http://usademocracy.com/main/main.asp
More than simply another petition site, USA Democracy lets you keep
track of legislation proposed in Congress according to subject. Plain-
English summaries of proposed legislation are provided with the

bills, so that you can analyze the bills without a law degree. The site
then lets you "vote" on these bills and will notify your elected officials of your position. The
site's voting feature is a cross between an on-line poll and an on-line petition. Neither is
particularly compelling in the eyes of most elected officials, but USA Democracy at least
allows you to access a list of real bills with ease.

SKILLS

http://usademocracy.com/legislator/mbrreps.asp   ⋆ Skill 1: Federal Districting
http://usademocracy.com/legislator/mbrreps.asp   ⋆ Skill 2: Bio and Contact
http://www.usademocracy.com/legislation/catsum.asp   ⋆ Skill 3: Current Legislation
http://www.usademocracy.com/legislation/catsum.asp   ⋆ Skill 4: Bill Tracking
http://www.usademocracy.com/legislator/mbrreps.asp   ⋆ Skill 5: Congressional E-mail
http://www.usademocracy.com/legislation/catsum.asp   ⋆ Skill 6: Votes
http://usademocracy.com/links/links.asp   ⋆ Skill 7: Links

UNIQUE FEATURES

http://usademocracy.com/news/news.asp   ⋆ "Political News" and "Election News" are
  available on the site.
http://usademocracy.com/poll/polls.asp   ⋆ "Polls" provides polling data on a list of
  current topics.

VOTE.com
http://www.vote.com
This is a minimal impact, petition-style web site (see

"The truth About On-Line Petitions"). VOTE.com
allows you to vote up or down on current topics and sends your E-mail address and opinion to your members of Congress and the president. Pro and con of each issue is provided
to foster some reflection before voting. And a "Discussion," feature allows users to post
their own viewpoints.

SKILLS

http://www.vote.com/   ⋆ Skill 5: Congressional E-mail
http://www.vote.com/   ⋆ Skill 6: Votes

Project Vote Smart (voting records)
http://www.vote-smart.org
Project Vote Smart researches, tracks and, provides to the public independent factual information on over thirteen thousand candidates and elected officials. Voting records, campaign issue positions, performance evaluations by special interests, campaign contributions, backgrounds, previous experience, and contact information are available on its web site.

SKILLS

http://www.vote-smart.org/state/Topics/register.phtml?checking= ★ Skill 1: Federal Districting
http://www.vote-smart.org/about/help/membership.phtml?checking= ★ Skill 6: Votes
http://www.vote-smart.org/about/help/vol_int.phtml?checking= ★ Skill 7: Links

CONGRESS.ORG
http://www.congress.org
Congressional supersite features a popular search engine that provides districting, an E-mail interface, recent voting records, and congressional schedules.

SKILLS

http://congress.org/search.html ★ Skill 1 Federal Districting
http://congress.org/capdir.html ★ Skill 2: Bio and Contact
http://congress.org/legis.html ★ Skill 3: Current Legislation
http://congress.org/search.html ★ Skill 5: Congresssional E-mail

UNIQUE FEATURES

http://policy.net/scorecard ★ "Scorecard" provides voting reports cards by various organisations from extremely conservative to extremely liberal.

Library of Congress Legislative Branch Pages

The **LIBRARY** *of* **CONGRESS**

http://lcweb.loc.gov/global/legislative/congress.html#legbranch
Library of Congress's legislative branch pages provide extensive links to congressional business, people, and history.

SKILLS

http://lcweb.loc.gov/global/legislative/congress.html#legbranch ★ Skill 7 Links

Five

The Supreme Court
of the United States

Introduction

The Supreme Court of the United States resides in a dignified marble building in Washington, D.C., directly across the street from the Congress—an architectural parent patrolling the playground of democracy. Ascending the steps of the Supreme Court in the light of midday, the marble walls and steps can meld together and give the sensation of stepping down into an empty pool rather than climbing a stairway to ultimate justice. Inside, nine black-robed justices consider the most difficult, the most vexing, and the most portentous cases of the day—cases of national import and cases that have not been sufficiently resolved by lower courts.

A term of the Supreme Court begins the first Monday in October and usually continues through the following summer. During that time, the justices divide their time between "sittings," when they hear the cases they have decided to hear, and scheduled recesses. Cases are added to the docket according to the *Rule of Four*, that is, if four of the nine Supreme Court justices agree that a case should be heard—it is. Only a small fraction of the thousands of cases that petition the Supreme Court are added to the docket. Once a case is added to the docket, written briefs, petitions, and other records are submitted to be considered by the judges along with current law. Each side is allowed to supplement the prior record of the case with brief, thirty-minute oral arguments to present the strongest justification for their position. And then the justices formulate, write, and release their opinions.

Since the justices of the Supreme Court rely almost solely on review of previous court documents and a brief argument from both sides, their proceedings completely lack the ingredients for a good Perry Mason potboiler. There are no surprise witnesses, no surprising admissions of evidence, no agonizing confessions, no shameless manipulations of the jury.

Which is not to say the Supreme Court is lacking in drama. The very nature of the Supreme Court makes the cases it decides to hear and the decisions it makes on those cases resonate far beyond the individual parties that brought forth the original actions. The justices, free of popular elections and term limits, decide where to draw the line between the governmental prerogatives and the inalienable rights of individuals, among other important roles. Their pronouncements are binding and almost impossible to overturn.

There is much for Americans to learn by simply having access to the work of the Supreme Court, even if you can't vote for Supreme Court justices or work to unseat them if you disagree with the majority opinion.

Reasons Why Everyday Citizens Might Take an Interest in the Decisions of the Supreme Court of the United States

The Supreme Court presents a special challenge for cybercitizens. The Court is supposed to be removed from them—immune, beyond the reach of an organized or outraged populous, separate from the circuslike fracas of politics in Congress—a place of quiet reflection, structured debate, and somber administration of its awesome power of *judicial review*, that is, the ability to declare any law, even popularly supported laws, unconstitutional and effectively void. And only impeachment can remove a Supreme Court justice. There are, however, reasons why the citizen-activist might take interest in the proceedings of the Supreme Court:

Supreme Court Decisions Help Define the Acceptable Parameters of Action on a Given Issue

In the heat of writing legislation, it can be difficult to adequately consider the rights of all of those parties affected. The Supreme Court lets Congress and other state and local governments know when the laws they passed go too far.

Supreme Court Cases Provide Strong Arguments on Both Sides of an Issue

The arguments and opinions of Supreme Court cases can be used to fortify your positions on the issues they address. When somebody argues a case before the highest court in the land, a lot of time is spent making sure the most compelling arguments are eloquently and succinctly advanced. The same thing is true with the opposition—their arguments are as good as they are gonna get in front of the Supreme Court.

The Long and Winding Road: Some Paths to the U.S. Supreme Court

United States District Courts ↓ United States Court of Appeals		Lower State Courts ↓ State Supreme Courts

The Supreme Court of the United States

↑

Special Federal Courts, e.g., United States Court of Federal Claims United States Court of Appeals for the Armed Forces

Skill 1: Review Supreme Court decisions.

Searching any of the following web sites by keyword will provide a list of opinions rendered by the Supreme Court of the United States. The *Opinion of the Court* announces why a case was decided in a particular way. It is sometimes not signed, but more often identifies a judge on the

Supreme Court as its author. The Opinion of the Court is binding law on future cases and lower courts, but a fractious court can produce a number of dissenting opinions. Such dissenting opinions take two forms: *concurring opinions,* in which the author agrees with the conclusion reached in the Opinion of the Court but for different reasons, and *dissenting opinions,* in which the author explains how he or she would have disposed of the case differently. It also summarizes the case and the reason for action. A dissenting opinion (or several) is usually provided and likewise becomes a matter of public record so that no voice is squelched and different aspects of difficult issues are preserved for future scrutiny and review.

Skill 2: Download transcripts of oral arguments presented before the Supreme Court and review "Friends of the Court" briefs.

The Supreme Court of the United States represents an interesting phenomenon in the advent of the Internet. Although *technically* in America, all U.S. government business should be available to any citizen, *historically,* government entities, such as the Supreme Court, have developed working relationships with businesses, law firms, journalists, and universities. This made sense when information was not easily disseminated—if you had to travel to Washington to get it—or easily digested—as can be the case with oral arguments made before the Supreme Court. The availability of information on the Internet and the increasing sophistication of everyday Americans in their understanding of public documents may force our Washington institutions to reevaluate their concept of clientele.

Transcripts of the oral arguments made before the Supreme Court are a prime example of documents that should be posted and available for the general public sometime in the near future as the Supreme Court gets its web site up and running. Currently, such transcripts are available to the public in Washington about five business days after the transcripts are made. The actual tape recordings of the arguments are turned over to the Library of Congress a year after they are made. Transcripts are not only difficult to obtain if you do not work for a law firm, they are costly. The company that transcribes the arguments charges over two dollars a page, and oral arguments can run to fifty or more pages. Commercial on-line services such as WestLaw also make the transcripts available, but for a hefty subscription price aimed at attracting the business of well-heeled law firms, and not the cybercitizen who may be curious about a few cases on the docket of the Supreme Court.

Another aspect of Supreme Court cases that should one day be available on the World Wide Web takes the form of what are called *Amicus Curiae* briefs, which means "Friends of the Court" in Latin. These briefings

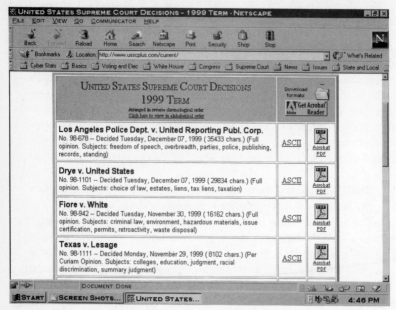

are legal arguments by interested third parties who wish to comment on the legal or constitutional issues at stake in a given case, but who are not directly involved in the originating lawsuit.

Although it may seem like an *Amicus* brief might serve as a grass-roots vehicle for everyday citizens to make their voices heard in the court system, the fact is that the filing of such documents, in an institution so steeped in tradition, involves extensive and complex guidelines that must be adhered to. The court is not structured to accommodate lobbying on the cases it hears, so *Amicus* briefs tend to be filed by organizations that have some depth of expertise in constitutional theory rather than mere positions on the issues at stake. Don't expect there to be an on-line form allowing you to file an *Amicus* brief with a few clicks.

However, *Amicus* briefs are reviewed by the Supreme Court prior to rendering their opinions. They are, officially, part of the public record and, like the oral arguments made before the Supreme Court, can offer a fascinating look at the arguments presented to the highest court in the land. For that reason, *Amicus* briefs should also be available online for the interested citizen to peruse and learn from.

Until the public documents that you are interested in reviewing are truly . . . well, public . . . analysis provided via the media or through scholarly journals may be a welcome resource to you.

Cybercitizen Web Listings

U.S. Judiciary
http://www.uscourts.gov
Federal judiciary homepage provides information about the organization of the U.S. courts systems and links to courts where they exist.

THE
FEDERAL
JUDICIARY
HOMEPAGE
— About the U.S. Courts

SKILLS

http://www.uscourts.gov/links.html ★ Skill 3: Links

USA TODAY Supreme Court Index
http://www.usatoday.com/news/court/nscotooo.htm
A chronological index of stories related to the U.S. Supreme Court is provided here.

Supreme Court

SKILLS

http://www.usatoday.com/news/court/nscotooo.htm ★ Skill 1: Decisions

Supreme Court of the United States
http://www.supremecourtus.gov
Taking its time to get online, the Supreme Court finally has a handsome web site that provides docket information, opinions, and calendars.

Supreme Court of the United States

SKILLS

http://www.supremecourtus.gov/websites/websites.html ★ Skill 3: Links

DECISIONS

FindLaw Supreme Court Center
http://supreme.findlaw.com/Supreme_Court/index.html
A division of the Findlaw site, the Supreme Court Center provides an organized interface to the Supreme Court Docket

SKILLS

http://supreme.findlaw.com/Supreme_Court/decisions/index.html ★ Skill 1: Decisions

http://supreme.findlaw.com/Supreme_Court/briefs/index.html ★ Skill 2: Oral

http://supreme.findlaw.com/Supreme_Court/landmark.html ★ "Landmark Cases" are summarized.

http://supreme.findlaw.com/Supreme_Court/supcthist.html ★ "A History of the Supreme Court" provides an illustrated overview.

http://supreme.findlaw.com/Supreme_Court/docket/octdocket.html ★ "Court Docket" provides list of upcoming cases and issues.

The Oyez Project Northwestern University

http://oyez.nwu.edu

The Oyez Project takes its  name from the phrase by which the marshal of the Court calls the courtroom to order. This site provides a multimedia database of the arguments made before the U.S. Supreme Court. It takes about ten months for an argument or decision to be released, edited, and digitized, but then cases can be searched here by title, citation, or subject matter. Oral arguments, abstracts, voting, and annotations are provided. Links to FindLaw provide written decisions.

http://oyez.nwu.edu/ ★ Skill 1: Decisions
http://oyez.nwu.edu/ ★ Skill 2: Oral

UNIQUE FEATURES

http://oyez.nwu.edu/justices/justices.cgi ★ "The Current Justices" provides biographical sketches and other information about present and past Supreme Court justices.

The Supreme Court Collection at Cornell University

http://supct.law.cornell.edu/supct

The Legal Information Institute at Cornell has assembled U.S. Supreme Court decisions that can be easily searched by date, topic, keyword, or the names of involved parties.

Supreme Court Collection

SKILLS

http://supct.law.cornell.edu/supct/ ★ Skill 1: Decisions

UNIQUE FEATURES

http://supct.law.cornell.edu/supct/cases/historic.htm ★ "Selected Historic Decisions of the Supreme Court" provides opinions of seminal Supreme Court cases.

USSC+

http://www.usscplus.com

This commercial web site provides current Supreme Court opinions for free.

SKILLS

http://www.usscplus.com/current/ ★ Skill 1: Decisions

usscplus.com

UNIQUE FEATURES

http://www.usscplus.com/topk/ ⋆ "The 1000 Cases Most Cited by the Court Itself" is a database of frequently cited cases.

http://www.usscplus.com/ecase/ ⋆ "Case Locator" allows you to search decisions by an extensive number of indexed subjects or your own keyword.

LAW

FindLaw (Home Page)
http://findlaw.com

FindLaw is the legal information super-site for lawyers, students, business, and the general public. Searchable databases provide access to legal code, briefs, decisions, and other web sites.
http://findlaw.com/ ⋆ Skill 3: Links

U.S. Code via GPO Access
http://www.access.gpo.gov/congress/congo13.html

The general and permanent laws of the United States can be found here as prepared by the Office of the Law Revision Counsel, U.S. House of Representatives.

U.S. Code via University of California's GPO Gate
http://www.gpo.ucop.edu/search/uscode.html

Search interface allows you to enter keywords or section numbers to locate the piece of the U.S. Code you are interested in.

U.S. House of Representatives Office of the Law Revision Counsel
http://uscode.house.gov
Searching "U.S. Code" on the House web site allows you to enter key-words, an easy way to find issues you are interested in, including Inter-net-related law that Congress has passed.

SUPERSITE

Library of Congress Judicial Branch Pages
The **LIBRARY** *of* **CONGRESS**

http://lcweb.loc.gov/global/judiciary.html
Library of Congress's judicial branch pages provide links to available information about America's justice system.

SKILLS

http://lcweb.loc.gov/global/judiciary.html ⋆ Skill 3: Links

Chapter Six

The News Media

★

Introduction

Legislators and advocates alike have courted the all-powerful news media, that "fourth estate" of American government, like lovesick Romeos in pursuit of the intoxicating gift that is better than love—exposure. While someone running for elected office will benefit from the mentioning of their name early and often, the relationship between advocates and the news media tends to be overrated in much the same way that the Internet is overrated. The media should be considered part of the journey of the cybercitizen—another tool at his or her disposal. It is not the destination.

Advocates spend much of their time and energy hoping to get on the news, as if a quote in the newspaper or a sound bite on the evening news will make everyone drop what they are doing, pick up a sign, and join the march for . . . whatever it is you are marching for. If you are lucky, people will mention the story the next day at the office, and even then, by that evening's broadcast, your issue is likely to be bumped back into public awareness oblivion. Except for some high-profile issues that are important enough to be followed regularly by the news media, the impression that your average news story gives is more *reassuring* than it is *motivating*—it seems that somebody is working on the issue, taking care of it—but the story does not necessarily make your average couch potato run out into the street waving a flag for your cause.

A blurb in the local newspaper is not ultimately how laws get passed. Laws are made when your local elected officials vote for them; they fail when your local elected officials ignore them or vote against them. The news media can play an important role in educating both you and your elected officials about the issues and even exert pressure on our lawmakers at critical junctures; but media exposure, in and of itself, should not be confused with a legislative victory on your issues.

How the Internet Complements Broadcast and Print Media

There were battles in Congress over the televised broadcast of daily House and Senate proceedings. Even the grassroots-oriented speaker, Tip "All politics is local" O'Neill, worried that televised coverage would demean the "greatest legislative body in the world." Nowadays, we know that those concerns were unfounded.

Just as fears of beaming Congress over the airwaves were exaggerated, so too were promises that it would result in an enlightened, involved democracy. Internet access to the archives of all media outlets in this country is not going to automatically make us all political advocates. It does have the potential of making those of us who are inclined to be involved more sophisticated, more effective, and, therefore, more relevant to the process of politics and news about politics in America.

Creation of a Timeline and Continuity

It is easy to get disoriented in the midst of an ongoing news story that occasionally bobs to the surface in the local media. News media web sites allow you to collect, in chronological order, all of the stories related to a specific issue, helping you to understand what happened and when.

Accommodation of Your Personal Schedule

With our busy lives, we don't always have time to scour our favorite publications on a daily basis, and sometimes we miss groundbreaking news. You can use the World Wide Web to search for any news stories you have missed or subscribe to news servers that will automatically send you articles of interest.

Collecting Missed Exclusives or
Interesting Thought Pieces

The news is not the same in every paper or on every television station. Different news outlets provide changes in perspective and rely on different sources. Often, if someone prints a thoughtful editorial, it will appear in a single paper or magazine, and it may not be one that you have a subscription to. Internet web sites allow you to comb through numerous media outlets to locate any stories you may have missed.

Spin-off Stories

Good news stories often provide leads on related stories or spark interest in a variety of related topics. The impeachment of President Clinton found its genesis in the less-than-scandalizing Whitewater investigation. You may be interested in following these on-line threads to the stories that really matter.

Availability of Additional Information

Electronic media often have severe time limitations that preclude them from presenting every interesting facet of a news story, and yet their reporters may have obtained interesting *primary documents* and other materials that provide depth and background to the story they are covering. Print media often have the space to present more in-depth coverage of news stories, but they have a bias for analysis, meaning your local newspaper is more likely to describe proposed legislation or public reaction to it rather than simply printing the bill verbatim. The Internet is often used to post supplementary documents for readers and viewers who are interested in reviewing primary documents for themselves.

Providing a Way to Bring Yourself Up to Speed

Interest in a specific issue may develop as a result of personal experience: maybe a close friend of yours develops a rare disease, or your son, the marine, finds himself fighting in a foreign land. New advocates are born every day with the potential to become active, articulate soldiers on the issues they care about, and one of the initial challenges is to develop a base of knowledge on an issue that is new to you but that has been in the news for some time. A review of past news stories can provide a solid foundation for the fledgling activist.

The Difference Between Broadcast and Print Media

Broadcast Media

Broadcast media are television and radio, also called electronic media. Such news outlets can reach millions of viewers at one time and for that reason play an incredibly important role in communicating the day-to-day news of this country. In addition, the images of the electronic media can be indelible—the confidence that a candidate is able (or unable) to project in response to a difficult question on the campaign trail can sometimes tell the would-be voter more about their suitability for office than a hundred printed editorials. The pictures that make broadcast media so effective also make them hard to transport, to share. In most cases, broadcast media must be viewed or listened to by everyone at a specific time, or they are missed. In addition, broadcast media usually have strict time limits on the amount of time they can devote to any given issue. Broadcast media reporters usually rely on what is called an "assignment desk" to receive story assignments.

Print Media

Print media are newspapers, magazines, and other publications. The advantages of print media are, in many ways, the limitations of broadcast media. Print media are easily shared; they can be photocopied, mailed, filed. Print media are not tied to the same time constraints as broadcast media—articles can run many pages and a thorough airing of the issue in question provided. Print media can also be read at the leisure of the individual, almost anywhere that's convenient. It is, however, more difficult to gauge the sincerity of a lawmaker from a quote in the print media than it is from the evening news. Print media reporters usually rely on a "news editor" to receive story assignments.

Skill 1: Research the news.

Nearly all of the media web sites that are online provide some sort of search engine that allows you to dig through their recent archives by keyword. The only question that needs to be answered is—is it free? Increasingly, media search engines have begun to charge a fee for the information they provide. The fee is usually nominal and can be immediately paid online via a credit card, but it is not unthinkable for you to peruse a hundred articles looking for the few that are really useful. That can quickly add up if you don't keep a close eye on your charges.

As media web sites become more sophisticated, they will regularly offer you the ability to customize the news you receive online or via your on-line mailbox. Remember, only use automated "clipping services," if you have the time to go through the number of responses you will get. Otherwise, the search engine is your best bet.

What to Search the Media For

Topic

The keyword that describes the issue you are interested in, e.g., "gun control" or "social security" or "John Smith for Governor." Remember to put it in quotes if it involves more than one word, or you may have to fish through many unrelated articles that match only one of your key words (see Appendix, "Boolean Commands," for more).

Key Lawmakers

This might lead you to stories that cover both the issues you are interested in and the lawmakers who represent you. Such articles might provide an indication of how your member will vote or at least the types of issues and arguments that interest him or her.

Key Players

Executive directors of influential associations, community leaders, and individuals who have grabbed media attention on an issue can all be fruitful subjects to search for. Sometimes key players will reveal their legislative strategies in the media or float key arguments for you to refute or adopt.

Related Stories

It is easy for an issue to run out of steam in the media—most last for only a day or two. Meanwhile, legislators considering a controversial piece of legislation can take weeks or even months to pass the bill. The media sometimes follow a legislative issue by covering a number of related stories. You can use news-related web sites to investigate stories related to your issues that you may not have thought of.

Media Products

There are a variety of media products available on news-related web sites. Just as your morning newspaper is a mixture of news, essays, letters, comics, and advertising, media web sites provide a number of different types of media products in response to keyword searches. Some of the products you will find:

News Stories

The days events told in objective, straightforward fashion with equal time given to all sides and a penchant for hard facts and objective reporting.

Columnists

Can be political, or humorous, technical or general, or of nearly any other bent. Columnists usually supply an analysis of the days' events. They can focus broadly on the news or pick apart some small aspect of a recent news story. The identifying characteristic of a columnist is that they are subjective—one person's educated opinion.

Letters to the Editor

These are responses to news stories from the general readership of a newspaper or magazine. The respondents are not necessarily experts, but they do have thoughts or feelings regarding a recent news story that they would like to share. Letters are usually very brief and come from local readers.

Editorials

Editorials usually take the form of essays in the printed media and are almost always written by an expert with a sophisticated insight into some issue. When done well, an editorial educates the reader about an issue. In addition to outside experts, most newspapers convene an Editorial Board consisting of their own staff of reporters, researchers, editors, and other experts, who also write editorials that express the internal sentiments of the newspaper.

Features

Features usually focus on an individual or an emotional event and tell a "human interest" story. Features may be interviews, photo essays, and sometimes "fluffy" news pieces. They focus on the lives of real people who are faced with a significant challenge, who make a difference through their work, or who are just plain colorful and interesting.

Transcripts

Transcripts are the written record of broadcast news stories. If you do not have on-line multimedia capabilities, or if you want to quickly review a news piece that you heard on the radio or saw on television, you may want to download and look at the transcript if it is available.

Paid Political Ads

Some organizations don't wait around to be interviewed in order to get their arguments out to the general public. Both the print and broadcast media take paid political ads that argue a position within the borders of paid advertising space.

Skill 2: Write a letter to the editor.

Lawmakers spend an awful lot of time trying to get their names, faces, wise thoughts, and predictions into the local media where Joe Voter can appreciate them. Public office attracts media interest more easily than simply being a constituent—but nearly every print media publication has a forum where readers can give feedback on published news stories. Many media web sites provide E-mail interfaces that allow you to send letters to the editor from your own computer. Specific guidelines vary by publication and are usually available online, but some general rules are as follows:

Keep it short. You have about two paragraphs to make your point. Anything longer is likely to be edited down to that length and your point might get distorted.

Don't paraphrase the entire article. Simply refer to it by date, author, or title, and then get on with your thoughts. Don't waste your two paragraphs rewriting what has already been written.

Don't address every single argument you can think of. Just address the one that you think makes the strongest point or that reveals the most glaring weakness in the original piece.

Don't take cheap shots. What may seem like witty repartee in a pub over a beer will be inane in a short letter that does not address the subject in a dignified manner.

Don't lie to make your case. As is the case with lawmakers, a fabricated story almost always reveals itself to the seasoned news editor. Your credibility is your calling card—don't squander it with lies.

Put your name, address, phone number, and E-mail address on the letter. This is so the editor can confirm that the letter is from a legitimate source and can contact you about making any editorial changes.

If you send a hard copy, send an electronic version on disk. Now that most newspapers are edited on computers, it is a big help if they can reprint your letter without retyping it.

Cut it out if it gets published. Congratulations, you are a citizen with something valuable to say. Lawmakers should pay more attention to you because when you open your mouth, others listen.

Skill 3: Write an opinion/editorial (op/ed).

If you are personally affected by an issue, or if you have formal or specialized training in a related area, e.g., if you are a doctor, or a researcher, or a lobbyist, and you know more about the complexities of a given issue than the unenlightened lawmakers trying to pass magic bullet legislation, you have the opportunity, and you may have an obligation, to

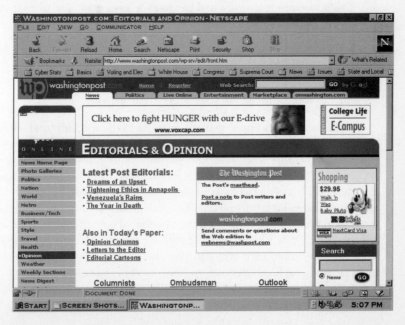

try your hand at an opinion/editorial for the local newspaper. Print media editorials tend to be longer in length than letters to the editor and take the form of an essay. An editorial usually focuses on an issue in general rather than a single article. In fact, it does not have to refer to a specific article at all. It must, however, argue a point sufficiently or enlighten the reader in some other way, and it must be well-written to make it into the paper.

As with letters to the editor, specific guidelines and contact information for editorials are usually available online, and they can sometimes be submitted via E-mail. Most of the tips from Skill 2 apply. In addition:

Although longer than a letter to the editor, an editorial is not that long. Generally it is no more than one thousand five hundred words (six typed, double-spaced pages).

Don't assume your reader has an extensive or formal background on the issue. Keep any necessary background information brief and don't be condescending. Don't use acronyms without fully spelling them out first.

Stay focused. It is far more effective to thoroughly address a single argument than to catalog every single argument and do justice to none of them. You want to provide an angle, not a laundry list.

Each sentence tends to be new paragraph in news print. Try to capture your ideas in single sentences.

Don't forget to include all of your contact information. This includes your E-mail address.

Skill 4: Contact the news editor (print) or assignment desk (broadcast).

The media does not, in general, consider itself especially interactive. There is a strong emphasis on objectivity that makes journalists wary of becoming too comfy with political organizations or individual advocates. On the other hand, the lifeblood of a journalist is his or her sources, and reporters are always on the lookout for people who can provide thoughtful analysis or dependable information. As with legislators, your concept of the Internet in relation to the media should be that of a relationship. You can use the World Wide Web to dialogue with the people who make the news decisions, the assignment editor at your local newspaper, or the Assignment Desk at your local television station, but not to badger them.

Keep in mind that once you develop a working relationship with your local editors and reporters, you may discover that certain editors prefer to be called, others prefer to receive faxes, still others may invite you to page them. Flexibility is key when you develop open lines of communication with your local media.

Reasons Why You May Want to Contact the Assignment Editor or News Desk

They Reported Some Aspect of a Story Inaccurately and You Want Them to Correct It

Reporters are often generalists working on deadline, and if they are being snowed by their interview subjects, they may need someone in the viewing audience to help bring them up to speed on an issue.

You Would Be an Especially Good Interview on the Issue in Question and You Want to Let Them Know You Exist

Again, reporters are always looking for interview subjects to file in their Rolodex, especially if they are credible, succinct, and willing to provide information promptly and without hassles.

You Thought a Story They Presented Was Well Done, Accurate, and Fair and Want to Encourage Their Reporters to Continue to Cover That Issue

The people who make the daily news decisions at your local paper and television stations respond to positive feedback as much as your lawmakers do. One news web master says his station is more likely to run follow-up stories when they get E-mails that indicate interest in a specific story from their viewers.

You Know There Is Going to Be a Local Event That They May Want to Cover

It must be "news," or do not even bother, e.g., an important announcement is going to be made, or there are strong visuals, such as a protest or a famous speaker. Remember, there is a different between an issue between an issue being important and an issue being "news."

How to Know If Your Event Is "Newsworthy"

Remember, none of this stuff guarantees that your local event is actually news. Very few events catch the attention of the news media, and your chances of coverage are pitted against everything else that is happening that day—what might have gotten covered on Sunday when nothing else was happening is not even worthy of consideration on Monday when the stock market crashes, a major earthquake hits, and your senator is caught with his pants down.

* You have a great video image for the electronic news media, such as people marching in protest, the unveiling of a work of art, or adorable children acting adorable—or something unusual and compelling, e.g., a strange contest.

* A celebrity will be present. Reporters like meeting movie stars and sports heroes as much as anyone else.

* It is the first time an event is going to happen, or the last time an event is going to happen, or some significant anniversary, like the fiftieth time an event is going to happen.

* You are making a major announcement that significantly affects what we know about an issue, or how we perceive it, such as a major scientific breakthrough on a disease or a press conference to explain a recent Supreme Court decision.

* You have access to an interview subject who is willing to share a personal story of struggle, or triumph, or justice—something that creates a local window on a newsworthy issue, such as a local person who has begun to take a new stroke treatment or a local business that is being hurt by burdensome new regulations.

* You have cultivated a relationship with a news reporter who is interested in covering your issues for the news and is willing to work with you on identifying newsworthy stories. (Note: Try not to cry wolf with a local reporter who is interested in your issue—develop a sophisticated sense of the types of stories he or she are willing to cover.)

* Something has changed—a new development in a criminal case or something that raises the stakes, a new group is formed, your neighbor announces his candidacy for office, etc.

* It is of legitimate interest to a significant portion of the local audience (not to be confused with your feeling that it *should be* of interest to a significant portion of the local audience).

* You have scheduled your event to allow news reporters to meet their deadlines.

Cybercitizen Web Listings

ABCNEWS.com
http://www.abcnews.go.com
ABCNEWS site, including *World News Tonight*, *20/20,* and *Nightline* web sites.

SKILLS

http://www.abcnews.go.com/ ★ Skill 1: News Search

http://www.abcnews.go.com/onair/**WorldNewsTonight/WNT_email.form.html**
★ Skill 2: Letter to Editor

UNIQUE FEATURES

http://www.abcnews.go.com/ ★ Live message boards allow you to interact with other viewers and post your comments on the current topics of the day.

http://www.abcnews.go.com/onair/nightline/**NightlineIndex.html** ★ *Nightline* link recaps nightly programs, solicits viewer feedback, and provides online discussions with *Nightline* journalists and researchers.

http://www.abcnews.go.com/ ★ "White House 2000" link provides a multimedia look at the presidential hopefuls.

CNN Interactive
http://cnn.com
CNN news network web site.

SKILLS

http://cnn.com.SEARCH/ ★ Skill 1: News Search

http://cnn.com/feedback/ ★ Skill 2: Letter to Editor

UNIQUE FEATURES

http://cnn.com/SEARCH/quiz/ ★ "Daily News Quiz" allows you to impress yourself with current affairs.

http://cnn.com/almanac/daily/ ★ "Dailyalmanac" provides a look at today's events as well as upcoming news events that have been scheduled.

FoxNews.com
http://foxnews.com
The official web site of Fox News.

SKILLS

http://foxnews.com/ ★ Skill 1: News Search

http://foxnews.com/ ★ Skill 2: Letter to Editor

http://foxnews.com/ ★ Skill 4: Assignment Desk

http://foxnews.com/   ★ "Views" feature solicits E-mail comments from viewers on the issues of the day.

MSNBC
http://msnbc.com
NBC network news web site, including *Today*, *Nightly News*, and *Dateline NBC*.

http://msnbc.com/news/default.asp?cp1=1   ★ Skill 1: News Search
http://msnbc.com/tools/nm/nm1.asp?t=Opinions&p=/news/OP_Front.asp
   ★ Skill 2: Letter to Editor

http://msnbc.com/tools/nm/nm1.asp?t=Opnions&p=/newslop_Front.asp
   ★ Commentary provided in "Opinions" section provides links to the authors for direct comments and links to the editor for public comments.

National Public Radio Online
http://npr.org
The official web site of nonprofit National Public Radio.

http://npr.org/   ★ Skill 1: News Search
http://www.npr.org/inside/contactnpr/   ★ Skill 2: Letter to Editor
http://www.npr.org/inside/contactnpr/   ★ Skill 4: Assignment Desk

http://npr.org/yourturn/   ★ "Your Turn" allows you to post opinions on the day's topics.

ON-LINE MEDIA

AMERICAN POLITICS JOURNAL
http://www.american-politics.com
On-line political news magazine provides editions in several languages, and an eclectic array of political columnists, commentary, humor, and political news.

http://www.american-politics.com/search.html   ★ Skill 1: News Search
http://www.american-politics.com/whereweare.html
   ★ Skill 2: Letter to Editor
http://www.american-politics.com/submit.html   ★ Skill 3: Op/Ed Guidelines
http://www.american-politics.com/submit.html   ★ Skill 4: Assignment Desk

http://www.american-politics.com/chat.html ★ "Chat Room" allows readers to discuss the issues.

Salon.com

http://salon.com
Available only online, this hip Internet 'zine combines a newswire service with original content by established writers and offers provocative political thought and commentary.

salon.com

SKILLS

http://salon.com/ ★ Skill 1: News Search
http://salon.com/contact/letters/ ★ Skill 2: Letter to Editor
http://salon.com/contact/submissions/ ★ Skill 3: Op/Ed Guidelines
http://salon.com/contact/staff/ ★ Skill 4: Assignment Desk

Slate

http://www.slate.com
On-line 'zine combines a daily news briefing with features written by established writers and columnists. Full access requires subscription.

SKILLS

http://www.slate.com/ ★ Skill 1: News Search
http://www.slate.com/code/fray/theFray.asp ★ Skill 2: Letter to Editor

UNIQUE FEATURES

http://www.slate.com/code/fray/theFray.asp ★ Extensive "the Fray" threads allow you to post your thoughts and comments related to on-line articles.

DRUDGE REPORT

http://www.drudgereport.com
The DRUDGE REPORT is rumor-central for political gossip and possible insider information as col-

lected and posted by cybermaven Matt Drudge and other columnists. Site also has extensive links to other news media.

SKILLS

http://www.drudgereport.com/ ★ Skill 1: News Search
http://www.drudgereport.com/ ★ Skill 2: Letter to Editor
http://www.drudgereport.com/ ★ Skill 4: Assignment Desk

UNIQUE FEATURES

http://www.drudgereport.com/ ★ Search the news wires from the DRUDGE REPORT's home page.

POLITICAL NEWS

ROLL CALL
http://www.rollcall.com
The newspaper of Capitol Hill politics, *ROLL CALL*, provides inside information on the machinations and maneuvers of Congress and no-nonsense analyses of election races.

SKILLS

http:sh/www.rollcall.com/aboutrc/aboutrc.html ★ Skill 2: Letter to Editor

UNIQUE FEATURES

http://www.rollcall.com/forums/ ★ "Commentary" allows you to post opinions on the topic of the day.

http://www.rollcall.com/election/map.html ★ Roll Call "Interactive Election Map" provides state-by-state coverage of congressional elections.

The Hill on the Web
http://www.hillnews.com
The newspaper of Capitol Hill documents the trials and toil of Capitol Hill lawmakers and the elections that keep them in office.

SKILLS

http://www.hillnews.com/htdig/search.html ★ Skill1: News Search
http://www.hillnews.com/features/editorial.html ★ Skill 2: Letter to Editor

PRINT MEDIA

CRAYON
http://crayon.net
CRAYON stands for "Create Your Own Newspaper." This site allows you to customize your news page from a variety of on-line news providers.

George Magazine
http://georgemag.com
Magazine started by JFK Jr. attempts to weave politics, fashion, and living in a variety of features written by journalists and politicos from every band of the ideological spectrum. On-line site provides a taste of *George*'s content with limited search capabilities.

NATIONAL REVIEW Online

http://nationalreview.com
Political magazine provides thought pieces and commentary on domestic and international public policy and the views of a variety of well-respected columnists.

SKILLS

http://www.nationalreview.com/contact/contact.html ★ Skill 1: Letter to Editor
http://www.nationalreview.com/contact/contact.html ★ Skill 2: Op/Ed Guidelines
http://www.nationalreview.com/contact/contact.html ★ Skill 3: Assignment Desk

UNIQUE FEATURES

http://www.nationalreview.com/soapbox/soapbox.html ★ "Soapbox" provides an interactive reader's forum that tends toward the more theoretical.

Newsweek.com

http://www.newsweek.com
The official web site of *Newsweek* magazine.

SKILLS

http://www.newsweek.com/ ★ Skill 1: News Search
http://www.newsweek.com/nw-srv/common/services/nwinfo.htm#contact
★Skill 2: Letter to Editor
http://www.newsweek.com/nw-srv/common/services/nwinfo.htm#my_turn
★ Skill 3: Op/Ed Guidelines
http://www.newsweek.com/nw-srv/common/services/nwinfo.htm#contact
★ Skill 4: Assignment Desk

UNIQUE FEATURES

http://www.newsweek.com/nw-srv/talk/cover/front.htm ★ "Live Talk" provides interactive discussions on the topics covered in the most recent issue.

The Economist

http://www.economist.com
Well-respected international magazine is the foremost authority on foreign relations.

SKILLS

http://www.economist.com/tfs/aarchive_tframeset.html ★ Skill 1: News Search

The Nation.

http://www.thenation.com
Political magazine publishes features and commentary by some of the most respected writers in Washington and across the country.

SKILLS

http://www.thenation.com/   ★ Skill 1: News Search
http://www.thenation.com/   ★ Skill2: Letter to Editor

THE NEW REPUBLIC
http://www.thenewrepublic.com
Political magazine devoted to politics and the arts provides in-
depth features and political commentary.

SKILLS

http://www.thenewrepublic.com/magazines/tnr/archive/search.html   ★ Skill 1: News
   Search

http://www.thenewrepublic.com/   ★ Skill 2: Letter to Editor

The New York Times
http://nytimes.com
The official web site of *The New York Times*.

SKILLS

http://www.nytimes.com/   ★ Skill 1: News Search
http://www.nytimes.com/subscribe/help/letters.html   ★ Skill 2: Letter to Editor
http://www.nytimes.com/subscribe/help/opedsubmit.html   ★ Skill 3: Op/Ed Guidelines
http://www.nytimes.com/subscribe/help/paper.html   ★ Skill 4: Assignment Desk

UNIQUE FEATURES

http://forums.nytimes.com/webin/WebX?14@191.akRjacyJifno@/   ★ "Forums" provides
   interactive discussion on the day's news headlines.

THE WALL STREET JOURNAL
Interactive Edition
http://interactive.wsj.com
The official web site of *The Wall Street Journal* newspaper requires that you subscribe to the web site to
access search and other features.

TIME.Com
http://www.pathfinder.com/time
The official web site of *Time* magazine.

SKILLS

http://www.pathfinder.com/time/magazine/archive/text/0,2647,0,00.html   ★
   Skill 1: News Search
http://www.pathfinder.com/time/writetous/   ★ Skill 2: Letter to Editor

UNIQUE FEATURES

http://www.pathfinder.com/time/community/0,2637,0,00.html ★ "Boards & Chat" provides interactive discussions on the topics covered in the most recent issue.

USA TODAY
http://www.usatoday.com
The official web site of *USA Today* newspaper.

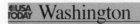

SKILLS

http://usatoday.com/ ★ Skill 1: News Search
http://www.usatoday.com/news/comment/debate.htm ★ Skill 2: Letter to Editor
http://survey.usatoday.com/cgi-bin/feedback.cgi ★ Skill 4: Assignment Desk

UNIQUE FEATURES

http://www.usatoday.com/news/comment/debate.htm ★ "Online Discussion" allows you to post your opinion on today's current issue.

http://www.usatoday.com/news/e98/ecentral.htm ★ "Election Guide" provides state-by-state and national coverage of elections and related issues. "State-by-state preview" can be found at http://www.usatoday.com/news/e98/preview/main.htm.

Washingtonpost.com
http://www.washingtonpost.com
The web site of *The Washington Post*.

SKILLS

http://search.washingtonpost.com/wp-srv/searches/mainsrch.htm ★ Skill 1: News Search

http://www.washingtonpost.com/wp-srv/interact/longterm/stfbio/wpemail.htm ★ Skill 2: Letter to Editor

http://www.washingtonpost.com/wp-dyn/opinion/ ★ Skill 3: Op/Ed Guidelines

http://www.washingtonpost.com/wp-srv/interact/longterm/stfbio/wpemail.htm ★ Skill 4: Assignment Desk

UNIQUE FEATURES

http://washingtonpost.com/wp-srv/liveonline/front.htm ★ "Live Online" provides on-line discussions with *Post* editors, journalists, and interviewees.

http://www.washingtonpost.com/wp-dyn/politics/ ★ "Campaign 2000 Video Search Engine" allows you to access video campaign footage based on name, party, or keyword.

http://www.washingtonpost.com/wp-srv/politics/special/special.htm ★ "The Issues" provides links to news stories organized according to campaign issues.

AMERICAN JOURNALISM REVIEW
NewsLink

http://ajr.newslink.org/news.html
This supersite contains literally thousands of links to newspapers, magazines, radio, and television news sources on the Internet, big and small, local, national, and international.

SKILLS

http://ajr.newslink.org/searchn.html ★ Skill 1: News Search

Democracy Network (Media Listings)
http://www.dnet.org
The Democracy Network provides links to local news media organized by state.

E&P ONLINE MEDIA
DIRECTORY
http://emedia1.mediainfo.com/emedia
Editor & Publisher magazine provides this extensive media database, which can be searched by region or format including newspapers, magazines, radio, and television.

NewsMax
http://newsmax.com/
Straightforward news supersite collects news links from various sources and organizes them by subject. NewsMax is an easy way to search multiple on-line news providers without getting bogged down in extensive mulimedia plug-ins.

SKILLS

http://newsmax.com/ ★ Skill 1: News Search

UNIQUE FEATURES

http://newsmax.com/commentmax/commentmax.shtml ★ "Columnists" provides links to pundits, political and otherwise.

http://www.newsmax.com/cartoons/ ★ On-line cartoon bank is provided here. Late Night jokes are also collected on the site.

News and Newspapers Online
http://library.uncg.edu/news
The University of North Carolina at Greensboro news
provides web site links by state.

Grassroots.com Political
Columnists Links
http://www.grassroots.com/scripts/
staticpage.dll?spage=cg/opinion.ht

Grassroots.com combines news media, election, and
E-mail technology to help educate citizens about spe-
cific issues, connect them with the organizations that fight on their behalf, and put them in
touch with their elected officials. The home page features political headlines. On-line opinions are available from a variety of pundits and columnists.

UNIQUE FEATURES

http://www.grassroots.com/scripts/staticpage.dll?spage=cg/funstuff.htm&ck=&ver=hb
  1.2.20 ★ On the lighter side, a selection of political cartoons is also available.

TotalNEWS
http://totalnews.com
"All the news on the net all the time...." TotalNEWS provides
hyperlinks to all major news sites and the ability to search
multiple sites using a single keyword.

SKILLS

http://totalnews.com/ ★ Skill 1: News Search

Chapter Seven

State and Local Government

Introduction

Ever mindful of us, our forefathers attempted to limit the size and authority of the federal government by encouraging a slew of sister governments to do their damndest to make sure "big brother" didn't get too bossy. They may have succeeded, but at the same time the number of lawmakers who represent you—people you theoretically should know and follow the actions of—was multiplied exponentially.

In addition to the fifty state governments in our country, there are literally hundreds of local governments and thousands of special government bodies, such as boards of education and water districts, with elected officials that you can vote for, monitor, and influence. The good news is that once you have mastered communicating with your federal officials, you can use many of these same skills with state and local officeholders. The bad news is that web sites and on-line services vary greatly by locale and are unlikely to be coordinated in any way.

As a cybercitizen, don't be content with state and local web sites that adopt an "aw shucks!" attitude to their on-line presence. Don't let your local governments get away with providing little current information online and few opportunities for interaction. Whatever the level of government you are dealing with, you should demand access to the information you need to foster a productive on-line relationship with your elected representatives. The key pieces of information that you need from your state and local governments are as follows:

Reasons to Go Local

Jurisdiction

Your state and local governments are the primary source of funding, regulation, and lawmaking for some critical areas that may be of interest to you. As a general rule, the closer the issue is to home, the more likely that a local legislator should be contacted to deal with it. In fact, it is futile to contact the wrong level of government to deal with a problem it has no jurisdiction over. Your state and local governments are probably responsible for the following services:

* **Education, schools, teachers, and curricula**
* **Health facilities and management of public health programs**
* **Police protection**
* **Water quality and utilities**
* **Garbage and recycling**
* **Transportation, including most roads, public parking, waterways, train stations, and airports**

State Legislation Laboratories

Many times before a law is passed on the national level, it has been, in effect, tested by being implemented in a few states. This helps a new law demonstrate its efficacy and builds support across the nation. If you are interested in passing a piece of landmark or controversial legislation, your best bet may be to try and pass it on the state or local level before you attempt to get it introduced in the hallowed halls of the U.S. Congress.

Direct Democracy

Many states allow ballot initiatives to qualify for the general election if organizers gather enough qualifying signatures. This is a way that the people, through majority vote, can directly pass laws themselves in addition to electing their representatives on Election Day. When state and local legislators refuse to address an important issue, such as campaign finance reform or term limits, direct democracy allows "the people" to pass the law for themselves. Keep in mind that sometimes even popularly supported legislation does not get passed because it is not a good idea or not constitutional, and many times direct democracy campaigns offer simplistic solutions to complex problems and build support through knee-jerk emotional arguments.

Access to Lawmakers

Your state and local lawmakers, in general, have fewer constituents than your federal representatives. State and local legislators generally address more discrete issues and do not need to spend so much time traveling between the home district and Washington, D.C. They also have less visibility in the media than their national counterparts and consequently reserve less time for interviews and press conferences. All of this makes your state and local elected officials more accessible than your U.S. senators in Washington. Forging a working relationship with the staff and the lawmakers of state and local elected offices may be considerably easier

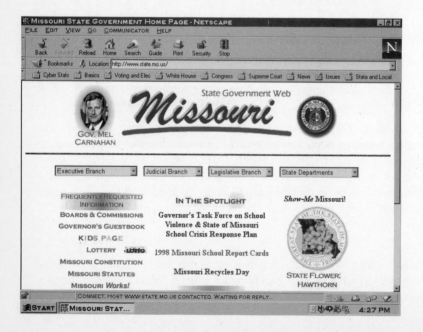

than forming a working relationship with your national representatives. District organizing will tend to get noticed quicker by local lawmakers who are always in town.

The Internet has been lauded for forming communities without boundaries and being able to connect people who live in all corners of the galaxy. Become a savvy advocate on your local issues—from water quality to zoning laws to police protection and schools—and you just might discover that the Internet has led you back into your own neighborhood and helped you solidify relationships with the people who live on your block.

Once Americans realize that the Internet has not replaced the geographic organization of our government, the World Wide Web, which has been lauded for establishing dispersed virtual communities, might begin to be used to reaffirm the connection between residents of local communities across the previously insurmountable divide of apartment hallways and side streets.

Skill 1: Identify your state and local legislators (districting).

As with the federal government, representation in this country is a geographic phenomenon. It is not based on issue interest, or race, or religion, or political party. That means you must talk to the person who repre-

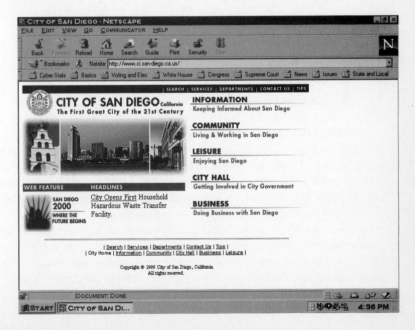

sents your neighborhood and you cannot do that unless you know what district you are in. To make things difficult, state and local district boundaries may be drawn completely differently from your congressional district lines.

While there are numerous web sites that can identify your *federal* representatives by zip code, you will most likely have to log on to your secretary of state's web site or call your local registrar of voters to find a zip-districting interface that reveals your state and local representatives.

As with your members of Congress, once you find out who represents you, the next important task is to gather contact information, including as much of the following as you can find:

* ★ Correct spelling of the names of your lawmakers
* ★ Addresses (both district office and state capital address for state representatives)
* ★ Phone numbers
* ★ Fax numbers
* ★ E-mail
* ★ Key staff
* ★ Party affiliation
* ★ Interesting biographical information
* ★ Campaign contribution information
* ★ Voting records
* ★ Election results
* ★ Committee assignments

Skill 2: Find out election dates and locations.

As long as you are asking local authorities who represents you, you might as well ask when the next election is. Your secretary of state may have a sample ballot prepared that lists the federal, state, and local offices that are up for election and any initiatives that have qualified for the ballot. No, you will probably not be able to cast your votes online, but request an absentee ballot if you know that you will be away on Election Day. In all other cases, you are going to have to find that little elementary school you never knew existed or that obscure community center. Hey, you pay for them, you might as well stop by once every so often to use the water fountain and vote.

Skill 3: Know your governor.

Just as the president helps establish and communicate the legislative agenda for the nation, your governor plays a significant role when it comes to establishing local priorities. In addition to agenda setting, your governor is likely to have a modest army of economic and other experts at his or her disposal, and a large state bureaucracy that oversees state issues such as your schools and teachers, local health-care delivery, and other local services such as police, water quality, and utilities (although these issues may be handled by your local government with state funding).

Your governor is a good place to start getting to know the politics of your state, and most have taken advantage of a governor's web page on the state web site to let you know just what issues they feel are important and what they are going to do about them.

One difference between the state and federal levels of government is that, whereas the president appoints leaders to federal departments, state department heads are often elected offices. In some states, even the equivalent of the vice president—the lieutenant governor—is an elected office separate from the governor. Because of this, forging a unified agenda on the state level can be a difficult task indeed, and unraveling the many threads is a challenge for any citizen.

Skill 4: Learn about your state legislature.

Most states emulated the federal government and established a state constitution with a bicameral government consisting of an upper and a lower house and a governor. Alternatively, many local governments, perhaps your city council, are *unicameral,* meaning there is just one legislative body. A unicameral city council or county board of supervisors may appoint a *city manager* who is responsible for the day-to-day management of your local government, but who is not elected—and legislation merely has to pass through one elected body to become law.

The problem is that each state has formed its own individual government in a different way, unmistakably underscoring the fact that America is a republic—a collection of states that are allowed, to some extent, to set their own destiny and manage their own citizens.

Your state constitution can tell you a lot about how your state government is organized, the elected offices, and other structural considerations. Background information on the organization of your state legislature is often available on a legislative home page.

Skill 5: Identify and track state bills.

Is legislation considered once a week and passed by voice vote on city council? Is legislation divvied up among various committees who fine-tune it? Do special commissions hold public hearings and then make recommendations back to the state and local government? It is annoying to have more than one way to pass legislation in this country, but that's what you get for safeguarding against tyranny—you get all of the frustrations without the oppression.

Aside from identifying any differences in process, most state legislatures use computers now to keep track of and disseminate proposed legislation, amendments, calendars, and the like, and in many cases this information is available on the Web, so that you can identify and follow politics on the state level. Remember, there is not one unified search engine, or web-site design, employed to track state legislation, so you must develop a feeling for your own state legislative information system. If it is unduly cumbersome or unreliable that is a legitimate complaint to lodge with your state officials.

Skill 6: Read the budget.

As with everything in America, even the work of our governments often comes down to shopping—how the government decides to spend your money. Will it be health care or roads? Police or fire? New textbooks or new paint for classrooms? New fire engines or new safety equipment for firefighters? As with the federal budget, an accounting of how your state and local governments spend their money can tell you more about the actual consequences of their work than a thousand silver-lining press releases.

The governor and the state legislature work to produce a state budget. The governor's web link to state financial information is usually provided in the listings, although additional fiscal information may be available on the state legislative web site. The governor often relies on local economic projections to determine the size of the state budget, and some of these studies can tell you a lot about the local economy and the local needs of the state where you live and work.

Skill 7: Review voting records.

Voting records are the final act of your state legislators on an issue in question. Your lawmakers can and should be held accountable for their votes, and any excuses or pleas for mercy should be discounted. As such, your state and local governments owe it to you to provide information on the proposals that your local government is considering and how your legislators voted on them.

Most state governments make votes available, after a fashion—they are often amended into the text of legislation. It is sometimes difficult to download specific pieces of legislation and hunt for the votes, and for that reason, our state governments should be pushed to provide search engines for voting records.

Legislators on the state level are as reluctant as federal legislators to simply post voting records, as the votes themselves do little to explain the context in which the vote was cast. A lawmaker who supports an alternate bill, or who spots a "poison pill" clause in a proposed piece of legislation, can, at a glance, seem to oppose an issue that they do, in fact, support. Even so, the finality and the consequences are such that as a voter, you should not only have voting records available, but have them easily accessible. That means that voting records should be linked on the legislative home page, and a convenient search engine that allows you to peruse votes by issue, by dates, or by legislator should be embedded in the web site. No state in the union currently provides an intuitive search engine to facilitate vote research, although you may be able to gather up voting records piece by piece by viewing individual pieces of legislation.

Skill 8: Send E-mail to state and local officials.

Once you have armed yourself with state and local legislative information, you are ready to send E-mail to your state officials as a concerned constituent. The same rules apply here as apply to corresponding with your federal representatives in Congress.

Note: When corresponding with your state or local officials, the titles you use may be different, e.g., state assembly member instead of member of the U.S. House of Representatives, or governor of the State of Massachusetts instead of president of the United States, but the salutation is always the same: "Honorable," in the place of Mr. or Mrs. or Ms. Your elected officials are always addressed as honorable whether they really are in your opinion or not.

Skill 9: Read the state constitution.

Most state and local governments have ratified a state constitution to establish their governments, but there are almost always important distinctions between your state and local governments and the federal government.

Key pieces of information to find are the dates and duration of state and local legislative sessions. Your local government may hold a weekly public meeting to handle all business, whereas your state government may only meet a few months out of the year. Other state and local governments, like the federal government, are open year-round, with staff to handle inquiries and problems from constituents any time of the year.

Your state and local governments are likely to have created various departments and committees to help them carry out their work. These departments are responsible for the delivery of services and are staffed by people who should provide you with information and with courteous, efficient service. If you have trouble accessing an existing state program (as opposed to a legislative problem), your first step may be to go to the city or state employee who is in charge of the program directly.

Skill 10: Download state statutes, laws, and codes.

Just as it is premature to take a strong stand on federal legislation until you are familiar with the current laws that have been passed, what they provide, where they have succeeded, and where they have failed, so, too, is it important that you be able to search your state laws to familiarize yourself with the rules that govern your city or town. State statutes, laws, and codes are available online for many states, in many different formats. Again, the posting of state law without a subject index for the layperson does little to help you locate any of the information you are interested in. Keep in mind that our state governments are grappling with this emerging resource and trying to discover and provide the information that is most valued by their constituents. You may want to send a polite and encouraging note to the state web master if you have any ideas for useful information that they could post or suggestions on how to make posted information more user friendly.

Cybercitizen Web Listings   SUPERSITE

Grassroots.com State Districting
http://congress.nw.dc.us/gr/

Grassroots.com
Your political action network.

Grassroots.com combines news media, election, and E-mail technology to help educate citizens about specific issues, connect them with the organizations that fight on their behalf, and put them in touch with their elected officials. "Legislative Action Center" provides zip-code districting for state officials.

http://congress.nw.dc.us/gr/ ⋆ Skill 1: State Districting

Library of Congress State and Local Government Pages

The **LIBRARY** *of* **CONGRESS**

http://lcweb.loc.gov/global/state/
stategov.html

Library of Congress's "State and Local Governments" pages provide extensive links to state and local government web sites and resources.

Project Vote Smart (State and Local Information)

http://www.vote-smart.org

Project Vote Smart researches, tracks and, provides to the public independent factual informa-

tion on over thirteen thousand candidates and elected officials. Voting records, campaign issue positions, performance evaluations by special interests, campaign contributions, backgrounds, previous experience, and contact information are available on its web site.

http://www.vote-smart.org/state/Topics/register.phtml?checking= ⋆ Skill 1: State Districting

E The People (E-mail Interface)

http://www.e-thepeople.com/affiliates/national

Although the efficacy of their petitions is suspect, E The People also provides links to any of 170,000 elected officials, including state and local lawmakers.

THE PEOPLE
An Alex Sheshunoff Initiative

http://www.e-thepeople.com/affiliates/national/ ⋆ Skill 1: State Districting
http://www.e-thepeople.com/affiliates/national/ ⋆ Skill 7: State Votes

Alabama

http://www.state.al.us

http://www.legislature.state.al.us/misc/zipsearch.html ⋆ Skill 1: State Districting
http://www.sos.state.al.us/ ⋆ Skill 2: Voting and Polling Info
http://www.governor.state.al.us/ ⋆ Skill 3: Governor

http://www.legislature.state.al.us/ ★ Skill 4: State Legislature
http://www.legislature.state.al.us/ALISHome.html ★ Skill 5: State Bills
http://www.budget.state.al.us/stgovfin.html ★ Skill 6: State Financial Info
http://www.legislature.state.al.us/ ★ Skill 8: State E-mail
http://www.legislature.state.al.us/misc/history/constitutions/ ★ Skill 9: State
Constitution
http://www.alalinc.net/library/index.cfm ★ Skill 10: Statutes, Laws, Code

LOCAL WEB SITES

City	Birmingham	http://www.bham.net/bhamcity.html
City	Huntsville	http://www.ci.huntsville.al.us/
City	Mobile	http://www.mobile.org/
City	Montgomery	http://montgomery.al.us/
County	Montgomery	http://montgomery.al.us/
County	Maricopa	http://www.maricopa.gov/
Newspaper	*alabama live*	http://www.al.com/
Newspaper	*Birmingham Post-Herald*	http://www.postherald.com/
Newspaper	*The Huntsville Times*	http://www.traveller.com/htimes/

Alaska
http://www.state.ak.us

SKILLS

http://www.gov.state.ak.us/ltgov/elections/homepage.html ★ Skill 2: Voting and Polling
Info
http://www.gov.state.ak.us/ ★ Skill 3: Governor
http://www.legis.state.ak.us/ ★ Skill 4: State Legislature
http://www.legis.state.ak.us/basis21.htm ★ Skill 5: State Bills
http://www.gov.state.ak.us/omb/akomb.htm ★ Skill 6: State Financial Info
http://www.legis.state.ak.us/ ★ Skill 8: State E-mail
http://www.gov.state.ak.us/ltgov/akcon/table.html ★ Skill 9: State Constitution
http://www.legis.state.ak.us/FOLHOME.HTM ★ Skill 10: Statutes, Laws, Code

LOCAL WEB SITES

City	Anchorage	http://www.ci.anchorage.ak.us/
City	Juneau	http://www.juneau.lib.ak.us/
Newspaper	*Anchorage Daily News*	http://www.adn.com/

Arizona
http://www.state.az.us

SKILLS

http://www.azleg.state.az.us/maps/state.htm ★ Skill 1: State Districting
http://www.sosaz.com/ ★ Skill 2: Voting and Polling Info
http://www.governor.state.az.us/ ★ Skill 3: Governor

http://www.azleg.state.az.us/ ★ Skill 4: State Legislature
http://www.azleg.state.az.us/ ★ Skill 5: State Bills
http://www.state.az.us/ospb/ ★ Skill 6: State Financial Info
http://www.azleg.state.az.us/ ★ Skill 8: State E-mail
http://www.azleg.state.az.us/ars/const/const.htm ★ Skill 9: State Constitution
http://www.dlapr.lib.az.us/law/resources.htm ★ Skill 10: Statues, Laws, Code

LOCAL WEB SITES

City	Glendale	http://www.ci.glendale.az.us/
City	Mesa	http://www.ci.mesa.az.us/
City	Phoenix	http://www.ci.phoenix.az.us/
City	Scottsdale	http://www.ci.scottsdale.az.us/
City	Temple	http://www.tempe.gov/
City	Tucson	http://www.ci.tucson.az.us/
County	Pima	http://www.co.pima.az.us/
Newspaper	*The Arizona Republic*	http://www.azcentral.com/

Arkansas
http://www.state.ar.us

SKILLS

http://www.sosweb.state.ar.us/legmaps/ ★ Skill 1: State Districting
http://www.sosweb.state.ar.us./elect.html ★ Skill 2: Voting and Polling Info
http://www.state.ar.us/governor/governor.html/ ★ Skill 3: Governor
http://www.arkleg.state.ar.us/ ★ Skill 4: State Legislature
http://www.arkleg.state.ar.us/ ★ Skill 5: State Bills
http://www.state.ar.us/dfa/revenue_budgets.html ★ Skill 6: State Financial Info
http://www.arkleg.state.ar.us/scripts/ABLR/members/memb ★ Skill 8: State E-mail
http://www.arkleg.state.ar.us/data/constitution/index.html ★ Skill 9: State Constitution
http://www.arkleg.state.ar.us/lpbin/lpext.dll ★ Skill 10: Statutes, Laws, Code

LOCAL WEB SITES

City	Little Rock	http://www.littlerockinfo.com/
Newspaper	*Arkansas Democrat-Gazette*	http://www.ardemgaz.com/

California
http://www.ca.gov

SKILLS

http://www.calvoter.org/maps/index.html ★ Skill 1: State Districting
http://www.ss.ca.gov/ ★ Skill 2: Voting and Polling Info
http://www.governor.ca.gov/s/ ★ Skill 3: Governor
http://www.leginfo.ca.gov/ ★ Skill 4: State Legislature
http://www.leginfo.ca.gov/ ★ Skill 5: State Bills
http://www.ca.gov/s/issues/budget/index.html ★ Skill 6: State Financial Info

http://www.ca.gov/s/govt/letigisca.html ★ Skill 8: State E-mail
http://www.leginfo.ca.gov/const.html ★ Skill 9: State Constitution
http://www.leginfo.ca.gov/calaw.html ★ Skill 10: Statutes, Laws, Code

LOCAL WEB SITES

City	Anaheim	http://www.anahiem.net/
City	Berkeley	http://www.ci.berkeley.ca.us/
City	Burbank	http://burbank.acityline.com/
City	Chula Vista	http://www.ci.chula-vista.ca.us/
City	Fremont	http://www.ci.fremont.ca.us/
City	Garden Grove	http://www.ci.garden-grove.ca.us/
City	Glendale	http://www.keyconnect.com/glendale/
City	Huntington Beach	http://www.ci.huntington-beach.ca.us/
City	Long Beach	http://www.ci.long-beach.ca.us/
City	Los Angeles	http://www.ci.la.ca.us/
City	Modesto	http://www.ci.modesto.ca.us
City	Oakland	http://oaklandnet.com/
City	Oceanside	http://www.ci.oceanside.ca.us/
City	Ontario	http://www.ci.ontario.ca.us/
City	Oxnard	http://www.ci.oxnard.ca.us/
City	Pasadena	http://www.ci.pasadena.ca.us/
City	Pomona	http://www.ci.pomona.ca.us/
City	Riverside	http://www.ci.riverside.ca.us/
City	Sacramento	http://www.sacto.org/
City	San Diego	http://www.sannet.gov/
City	San Francisco	http://www.ci.sf.ca.us/
City	San Jose	http://www.ci.san-jose.ca.us
City	Santa Barbara	http://www.ci.santa-barbara.ca.us/
City	Stockton	http://www.stocktongov.com/
City	Torrance	http://www.ci.torrance.ca.us/
County	San Francisco	http://www.ci.sf.ca.us/
County	Alameda	http://www.ci.alameda.ca.us/
County	Contra Costa	http://www.co.contra-costa.ca.us/
County	Fresno	http://www.fresno.ca.gov/
County	Kern	http://www.kerncounty.com/
County	Los Angeles	http://www.co.la.ca.us/bos/bos/bos.htm/
County	Merced	http://www.co.merced.ca.us/
County	Monterey	http://www.co.monterey.ca.us/
County	Orange	http://www.oc.ca.gov/
County	Riverside	http://www.co.riverside.ca.us/
County	Sacramento	http://www.co.sacramento.ca.us/
County	San Bernadino	http://www.co.san-bernadino.ca.us/
County	San Diego	http://www.co.san-diego.ca.us/
County	San Joaquin	http://www.co.san-joaquin.ca.us/
County	San Mateo	http://www.co.sanmateo.ca.us/
County	Santa Barbara	http://www.co.santa-barbara.ca.us/
County	Santa Clara	http://claraweb.co.santa-clara.ca.us/
County	Sonoma	http://www.sonoma-county.org/
County	Stanislaus	http://www.co.stanislaus.ca.us/
County	Ventura	http://www.ventura.org/vencnty.htm/
Newspaper	*Los Angeles Times*	http://www.latimes.com/
Newspaper	*The Sacramento Bee*	http://www.sacbee.com/

Newspaper	*The San Diego Union-Tribune*	http://www.uniontrib.com/
Newspaper	*San Francisco Chronicle*	http://www.sfgate.com/
Newspaper	*San Francisco Examiner*	http://www.examiner.com/
Newspaper	*San Jose Mercury News*	http://www.mercurycenter.com/

Colorado
http://www.state.co.us

SKILLS

http://www.state.cp.us/gov_dir/stateleg.html ★ Skill 1: State Districting
http://www.sos.state.co.us/elections/electioninfo.html ★ Skill 2: Voting and Polling Info
http://www.state.co.us/gov_dir/governor_office.html ★ Skill 3: Governor
http://www.state.co.us/gov_dir/stateleg.html ★ Skill 4: State Legislature
http://www.state.co.us/gov_dir/stateleg.html ★ Skill 5: State Bills
http://www.state.co.us/gov_dir/govnr_dir/osph/stateplan_g ★ Skill 6: State Financial Info
http://www.state.co.us/gov_dir/govmenu.html#elected ★ Skill 8: State E-mail
http://www.state.co.us/gov_dir/gss/archives/constitution/ind ★ Skill 9: State
    Constitution
http://165.212.243.216/stat99/ ★ Skill 10: Statutes, Laws, Code

LOCAL WEB SITES

City	Aurora	http://www.ci.aurora.co.us/
City	Boulder	http://www.ci.boulder.co.us/
City	Colorado Springs	http://www.colorado-springs.com/
City	Fort Collins	http://www.ci.fort-collins.co.us/
City	Lakewood	http://www.lakewood.org/
County	Arapahoe	http://www.co.arapahoe.co.us/
County	El Paso	http://www.co.el-paso.co.us/
Newspaper	*DenverPost*	http://www.denverpost.com/
Newspaper	*RockyMountainNews*	http://www.denver-rmn.com/

Connecticut
http://www.state.ct.us

SKILLS

http://www.cga.state.ct.us/maps/map.htm ★ Skill 1: State Districting
http://www.sots.state.ct.us/ ★ Skill 2: Voting and Polling Info
http://www.state.ct.us/governor/ ★ Skill 3: Governor
http://www.cga.state.ct.us/ ★ Skill 4: State Legislature
http://www.cga.state.ct.us/three/legislative_info.asp ★ Skill 5: State Bills
http://www.opm.state.ct.us/ ★ Skill 6: State Financial Info
http://www.cga.state.ct.us/ ★ Skill 8: State E-mail
http://www.state.ct.us/sots/RegisterManual/ctconstit.htm ★ Skill 9: State Constitution
http://www.cga.state.ct.us/three/asp/SearchCurrent.asp ★ Skill 10: Statutes, Laws, Code

LOCAL WEB SITES

City	Danbury	http://www.danbury.lib.ct.us/
City	Hartford	http://ci.hartford.ct.us/
City	New Haven	http://www.cityofnewhaven.com/
Newspaper	*The Hartford Courant*	http://www.courant.com/
Newspaper	*News-Times*	http://www.newstimes.com/

Delaware
http://www.state.de.us

SKILLS:

http://www.state.de.us/election/index.htm ★ Skill 1: State Districting
http://www.state.de.us/election/index.htm ★ Skill 2: Voting and Polling Info
http://www.state.de.us/governor/index.htm ★ Skill 3: Governor
http://www.state.de.us/delegis.htm ★ Skill 4: State Legislature
http://Aosta.state.de.us/Lis/LIS140.nsf/$$WebHome?openf ★ Skill 5: State Bills
http://www.state.de.us/budget.htm ★ Skill 6: State Financial Info
http://www.state.de.us/contacts.htm ★ Skill 8: State E-mail
http://www.state.de.us/facts/constit/de_const.htm ★ Skill 9: State Constitution
http://www.state.de.us/research/dor/code.htm ★ Skill 10: Statutes, Laws, Code

UNIQUE FEATURES

http://www.state.de.us/facts/ushist/ ★ "Little Known Facts About the Revolution"
provides historic tidbits such as the "other" Boston Tea Party, and the fact that
Americans had the lowest taxes in the Western Hemisphere when we revolted.

District of Columbia
http://www.ci.washington.dc.us

SKILLS

http://dcboee.org/ ★ Skill 2: Voting and Polling Info
(Mayor)http://www.washingtondc.gov/mayor/index.htm ★ Skill 3: Governor
http://www.dccouncil.washington.dc.us/ ★ Skill 4: State Legislature
http://www.dccouncil.washington.dc.us/ ★ Skill 5: State Bills
http://www.dcfra.gov/budget.html ★ Skill 6: State Financial Info
http://www.dccouncil.washington.dc.us/ ★ Skill 8: State E-mail
http://www.lexislawpublishing.com/sdCGI-BIN/om_isapi.dll ★ Skill 9: State
    Constitution
http://www.lexislawpublishing.com/sdCGI-BIN/om_isapi.dll ★ Skill 10: Statutes, Laws,
    Code

LOCAL WEB SITES

Newspaper	*The Washington Post*	http://www.washingtonpost.com/
Newspaper	*Washington Times*	http://www.washtimes-weekly.com/

Florida
http://www.state.fl.us

SKILLS

http://www.leg.state.fl.us/citizen/findleg/index.html ⋆ Skill 1: State Districting
http://election.dos.state.fl.us/online/index.shtml ⋆ Skill 2: Voting and Polling Info
http://www.eog.state.fl.us/ ⋆ Skill 3: Governor
http://www.leg.state.fl.us/ ⋆ Skill 4: State Legislature
http://www.leg.state.fl.us/ ⋆ Skill 5: State Bills
http://www.state.fl.us/eog/budget/99-00/budget_material.html ⋆ Skill 6: State
  Financial Info
http://www.leg.state.fl.us/ ⋆ Skill 8: State E-mail
http://www.leg.state.fl.us/citizen/documents/statutes/index.html ⋆ Skill 9: State
  Constitution
http://www.leg.state.fl.us/citizen/documents/statutes/index.html ⋆ Skill 10: Statutes,
  Laws, Code

LOCAL WEB SITES

City	Clearwater	http://www.ci.clearwater.fl.us/
City	Fort Lauderdale	http://info.ci.ftlaud.fl.us/
City	Gainesville	http://www.state.fl.us/gvl/
City	Hollywood	http://www.hollywoodfl.org/
City	Jacksonville	http://www.ci.ax.fl.us
City	Lakeland	http://www.lakeland.net/
City	Miami Beach	http://ci.miami-beach.fl.us/
City	Orlando	http://www.ci.orlando.fl.us/
City	Saint Petersburg	http://www.stpete.org/
City	Tallahassee	http://fcn.state.fl.us/citytlh/
City	Tampa	http://www.ci.tampa.fl.us/
County	Brevard	http://www.brev.lib.fl.us/
County	Broward	http://www.co.broward.fl.us/
County	Hillsborough	http://www.hillsboroughcounty.org/
County	Dade	http://www.metro-dade.com/
County	Orange	http://www.onetgov.net
County	Palm Beach	http://www.co.palm-beach.fl.us/
County	Pinellas	http://www.co.pinellas.fl.us/bcc/
County	Polk	http://www.polk-county.net/
County	Volusia	http://volusia.org/
Newspaper	*The Miami Herald*	http://www.herald.com/
Newspaper	*St. Petersburg Times*	http://www.sptimes.com/
Newspaper	*Sun-Sentinel*	http://www.sun-sentinel.com/
Newspaper	*The Tampa Tribune*	http://www.tampatrib.com/

Georgia
http://www.state.ga.us

SKILLS

http://www.sos.state.ga.us/elections/ ⋆ Skill 1: State Districting
http://www.sos.state.ga.us/elections/ ⋆ Skill 2: Voting and Polling Info

http://www.gagovernor.org/ ★ Skill 3: Governor
http://www2.state.ga.us./Legis/ ★ Skill 4: State Legislature
http://www2.state.ga.us/Legis/ ★ Skill 5: State Bills
http://www.opb.state.ga.us/ ★ Skill 6: State Financial Info
http://www2.state.ga.us/Legis/ ★ Skill 8: State E-mail
http://www.sos.state.ga.us/93%2D94register/93%2D94%20chapter%2001/
93%2D94%20 ★ Skill 9: State Constitution
http://www2.state.ga.us/Legis/Chapter%2001%20preamble.html ★ Skill 10: Statutes,
Laws, Code

LOCAL WEB SITES

City	Albany	http://www.albany.ga.us/
City	Atlanta	http://www.atlanta.org/
City	Columbus	http://www.columbusga.com/
County	Cobb	http://www.cobb-net.com/
County	DeKalb	http://www.co.dekalb.ga.us/
County	Fulton	http://www.co.fulton.ga.us/
County	Gwinnett	http://www.co.gwinnett.ga.us/
Newspaper	*The Atlanta Journal-Constitution*	http://www.accessatlanta.com/partners/ajc/

Hawaii
http://www.state.hi.us

SKILLS

http://166.122.126.181/site1/info/info.asp?press1=info ★ Skill 1: State Districting
http://www.state.hi.us/elections/ ★ Skill 2: Voting and Polling Info
http://gov.state.hi.us ★ Skill 3: Governor
http://166.122.126.181/site1/info/info.asp?Press1=info/ ★ Skill 4: State Legislature
http://166.122.126.181/site1/docs/docs.asp?press1=docs ★ Skill 5: State Bills
http://www.state.hi.us/budget/ ★ Skill 6: State Financial Info
http://166.122.126.181/site1/info/info.asp?press1=info ★ Skill 8: State E-mail
http://www.state.hi.us/lrb/con/ ★ Skill 9: State Constitution
http://166.122.126.181/site1/docs/docs.asp?press1=docs ★ Skill 10: Statutes, Laws, Code

LOCAL WEB SITES

City	Honolulu	http://www.co.honolulu.hi.us/

Idaho
http://www.state.id.us

SKILLS

http://www.state.id.us/legislat/map/ ★ Skill 1: State Districting
http://www.idsos.state.id.us/ ★ Skill 2: Voting and Polling Info

http://www.state.id.us/gov/govhmpg.htm ★ Skill 3: Governor
http://www.state.id.us/legislat/legislat.html/ ★ Skill 4: State Legislature
http://www3.state.id.us/legislat/legtrack.html ★ Skill 5: State Bills
http://www.state.id.us/dfm/dfm.htm ★ Skill 6: State Financial Info
http://www.state.id.us/legislat/legislat.html#const ★ Skill 8: State E-mail
http://www3.state.id.us/idstat/const/constTOC.html ★ Skill 9: State Constitution
http://www3.state.id.us/idstat/TOC/idstTOC.html ★ Skill 10: Statutes, Laws, Code

LOCAL WEB SITES

| County | Ada | http://adaweb.co.ada.id.us/ |
| Newspaper | *IdahoStatesman* | http://www.idahostatesman.com/ |

Illinois
http://www.state.il.us

SKILLS

http://www.state.il.us/legis/map.htm ★ Skill 1: State Districting
http://www.elections.state.il.us/VoteInfo/pages/welcome.asp ★ Skill 2: Voting and Polling Info
http://www.state.il.us/gov/ ★ Skill 3: Governor
http://www.state.il.us/legis/default.htm ★ Skill 4: State Legislature
http://www.state.il.us/budget/ ★ Skill 6: State Financial Info
http://www.state.il.us/legis/default.htm ★ Skill 8: State E-mail
http://www.state.il.us/gov/bio/const1.htm ★ Skill 9: State Constitution
http://www.legis.state.il.us/ilcs/chapterlist.html ★ Skill 10: Statutes, Laws, Code

LOCAL WEB SITES

City	Chicago	http://www.ci.chi.il.us/
City	Rockford	http://www.rockford.il.us/
City	Springfield	http://www.springfield-il.com/
County	Cook	http://www.co.cook.il.us/
County	DuPage	http://www.co.dupage.il.us/
Newspaper	*Chicago Sun-Times*	http://www.suntimes.com/
Newspaper	*Chicago Tribune*	http://www.chicago.tribune.com/
Newspaper	*The State Journal-Register*	http://www.sj-r.com/

Indiana
http://www.state.in.us

SKILLS

http://www.state.in.us/legislative/about.html ★ Skill 1: State Districting Info
http://www.state.in.us/sos/elections/ ★ Skill 2: Voting and Polling
http://www.state.in.us/gov/ ★ Skill 3: Governor

http://www.state.in.us/legislative/ ★ Skill 4: State Legislature
http://www.state.in.us/legislative/billwatch.html ★ Skill 5: State Bills
http://www.state.in.us/sba/index.html ★ Skill 6: State Financial Info
http://www.state.in.us/legislative/leg_staff.html ★ Skill 8: State E-mail
http://www.ai.org/icpr/webfile/consti/1816.html ★ Skill 9: State Constitution
http://www.state.in.us/legislative/ic/code/ ★ Skill 10: Statutes, Laws, Code

LOCAL WEB SITES

City	Evansville	http://www.evansville.net/eville/
City	Fort Wayne	http://www.ci.ft-wayne.in.us/
City	Indianapolis	http://www.indygov.org/
City	South Bend	http://www.ci.south-bend.in.us/
Newspaper	Evansville Courier & Press	http://www.evansville.net/
Newspaper	The Journal Gazette	http://www.fortwayne.com/
Newspaper	The Indianapolis Star	http://www.starnews.com/

Iowa
http://www.iowaccess.org

SKILLS

http://www.legis.state.ia.us/Members/78GA-members.html ★ Skill 1: State Districting
http://www.sos.state.legis.ia.us//new/sos/elections.html ★ Skill 2: Voting and Polling
Info
http://www.state.ia.us/government/governor/index.htm/ ★ Skill 3: Governor
http://www.legis.state.ia.us/ ★ Skill 4: State Legislature
http://www.legis.state.ia.us/GA/78GA/Legislation/index.htm ★ Skill 5: State Bills
http://www.state.ia.us/government/dom/state_government. ★ Skill 6: State Financial Info
http://www.legis.state.ia.us/Members/78GA-members.html ★ Skill 8: State E-mail
http:sh/www.legis.state.ia.us/Constitution.html ★ Skill 9: State Constitution
http://www.legis.state.ia.us/Code.html ★ Skill 10: Statutes, Laws, Code

UNIQUE FEATURES

http://www.legis.state.ia.us/RealAu ★ "Floor Debate Audio" allows you to listen to Iowa
House and Senate chambers.

LOCAL WEB SITES

City	Cedar Rapids	http://www.fyiowa.com/iowa/cityofcr/
City	Des Moines	http://www.ci.des-moines.ia.us/
Newspaper	The Des Moines Register	http://www.desmoinesregister.com/

Kansas
http://www.state.ks.us

SKILLS

http://www.kssos.org/elewelc.html ⋆ Skill 2: Voting and Polling Info
http://www.ink.org/public/governor/ ⋆ Skill 3: Governor
http://www.state.ks.us/public/legislative/ ⋆ Skill 4: State Legislature
http://www.ink.org/public/legislative/index.cgi ⋆ Skill 5: State Bills
http://da.state.ks.us/budget/ ⋆ Skill 6: State Financial Info
http://www.ink.org/public/legislative/main.html ⋆ Skill 8: State E-mail
http://skyways.lib.ks.us/ksl/ref/ks_const.html ⋆ Skill 9: State Constitution
http://www.ink.org/public/legislative/index.cgi ⋆ Skill 10: Statutes, Laws, Code

UNIQUE FEATURES

http://www.ink.org/public/legislative ⋆ Live legislative sessions on RealAudio.

LOCAL WEB SITES

City	Kansas City	http://www.wycokck.org
City	Lawrence	http://www.ci.lawrence.ks.us/
City	Topeka	http://www.topeka.org/
City	Wichita	http://www.ci.wichita.ks.us/
County	Wyandotte	http://www.wycokck.org
County	Sedgwick	http://www.sedgwick.ks.us/

Kentucky
http://www.state.ky.us

SKILLS

http://www.lrc.state.ky.us/#whoswho ⋆ Skill 1: State Districting
http://www.sos.state.ky.us/ElecDiv.htm ⋆ Skill 2: Voting and Polling Info
http://www.state.ky.us/patmsg.htm ⋆ Skill 3: Governor
http://www.lrc.state.ky.us/home.htm/ ⋆ Skill 4: State Legislature
http://www.lrc.state.ky.us/legislat/legislat.htm ⋆ Skill 5: State Bills
http://www.state.ky.us/ ⋆ Skill 6: State Financial Info
http://www.lrc.state.ky.us/whoswho/whoswho.htm ⋆ Skill 8: State E-mail
http://www.lrc.state.ky.us/legresou/constitu/intro.htm ⋆ Skill 9: State Constitution
http://www.lrc.state.ky.us/statrev/frontpg.htm ⋆ Skill 10: Statutes, Laws, Code

LOCAL WEB SITES

City	Frankfort	http://www.frankfortky.org/
City	Lexington	http://www.lfucg.com/
City	Owensboro	http://www.owensboro.org/
County	Fayette Urban	http://www.lfucg.com/
Newspaper	*The Courier-Journal*	http://www.courier-journal.com
Newspaper	*Lexington Herald-Leader*	http://www.kentuckyconnect.com/

Louisiana
http://www.state.la.us

SKILLS

http://www.legis.state.la.us/welcome.htm   ★ Skill 1: State Districting
http://www.laelections.org/   ★ Skill 2: Voting and Polling Info
http://www.gov.state.la.us/   ★ Skill 3: Governor
http://www.legis.state.la.us/welcome.htm   ★ Skill 4: State Legislature
http://www.legis.state.la.us/welcome.htm   ★ Skill 5: State Bills
http://www.state.la.us/opb/index.htm   ★ Skill 6: State Financial Info
http://www.legis.state.la.us/welcome.htm   ★ Skill 8: State E-mail
http://senate.legis.state.la.us/documents/constitution/   ★ Skill 9: State Constitution
http://www.state.la.us/osr/lac/lac.htm   ★ Skill 10: Statutes, Laws, Code

LOCAL WEB SITES

City	New Orleans	http://www.neworleans.com/
City	Shreveport	http://www.ci.shreveport.la.us/
County	Jefferson Parish	http://www.jeffparish.net/
Newspaper	*The Advocate*	http://www.theadvocate.com/

Maine
http://janus.state.me.us/homepage.asp

SKILLS

http://www.state.me.us/legis/   ★ Skill 1: State Districting
http://www.state.me.us/sos/sos.htm/   ★ Skill 2: Voting and Polling Info
http://www.state.me.us/governor/index.html   ★ Skill 3: Governor
http://www.state.me.us/legis/   ★ Skill 4: State Legislature
http://janus.state.me.us/legis/bills/   ★ Skill 5: State Bills
http://janus.state.me.us/spo/   ★ Skill 6: State Financial Info
http://www.state.me.us/legis/   ★ Skill 8: State E-mail
http://janus.state.me.us/legis/const/htframe.htm   ★ Skill 9: State Constitution
http://janus.state.me.us/legis/statutes/   ★ Skill 10: Statutes, Laws, Code

LOCAL WEB SITES

City	Augusta	http://www.ci.augusta.me.us
City	Lewiston	http://ci.lewiston.me.us/

Maryland
http://www.mec.state.md.us

http://mlis.state.md.us/ ★ Skill 1: State Districting

http://www.mdarchives.state.md.us/msa/mdmanual/41electp/html/oolist.html ★
Skill 2: Voting and Polling Info

http://www.gov.state.md.us/ ★ Skill 3: Governor

http://mlis.state.md.us/ ★ Skill 4: State Legislature

http://mlis.state.md.us/ ★ Skill 5: State Bills

http://www.mdarchives.state.md.us/msa/mdmanual/34bud/ ★ Skill 6: State
Financial Info

http://mlis.state.md.us/ ★ Skill 8: State E-mail

http://www.mdarchives.state.md.us/msa/mdmanual/43cons ★ Skill 9: State
Constitution

http://mlis.state.md.us/cgi-win/web_statutes.exe ★ Skill 10: Statutes, Laws, Code

City	Annapolis	http://www6.annap.infi.net/~city/
City	Baltimore	http://www.ci.baltimore.md.us/
County	Baltimore	http://www.co.ba.md.us/
County	Howard	http://www.co.ho.md.us/
County	Montgomery	http://www.co.mo.md.us/
County	Prince George's	http://www.co.pg.md.us/
Newspaper	*Sun Spot*	http://www.sunspot.net/

Massachusetts
http://www.state.ma.us

http://www.state.ma.us/legis/ ★ Skill 1: State Districting

http://www.state.ma.us/elc.htm ★ Skill 2: Voting and Polling Info

http://www.state.ma.us/gov/gov.htm ★ Skill 3: Governor

http://www.state.ma.us/legis/ ★ Skill 4: State Legislature

http://www.state.ma.us/legis/ltsform.htm ★ Skill 5: State Bills

http://www.state.ma.us/fin.htm ★ Skill 6: State Financial Info

http://www.state.ma.us/legis/ ★ Skill 8: State E-mail

http://www.state.ma.us/legis/const.htm ★ Skill 9: State Constitution

http://www.state.ma.us/legis/laws/mgl/index.htm ★ Skill 10: Statutes, Laws, Code

City	Boston	http://www.ci.boston.ma.us/
City	Brockton	http://www.brocktonmass.com/
City	Cambridge	http://www.ci.cambridge.ma.us/
City	Holyoke	http://www.holyoke.org/
City	Lowell	http://www.ci.lowell.ma.us/index.html
City	Medford	http://www.medford.org/
City	New Bedford	http://www.ci.new-bedford.ma.us/

City	Newton	http://www.ci.newton.ma.us/
City	Peabody	http://www.ci.peabody.ma.us/
City	Quincy	http://www.ci.quincy.ma.us/
City	Springfield	http://www.ci.springfield.ma.us/
City	Taunton	http://www.ci.taunton.ma.us/
City	Worcester	http://www.ci.worcester.ma.us/
Newspaper	*The Boston Globe*	http://www.boston.com/
Newspaper	*Boston Herald*	http://www.bostonherald.com/

Michigan
http://www.state.mi.us

SKILLS

http://www.state.mi.us/ ★ Skill 1: State Districting
http://www.sos.state.mi.us/election/elect.html ★ Skill 2: Voting and Polling Info
http://www.migov.state.mi.us/ ★ Skill 3: Governor
http://www.state.mi.us/ ★ Skill 4: State Legislature
http://www.michiganlegislature.org/ ★ Skill 5: State Bills
http://www.state.mi.us/dmb/ofm/ ★ Skill 6: State Financial Info
http://www.state.mi.us/ ★ Skill 8: State E-mail
http://www.state.mi.us/migov/Constitution/ConstitutionoftheStateofMichigan.htm
  ★ Skill 9: State Constitution
http://www.michiganlegislature.org/law/ ★ Skill 10: Statutes, Laws, Code

LOCAL WEB SITES

City	Ann-Arbor	http://www.ci.ann-arbor.mi.us/
City	Grand Rapids	http://www.grand-rapids.mi.us/
City	Lansing	http://ci.lansing.mi.us/
County	Oakland	http://www.co.oakland.mi.us/
County	Wayne	http://www.waynecounty.com/
Newspaper	*Detroit Free Press*	http://www.freep.com/
Newspaper	*The Detroit News*	http://www.detnews.com/

Minnesota
http://www.state.mn.us

SKILLS

http://www.sos.state.mn.us/election/maps.html ★ Skill 1: State Districting
http://www.sos.state.mn.us/election/index.html ★ Skill 2: Voting and Polling Info
http://www.state.mn.us/ebranch/governor/ ★ Skill 3: Governor
http://www.leg.state.mn.us/ ★ Skill 4: State Legislature
http://www.leg.state.mn.us/leg/legis.htm ★ Skill 5: State Bills
http://www.finance.state.mn.us/budget/ ★ Skill 6: State Financial Info
http://www.state.mn.us/ ★ Skill 8: State E-mail

http://www.house.leg.state.mn.us/cco/rules/mncon/preamble.htm ★ Skill 9: State
  Constitution
http://www.leg.state.mn.us/leg/statutes.htm ★ Skill 10: Statutes, Laws, Code

LOCAL WEB SITES

City	Duluth	http://www.ci.duluth.mn.us/
City	Minneapolis	http://www.ci.mpls.mn.us/
City	Saint Paul	http://www.stpaul.gov/
County	Hennepin	http://www.co.hennepin.mn.us/
County	Ramsey	http://www.co.ramsey.mn.us/
Newspaper	*Pioneer Planet*	http://www.pioneerpress.com/
Newspaper	*Star Tribune*	http://www.startribune.com/

Mississippi
http://www.state.ms.us

SKILLS

http://www.sos.state.ms.us/ ★ Skill 2: Voting and Polling Info
http://www.govoff.state.ms.us/ ★ Skill 3: Governor
http://www.ls.state.ms.us/ ★ Skill 4: State Legislature
http://billstatus.ls.state.ms.us/default.htm ★ Skill 5: State Bills
http://www.dfa.state.ms.us/ ★ Skill 6: State Financial Info
http://www.ls.state.ms.us/ ★ Skill 8: State E-mail
http://www.lexislawpublishing.com/sdCGI-BIN/om_isapi.dll ★ Skill 9: State Constitution
http://www.lexislawpublishing.com/sdCGI-BIN/om_isapi.dll ★ Skill 10: Statutes, Laws,
  Code

LOCAL WEB SITES

City	Jackson	http://www.city.jackson.ms.us/

Missouri
http://www.state.mo.us

SKILLS

http://www.house.state.mo.us/searchzp.htm ★ Skill 1: State Districting
http://mosl.sos.state.mo.us/sos-elec/soselec.html ★ Skill 2: Voting and Polling Info
http://www.gov.state.mo.us/ ★ Skill 3: Governor
http://www.moga.state.mo.us/ ★ Skill 4: State Legislature
http://www.house.state.mo.us/bills99/HOMESRCH.HTM ★ Skill 5: State Bills
http://www.oa.state.mo.us/bp/index.shtml ★ Skill 6: State Financial Info
http://www.moga.state.mo.us/ ★ Skill 8: State E-mail
http://www.moga.state.mo.us/homecon.htm ★ Skill 9: State Constitution
http://www.moga.state.mo.us/homestat.htm ★ Skill 10: Statutes, Laws, Code

LOCAL WEB SITES

City	Independence	http://www.ci.independence.mo.us/
City	Jefferson City	http://jeffcity.com/
City	Kansas City	http://www.kcmo.org/
City	Saint Louis	http://stlouis.missouri.org/
City	Springfield	http://www.ci.springfield.mo.us/
County	Saint Louis	http://www.co.st-louis.mo.us/
Newspaper	*Kansas City Star*	http://www.kansascity.com/
Newspaper	*St. Louis Post-Dispatch*	http://www.postnet.com/

Montana
http://www.state.mt.us

SKILLS

http://nris.state.mt.us/gis/legislat/legislat.html ★ Skill 1: State Districting
http://www.state.mt.us/sos/index.htm ★ Skill 2: Voting and Polling Info
http://www.state.mt.us/governor/governor.htm ★ Skill 3: Governor
http://leg.state.mt.us/ ★ Skill 4: State Legislature
http://leg.state.mt.us/index.htm ★ Skill 5: State Bills
http://www.state.mt.us/budget/index.htm ★ Skill 6: State Financial Info
http://leg.state.mt.us/index.htm ★ Skill 8: State E-mail
http://leg.state.mt.us/services/legal/laws.htm ★ Skill 9: State Constitution
http://leg.state.mt.us/services/legal/laws.htm ★ Skill 10: Statutes, Laws, Code

Nebraska
http://www.state.ne.us

SKILLS

http://www.unicam.state.ne.us/district.htm ★ Skill 1: State Districting
http://www.nol.org/home/SOS/Elections/election.htm ★ Skill 2: Voting and Polling Info
http://gov.nol.org/ ★ Skill 3: Governor
http://www.unicam.state.ne.us/ ★ Skill 4: State Legislature
http://www.unicam.state.ne.us/Bills.htm ★ Skill 5: State Bills
http://www.das.state.ne.us/das_budget/bud/homepg.htm ★ Skill 6: State Financial Info
http://www.unicam.state.ne.us/index.htm ★ Skill 8: State E-mail
http://www.unicam.state.ne.us/constitu.htm ★ Skill 9: State Constitution
http://www.unicam.state.ne.us/statutes.htm ★ Skill 10: Statutes, Laws, Code

LOCAL WEB SITES

City	Lincoln	http://interlinc.ci.lincoln.ne.us/
City	Omaha	http://www.ci.omaha.ne.us/
County	Douglas	http://www.co.douglas.ne.us/
Newspaper	*Lincoln Journal Star*	http://www.journalstar.com/

Nevada
http://www.state.nv.us

http://www.leg.state.nv.us/70th/Legislators/ ⋆ Skill 1: State Districting
http://sos.state.nv.us/nvelection/ ⋆ Skill 2: Voting and Polling Info
http://www.governor@govmail.state.nv.us/ ⋆ Skill 3: Governor
http://www.leg.state.nv.us/ ⋆ Skill 4: State Legislature
http://www.leg.state.nv.us/Bills/Bills.htm ⋆ Skill 5: State Bills
http://www.state.nv.us/budget/ ⋆ Skill 6: State Financial Info
http://www.leg.state.nv.us/70th/Legislators/ ⋆ Skill 8: State E-mail
http://www.leg.state.nv.us/web/Const/NVConst.html ⋆ Skill 9: State Constitution
http://www.leg.state.nv.us/law1.htm ⋆ Skill 10: Statutes, Laws, Code

LOCAL WEB SITES

City	Carson City	http://www.carson-city.nv.us/
City	Las Vegas	http://www.ci.las-vegas.nv.us/
City	Reno	http://www.reno.gov/
County	Clark	http://www.co.clark.nv.us/
Newspaper	*Las Vegas Review-Journal*	http://www.lvrj.com/

New Hampshire
http://www.state.nh.us

http://199.92.250.14/gencourt/whois.html ⋆ Skill 1: State Districting
http://www.state.nh.us/sos/ ⋆ Skill 2: Voting and Polling Info
http://www.state.nh.us/governor/index.html ⋆ Skill 3: Governor
http://www.state.nh.us/gencourt/gencourt.htm/ ⋆ Skill 4: State Legislature
http://www.state.nh.us/gencourt/gencourt.htm ⋆ Skill 5: State Bills
http://www.state.nh.us/governor/budget/ ⋆ Skill 6: State Financial Info
http://www.state.nh.us/gencourt/gencourt.htm ⋆ Skill 8: State E-mail
http://www.state.nh.us/constitution/constitution.html ⋆ Skill 9: State Constitution
http://199.92.250.14/rsa/ ⋆ Skill 10: Statutes, Laws, Code

LOCAL WEB SITES

City	Concord	http://www.ci.concord.nh.us/
Newspaper	*Concord Monitor*	http://www.cmonitor.com/
Newspaper	*The Union Leader*	http://theunionleader.com/

New Jersey
http://ww.state.nj.us

SKILLS

http://www.njleg.state.nj.us/htmllegdist.htm   ★ Skill 1: State Districting
http://www.state.nj.us/lps/elections/index.html   ★ Skill 2: Voting and Polling Info
http://www.state.nj.us/governor/   ★ Skill 3: Governor
http://www.njleg.state.nj.us/   ★ Skill 4: State Legislature
http://www.njleg.state.nj.us/   ★ Skill 5: State Bills
http://www.state.nj.us/treasury/omb/index.html   ★ Skill 6: State Financial Info
http://www.njleg.state.nj.us/   ★ Skill 8: State E-mail
http://www.njleg.state.nj.us/htmlconsearc.htm   ★ Skill 9: State Constitution
http://www.njleg.state.nj.us/html/chapter.htm   ★ Skill 10: Statutes, Laws, Code

LOCAL WEB SITES

City	Atlantic City	http://library.atlantic.city.lib.nj.us/ac/
City	Bayonne	http://www.bayonne.net/
City	Clifton	http://www.cliftononline.com/
City	Elizabeth	http://www.elizabethnj.org/
City	Jersey City	http://www.ci.jersey-city.nj.us/
City	Trenton	http://www.ci.trenton.nj.us/
County	Burlington	http://www.co.burlington.nj.us/
County	Camden	http://www.co.camden.nj.us/
County	Middlesex	http://co.middlesex.nj.us/
County	Monmouth	http://www.shore.co.monmouth.nj.us/
County	Morris	http://www.co.morris.nj.us/
County	Ocean	http://www.oceancountygov.com
County	Union	http://www.unioncountynj.org/
Newspaper	*Asbury Park Press*	http://www.injersey.com/
Newspaper	*Daily Record*	http://www.dailyrecord.com/
Newspaper	*Home News Tribune*	http://www.thnt.com/
Newspaper	*The Record*	http://www.bergen.com/
Newspaper	*The Star-Ledger*	http://www.starledger.com/
Newspaper	*The Times*	http://www.nj.com/times/

New Mexico
http://www.state.nm.us

SKILLS

http://legis.state.nm.us/   ★ Skill 1: State Districting
http://www.sos.state.nm.us/elect.htm   ★ Skill 2: Voting and Polling Info
http://www.governor.state.nm.us/   ★ Skill 3: Governor
http://www.legis.state.nm.us/   ★ Skill 4: State Legislature
http://legis.state.nm.us/scripts/FirstBillFinderForm.asp   ★ Skill 5: State Bills
http://www.stonm.org/   ★ Skill 6: State Financial Info
http://legis.state.nm.us/   ★ Skill 8: State E-mail
http://www.lexislawpublishing.com/resources   ★ Skill 9: State Constitution
http://www.lexislawpublishing.com/resources/   ★ Skill 10: Statutes, Laws, Code

City	Albuquerque	http://www.cabq.gov/
County	Barnalillo	http://www.bernco.gov/
Newspaper	*The Albuquerque Journal*	http://www.abqjournal.com/
Newspaper	*Santa Fe New Mexican*	http://www.sfnewmexican.com/

New York
http://www.state.ny.us

SKILLS

http://www.elections.state.ny.us/sboemaps/maps.htm ★ Skill 1: State Districting
http://www.elections.state.ny.us/ ★ Skill 2: Voting and Polling Info
http://www.state.ny.us/governor/ ★ Skill 3: Governor
http://www.senate.state.ny.us/ ★ Skill 4: State Legislature
http://www.senate.state.ny.us/ ★ Skill 5: State Bills
http://www.state.ny.us/dob/ ★ Skill 6: State Financial Info
http://www.senate.state.ny.us/ ★ Skill 8: State E-mail
gopher://Leginfo.LBDC.State.NY.US:70/11/.const/ ★ Skill 9: State Constitution
http://www.nylj.com/guide/ ★ Skill 10: Statutes, Laws, Code

LOCAL WEB SITES

City	Albany	http://www.albanyonline.com/
City	Buffalo	http://www.ci.buffalo.ny.us/
City	Hempstead	http://www.townofhempstead.org/
City	New York	http://www.ci.nyc.ny.us/
City	Rochester	http://www.ci.rochester.ny.us/
City	Syracuse	http://www.syracuse.ny.us/
County	Erie	http://www.erie.gov/
County	Monroe	http://www.co.monroe.ny.us/
County	Nassau	http://www.co.nassau.ny.us/
County	Onondaga	http://www.co.onondaga.ny.us/
County	Orange	http://orange-ctyny.com/
County	Rockland	http://www.co.rockland.ny.us/
County	Suffolk	http://www.co.suffolk.ny.us/
County	Westchester	http://www.co.westchester.ny.us/
Newspaper	*Buffalo News*	http://www.buffnews.com/
Newspaper	*Daily News*	http://www.nydailynews.com/
Newspaper	*NY Journal News*	http://www.nyjournalnews.com/
Newspaper	*New York Post*	http://www.nypost.com/
Newspaper	*The New York Times*	http://www.nytimes.com/
Newspaper	*Newsday*	http://www.newsday.com/
Newspaper	*Staten Island Advance*	http://www.silive.com/advance
Newspaper	*Times Union*	http://www.timesunion.com/
Newspaper	*The Village Voice*	http://www.villagevoice.com/

North Carolina
http://www.state.nc.us

SKILLS

http://www.ncga.state.nc.us/html1999/geography/html4Tran's/main.htm ★ Skill 1:
State Districting
http://www.sboe.state.nc.us/index.html ★ Skill 2: Voting and Polling Info
http://www.governor.state.nc.us ★ Skill 3: Governor
http://www.nega.state.nc.us/ ★ Skill 4: State Legislature
http://www.ncga.state.nc.us/ ★ Skill 5: State Bills
http://www.osbm.state.nc.us/osbm/index.html ★ Skill 6: State Financial Info
http://www.ncga.state.nc.us/ ★ Skill 8: State E-mail
http://statelibrary.dcr.state.nc.us/nc/stgovt/preconst.html ★ Skill 9: State Constitution
http://www.ncga.state.nc.us/Statutes/Statutes.html ★ Skill 10: Statutes, Laws, Code

UNIQUE FEATURES

http://www.ncga.state.nc.us/ ★ "Chamber Audio" allows you to listen to Assembly and
Senate when in session.

LOCAL WEB SITES

City	Asheville	http://www.asheville-nc.com/
City	Greensboro	http://www.ci.greensboro.nc.us/
City	High Point	http://www.high-point.net/
City	Raleigh	http://www.raleigh-nc.org/
City	Winston-Salem	http://www.ci.winston-salem.nc.us/
County	Cumberland	http://www.co.cumberland.nc.us/
County	Forsyth	http://www.co.forsyth.nc.us/
County	Guilford	http://www.co.guilford.nc.us/
County	Mecklenburg	http://www.mecklenburg.nc.us/
County	Wake	http://www.co.wake.nc.us/
Newspaper	*The Charlotte Observer*	http://www.charlotte.com/
Newspaper	*The News & Observer*	http://www.news-observer.com/

North Dakota
http://www.state.nd.us

SKILLS

http://www.state.nd.us/sec/ ★ Skill 1: State Districting
http://www.state.nd.us/sec/ ★ Skill 2: Voting and Polling Info
http://www.health.state.nd.us/gov/ ★ Skill 3: Governor
http://www.state.nd.us/lr/ ★ Skill 4: State Legislature
http://www.state.nd.us/lr/ ★ Skill 5: State Bills
http://www.state.nd.us/fiscal/ ★ Skill 6: State Financial Info
http://www.state.nd.us/lr/ ★ Skill 8: State E-mail
http://www.state.nd.us/lr/ ★ Skill 9: State Constitution
http://www.state.nd.us/lr/ ★ Skill 10: Statutes, Laws, Code

City	Bismarck	http://www.bismarck.org
County	Cass	http://www.co.cass.nd.us/
Newspaper	*Bismarck Tribune*	http://www.ndonline.com/

Ohio
http://www.ohio.gov

SKILLS

http://www.legislature.state.oh.us/ ★ Skill 1: State Districting
http://www.state.oh.us/sos/ ★ Skill 2: Voting and Polling Info
http://www.state.oh.us/gov/ ★ Skill 3: Governor
http://www.legislature.state.oh.us/ ★ Skill 4: State Legislature
http://www.legislature.state.oh.us/ ★ Skill 5: State Bills
http://www.ohio.gov/obm/proginf/budprog.htm ★ Skill 6: State Financial Info
http://www.legislature.state.oh.us/ ★ Skill 8: State E-mail
http://www.legislature.state.oh.us/constitution.cfm ★ Skill 9: State Constitution
http://www.ohio.gov/ohio/ohiolaws.htm ★ Skill 10: Statutes, Laws, Code

LOCAL WEB SITES

City	Akron	http://www.ci.akron.oh.us/
City	Canton	http://www.cityofcanton.com
City	Cincinnati	http://www.cinci.com/
City	Columbus	http://www.columbus.net/
City	Dayton	http://www.dayton.net/dayton
City	Toledo	http://www.ci.toledo.oh.us/
County	Lucas	http://commissioners.co.lucas.oh.us/
County	Montgomery	http://www.co.montgomery.oh.us/
Newspaper	*The Beacon Journal*	http://www.ohio.com/
Newspaper	*The Cincinnati Enquirer*	http://www.enquirer.com/
Newspaper	*The Plain Dealer*	http://www.plaind.com/
Newspaper	*The Columbus Dispatch*	http://www.dispatch.com
Newspaper	*The Blade*	http://www.toledoblade.com/index/index.html

Oklahoma
http://www.state.ok.us

SKILLS

http://www.lsb.state.ok.us/senate/SenDisMaps.html ★ Skill 1: State Districting
http://www.oklaosf.state.ok.us/~elections/ ★ Skill 2: Voting and Polling Info
http://www.state.ok.us/osfdocs/gvhp.html ★ Skill 3: Governor
http://www.lsb.state.ok.us/ ★ Skill 4: State Legislature
http://www.lsb.state.ok.us/ ★ Skill 5: State Bills
http://www.busn.ucok.edu/ole/ ★ Skill 6: State Financial Info
http://www.lsb.state.ok.us/ ★ Skill 8: State E-mail

http://oklegal.onenet.net/okcon/index.html ★ Skill 9: State Constitution
http://oklegal.onenet.net/index.html ★ Skill 10: Statutes, Laws, Code

LOCAL WEB SITES

| Newspaper | *The Oklahoman* | http://www.oklahoman.com/ |
| Newspaper | *Tulsa World* | http://www.tulsaworld.com/ |

Oregon
http://www.state.or.us

SKILLS

http://www.sos.state.or.us/elections/elechp.htm ★ Skill 2: Voting and Polling Info
http://www.governor.state.or.us/ ★ Skill 3: Governor
http://www.leg.state.or.us/ ★ Skill 4: State Legislature
http://www.leg.state.or.us/bills.html ★ Skill 5: State Bills
http://www.leg.state.or.us/lfo/ ★ Skill 6: State Financial Info
http://www.leg.state.or.us/ ★ Skill 8: State E-mail
http://www.leg.state.or.us/orcons/ ★ Skill 9: State Constitution
http://www.leg.state.or.us/ors/ ★ Skill 10: Statutes, Laws, Code

UNIQUE FEATURES

http://www.leg.state.or.us/listn/ ★ "Legislative Web Audio" allows you to listen to the Oregon Senate and House chambers when they are in session.

LOCAL WEB SITES

City	Eugene	http://www.ci.eugene.or.us/
City	Portland	http://www.ci.portland.or.us/
City	Salem	http://www.open.org/salem
County	Multnomah	http://www.multnomah.lib.or.us/cc/bev/
Newspaper	Portland *Press Herald* and *Maine Sunday Telegram*	http://www.portland.com/
Newspaper	*Statesman Journal*	http://www.statesmanjournal.com/

Pennsylvania
http://www.state.pa.us

SKILLS

http://www.legis.state.pa.us/WU01/VC/find/counties.htm ★ Skill 1: State Districting
http://www.dos.state.pa.us/election/election_night.htm ★ Skill 2: Voting and Polling Info
http://www.state.pa.us/PA_Exec/Governor/overview.html/ ★ Skill 3: Governor
http://www.legis.state.pa.us/ ★ Skill 4: State Legislature
http://www.legis.state.pa.us/WU01/LI/BI/billroom.htm ★ Skill 5: State Bills
http://www.budget.state.pa.us/ ★ Skill 6: State Financial Info

http://www.legis.state.pa.us/ ⋆ Skill 8: State E-mail
http://www.dgs.state.pa.us/pamanual/Section2/sec2.htm ⋆ Skill 9: State Constitution
http://www.pacode.com/ ⋆ Skill 10: Statutes, Laws, Code

LOCAL WEB SITES

City	Philadelphia	http://www.phila.gov/
City	Pittsburgh	http://www.city.pittsburgh.pa.us/
Country	Allegheny	http://info.co.allegheny.pa.us/
Country	Bucks	http://www.buckscounty.com/
Country	Chester	http://www.chesco.org/
Country	Delaware	http://www.co.delaware.pa.us/
Country	Lancaster	http://www.co.lancaster.pa.us/
Country	Montgomery	http://www.montcopa.org/
Newspaper	*The Morning Call*	http://www.mcall.com/
Newspaper	*The Philadelphia Daily News*	http://www.philly.com/
Newspaper	*The Inquirer*	http://www.philly.com/
Newspaper	*Pittsburgh Post-Gazette*	http://www.post-gazette.com/

Puerto Rico
http://www.fortaleza.govpr.org

Rhode Island
http://www.state.ri.us

SKILLS

http://www.state.ri.us/RIELEC/FINDOFF.htm ⋆ Skill 1: State Districting
http://www.sec.state.ri.us/ ⋆ Skill 2: Voting and Polling Info
http://www.state.ri.us/manual/data/queries/gen_.idc?Employee_ID=2 ⋆ Skill 3: Governor
http://www.rilin.state.ri.us/ ⋆ Skill 4: State Legislature
http://www.rilin.state.ri.us/gen_assembly/genmenu.html ⋆ Skill 5: State Bills
http://www.state.ri.us/legpages/sort.htm ⋆ Skill 8: State E-mail
http://www.rilin.state.ri.us/gen_assembly/RiConstitution/riconst.html ⋆ Skill 9: State Constitution
http://www.rilin.state.ri.us/Statutes/Statutes.html ⋆ Skill 10: Statutes, Laws, Code

LOCAL WEB SITES

City	East Providence	http://www.eastprovidence.com
City	Pawtucket	http://www.pawtucket.ri.us/
City	Providence	http://www.providence.ri.us/
Newspaper	*The Providence Journal*	http://www.projo.com/

South Carolina
http://www.state.sc.us

SKILLS

http://www.state.sc.us/scsec/ ★ Skill 2: Voting and Polling Info
http://www.state.sc.us/governor ★ Skill 3: Governor
http://www.state.sc.us/legislature.html ★ Skill 4: State Legislature
http://www.leginfo.state.sc.us/ ★ Skill 5: State Bills
http://www.state.sc.us/osb/ ★ Skill 6: State Financial Info
http://www.lpitr.state.sc.us/whoswho.htm ★ Skill 8: State E-mail
http://www.lpitr.state.sc.us/reports/sccnstoo.htm ★ Skill 9: State Constitution
http://www.lpitr.state.sc.us/code/statmast.htm ★ Skill 10: Statutes, Laws, Code

UNIQUE FEATURES

http://www.leginfo.state.sc.us/ ★ "LIS Web Coverage" provides live audio and video from the South Carolina legislature when in session.

LOCAL WEB SITES

City	Charleston	http://www.charleston.net/charlestoncity/
City	Columbia	http://www.columbiasc.net/
Newspaper	*The State*	http://www.thestate.com/

South Dakota
http://www.state.sd.us

SKILLS

http://www.state.sd.us/state/legis/lrc/general/general.htm ★ Skill 1: State Districting
http://www.state.sd.us/sos/sos.htm#Elections Information ★ Skill 2: Voting and Polling Info
http://www.state.sd.us/governor/welcome.htm ★ Skill 3: Governor
http://www.state.sd.us/state/legis/lrc.htm/ ★ Skill 4: State Legislature
http://www.state.sd.us/state/legis/lrc/lawstat/https/74/Billsrc ★ Skill 5: State Bills
http://www.state.sd.us/bfm/ba/ ★ Skill 6: State Financial Info
http://www.state.sd.us/state/legis/lrc/general/general.htm ★ Skill 8: State E-mail
http://www.state.sd.us/state/pride/con-indx.htm ★ Skill 9: State Constitution
http://www.state.sd.us/state/legis/lrc/statutes/lrcmenu.htm ★ Skill 10: Statutes, Laws, Code

LOCAL WEB SITES

City	Sioux Falls	http://www.sioux-fall.org/
Newspaper	*Indian Country Today*	http://www.indiancountry.com/

Tennessee
http://www.state.tn.us

SKILLS:

http://www.legislature.state.tn.us/ ★ Skill 1: State Districting
http://www.state.tn.us/sos/election.htm ★ Skill 2: Voting and Polling Info

http://www.state.tn.us/governor ★ Skill 3: Governor
http://www.legislature.state.tn.us/ ★ Skill 4: State Legislature
http://www.legislature.state.tn.us/ ★ Skill 5: State Bills
http://www.state.tn.us/finance/bud/budget.html ★ Skill 6: State Financial Info
http://www.legislature.state.tn.us/ ★ Skill 8: State E-mail
http://www.state.tn.us/sos/bluebook/tnconst.htm ★ Skill 9: State Constitution
http://www.lexislawpublishing.com/resources/ ★ Skill 10: Statues, Laws, Code

LOCAL WEB SITES

City	Chattanooga	http://www.chattanooga.gov/
City	Knoxville	http://www.ci.knoxville.tn.us/
City	Memphis	http://www.ci.memphis.tn.us/
City	Nashville	http://www.nashville.org/
County	Davidson	http://www.nashville.org/
County	Shelby	http://www.co.shelby.tn.us/
Newspaper	*The Commercial Appeal*	http://www.gomemphis.com/
Newspaper	*The Knoxville News-Sentinel*	http://www.knoxnews.com/
Newspaper	The Tennessean	http://www.tennessean.com/

Texas
http://www.state.tx.us

SKILLS

http://www.senate.state.tx.us/ ★ Skill 1: State Districting
http://www.sos.state.tx.us/function/elec1/ ★ Skill 2: Voting and Polling Info
http://www.gvoernor.state.tx.us/ ★ Skill 3: Governor
http://www.senate.state.tx.us/ ★ Skill 4: State Legislature
http://www.senate.state.tx.us/ ★ Skill 5: State Bills
http://www.governor.state.tx.us/Budget/budget_index.html ★ Skill 6: State Financial Info
http://www.senate.state.tx.us/ ★ Skill 8: State E-mail
http://www.capitol.tlc.state.tx.us/statutes/cntoc.html/ ★ Skill 9: State Constitution
http://www.capitol.tlc.state.tx.us/statutes/statutes.html ★ Skill 10: Statutes, Laws, Code

UNIQUE FEATURES

http://www.house.state.tx.us/ ★ Floor sessions for the Texas House and Senate are available on RealAudio.

LOCAL WEB SITES

City	Abilene	http://www.abilenetx.com
City	Amarillo	http://www.amarillo-tx.com
City	Arlington	http://www.ci.arlington.tx.us/
City	Austin	http://www.ci.austin.tx.us/
City	Beaumont	http://www.cityof beaumont.com/
City	Dallas	http://www.ci.dallas.tx.us/
City	Fort Worth	http://www.ci.fort-worth.tx.us/

City	Garland	http://www.ci.garland.tx.us/
City	Houston	http://www.ci.houston.tx.us/
City	Laredo	http://www.cityoflaredo.com/
City	Lubbock	http://www.ci.lubbock.tx.us/
City	Plano	http://ci.plano.tx.us/
City	San Antonio	http://www.ci.sat.tx.us/
County	Bexar	http://www.co.bexar.tx.us/
County	Harris	http://www.co.harris.tx.us/
County	Tarrant	http://www.tarrantcounty.com/
Newspaper	*Austin American-Statesman*	http://www.statesman.com/
Newspaper	*The Dallas Morning News*	http://www.dallasnews.com/
Newspaper	*Fort Worth Star-Telegram*	http://www.star-telegram.com/
Newspaper	*HoustonChronicle*	http://www.houstonchronicle.com/
Newspaper	*San Antonio Express-News*	http://www.express-news.net/

Utah
http://www.state.ut.us

SKILLS

http://www.le.state.ut.us/house/District_info/district_info.htm ★ Skill 1: State Districting

http://yeehaw.state.ut.us/ ★ Skill 2: Voting and Polling Info

http://www.governor.state.ut.us/ ★ Skill 3: Governor

http://www.state.ut.us/government/legislative.html ★ Skill 4: State Legislature

http://www.state.ut.us/government/legislative.html ★ Skill 5: State Bills

http://www.governor.state.ut.us/gopb/default.html ★ Skill 6: State Financial Info

http://www.state.ut.us/government/legislative.html ★ Skill 8: State E-mail

http://www.le.state.ut.us/%7Ecode/code.htm ★ Skill 9: State Constitution

http://www.le.state.ut.us/%7Ecode/code.htm ★ Skill 10: Statutes, Laws, Code

LOCAL WEB SITES

City	Salt Lake City	http://www.ci.slc.ut.us/
County	Salt Lake	http://www.co.slc.ut.us/
Newspaper	*desertnews*	http://www.desnews.com/

Vermont
http://www.state.vt.us

SKILLS

http://www.state.vt.us/vtmap/vtmap.htm ★ Skill 1: State Districting

http://www.sec.state.vt.us/ ★ Skill 2: Voting and Polling Info

http://www.state.vt.us/governor/index.htm/ ★ Skill 3: Governor

http://www.leg.state.vt.us/ ★ Skill 4: State Legislature

http://www.leg.state.vt.us/database/database2.cfm?Session7=2000 ★ Skill 5: State Bills

http://www.state.vt.us/fin/budget.htm ⋆ Skill 6: State Financial Info
http://www.leg.state.vt.us/legdir/legdir2.htm ⋆ Skill 8: State E-mail
http://www.leg.state.vt.us/statutes/const2.htm ⋆ Skill 9: State Constitution
http://www.leg.state.vt.us/statutes/statutes2.htm ⋆ Skill 10: Statutes, Laws, Code

Virginia
http://www.state.va.us

SKILLS

http://206.246.254.9/whosmy/constituent.asp ⋆ Skill 1: State Districting
http://www.sbe.state.va.us/ ⋆ Skill 2: Voting and Polling Info
http://www.state.va.us/governor/ ⋆ Skill 3: Governor
http://legis.state.va.us/ ⋆ Skill 4: State Legislature
http://leg 1.state.va.us/lis.htm ⋆ Skill 5: State Bills
http://www.state.va.us/dpb/ ⋆ Skill 6: State Financial Info
http://legis.state.va.us/vaonline/cg2.htm ⋆ Skill 8: State E-mail
http://legis.state.va.us/vaonline/li1.htm ⋆ Skill 9: State Constitution
http://legis.state.va.us/codecomm/codhome.htm ⋆ Skill 10: Statutes, Laws, Code

LOCAL WEB SITES

City	Alexandria	http://www.ci.alexandria.va.us/
City	Chesapeake	http://www.chesapeake.va.us/
City	Danville	http://www.ci.danville.va.us/
City	Norfolk	http://www.norfolk.va.us/
City	Petersburg	http://www.petersburg-va.org/
City	Richmond	http://www.ci.richmond.va.us/
City	Roanoke	http://www.co.roanoke.va.us/
City	Virginia Beach	http://www.virginia-beach.va.us/
County	Arlington	http://www.co.arlington.va.us/
County	Chesterfield	http://www.co.chesterfield.va.us/
County	Fairfax	http://www.co.fairfax.va.us/
County	Henrico	http://www.co.henrico.va.us/
County	Prince William	http://www.pwcgov.org/
Newspaper	*Richmond Times-Dispatch*	http://www.gatewayva.com/

Washington
http://access.wa.gov

SKILLS

http://dfind.leg.wa.gov/ ⋆ Skill 1: State Districting
http://www.secstate.wa.gov/ ⋆ Skill 2: Voting and Polling Info
http://www.wa.gov/governor/ ⋆ Skill 3: Governor
http://www.leg.wa.gov/ ⋆ Skill 4: State Legislature
http://search.leg.wa.gov/basic/textsearch/default.asp ⋆ Skill 5: State Bills

http://www.ofm.wa.gov/budget_toc.html ★ Skill 6: State Financial Info
http://www.leg.wa.gov/wsladm/default.htm ★ Skill 8: State E-mail
http://www.wa.gov/pub/other/washington_constitution.txt ★ Skill 9: State Constitution
http://www.leg.wa.gov/wsladm/rcw.htm ★ Skill 10: Statutes, Laws, Code

LOCAL WEB SITES

City	Bellevue	http://www.ci.bellevue.wa.us/
City	Seattle	http://www.ci.seattle.wa.us/
City	Tacoma	http://www.ci.tacoma.wa.us/
County	King	http://www.metrokc.gov/
County	Pierce	http://co.pierce.wa.us/
County	Snohomish	http://www.co.snohomish.wa.us/
County	Spokane	http://www.spokanecounty.org/
Newspaper	The Olympian	http://www.theolympian.com/
Newspaper	*Seattle Post-Intelligencer*	http://www.seattle-pi.com/
Newspaper	*The Seattle Times*	http://www.seattletimes.com/

West Virginia
http://www.state.wv.us

SKILLS

http://www.legis.state.wv.us/ ★ Skill 1: State Districting
http://www.state.wv.us/sec/default.htm ★ Skill 2: Voting and Polling Info
http://www.state.wv.us/governor/ ★ Skill 3: Governor
http://www.legis.state.wv.us/ ★ Skill 4: State Legislature
http://www.legis.state.wv.us/ ★ Skill 5: State Bills
http://www.state.wv.us/admin/finance/budget/ ★ Skill 6: State Financial Info
http://www.legis.state.wv.us/ ★ Skill 8: State E-mail
http://www.state.wv.us/cont/default.htm ★ Skill 9: State Constitution
http://www.legis.state.wv.us/ ★ Skill 10: Statutes, Laws, Code

LOCAL WEB SITES

Newspaper	*Charleston Daily Mail*	http://www.dailymail.com/

Wisconsin
http://www.state.wi.us

SKILLS

http://165.189.139.202/waml/ ★ Skill 1: State Districting
http://www.wisgov.state.wi.us/ ★ Skill 3: Governor
http://www.legis.state.wi.us/ ★ Skill 4: State Legislature
http://www.legis.state.wi.us/index.html ★ Skill 5: State Bills
http://www.doa.state.wi.us/debf/sbo/9901_state_budget.htm ★ Skill 6: State Financial Info

http://www.legis.state.wi.us/index.html ★ Skill 8: State E-mail
http://www.legis.state.wi.us/rsb/2wiscon.html ★ Skill 9: State Constitution
http://www.legis.state.wi.us/rsb/stats.html ★ Skill 10: Statutes, Laws, Code

UNIQUE FEATURES

http://www.legis.state.wi.us/index.html ★ "In Session" audio allows you to listen to
state government when in session.

LOCAL WEB SITES

City	Green Bay	http://www.ci.green-bay.wi.us/
City	Madison	http://www.ci.madison.wi.us/
City	Milwaukee	http://www.ci.mil.wi.us/
County	Dane	http://www.co.dane.wi.us/
Newspaper	*Milwaukee Journal Sentinel*	http://www.jsonline.com/
Newspaper	*Wisconsin State Journal*	http://www.madison.com/

Wyoming
http://www.state.wy.us

SKILLS

http://soswy.state.wy.us/director/kg/h-map.htm ★ Skill 1: State Districting
http://soswy.state.wy.us/election/election.htm ★ Skill 2: Voting and Polling Info
http://www.state.wy.us/governor/governor_home.html/ ★ Skill 3: Governor
http://legisweb.state.wy.us/ ★ Skill 4: State Legislature
http://legisweb.state.wy.us/sessions/legsess.htm ★ Skill 5: State Bills
http://www.state.wy.us/ai/budget.html ★ Skill 6: State Financial Info
http://legisweb.state.wy.us/email.htm ★ Skill 8: State E-mail
http://soswy.state.wy.us/informat/const.htm ★ Skill 9: State Constitution
http://legisweb.state.wy.us/titles/statues.htm ★ Skill 10: Statutes, Laws, Code

No sooner do you set foot on American soil than you find yourself in a sort of tumult . . . here the people of a district are assembled to discuss the possibility of building a church; there they are busy choosing a representative; further on, the delegates of a district are hurrying to town to consult about some local improvements; elsewhere it's the village farmers who have left their furrows to discuss the plan for a road or a school. One group of citizens assembles for the sole object of announcing that they disapprove of the government's course, while others unite to proclaim that the men in office are the fathers of their country.

—ALEXIS DE TOCQUEVILLE

Chapter Eight

Issues, Associations, Groups, and Coalitions

Introduction

Even if you aren't quite sure what they are, you are probably certain that "special interest groups" represent the opportunistic underbelly of American politics. Why did Tocqueville have such a drastically different view of special interest groups in our country? Far from being a cancer on the system, Tocqueville saw special interest groups as being an inextricable part of democracy—forming a vital link between the institutions that govern us and the experiences of those who are governed.

Tocqueville saw much of the frenetic pace of American life devoted to citizens forming new groups, disbanding others, and passing bylaws to address every conceivable community concern. To Tocqueville, it was the single most telling characteristic of America and her citizens.

So why do we look upon such narrowly focused groups with such disgust and distrust, as if anything but a general take on the whole gamut of issues that face us is a betrayal of the type of government that was founded here several hundred years ago? And why, if they are so disgusting, are they so effective?

A government that takes care of itself without any need for the input or expertise of its citizens is something other than a democracy and may be quite worse. The complexity of the problems that face us favor the development of special interest groups that can focus on a narrow issue and do it justice in the public arena, but often we think of special interest groups as corporate interests using their deep pockets to make the American government do their bidding.

And while for-profit corporate special interests often try to solidify their access to lawmakers through generous PAC contributions during election time—contributions that noncorporate, nonprofits are prohibited by law from also making—here we use the concept of special interest groups as interchangeable with trade associations and less formal political groups. Essentially the grassroots tools that any trade association uses are the same that are available to any group of Americans who want to organize themselves around a subject that they find mutually compelling—whether it be profits, tax breaks, civil rights, health care, national defense, or education.

You would do well to stop complaining and join a few of these groups because lots of other Americans have. In fact, over sixty-five million Americans belong to the twenty largest political associations alone—and there are literally thousands of others to choose from.

The fact is that political groups in the United States offer significant benefits to their members above and beyond their ability to monitor legislation at the federal, state, and local levels of government. A democracy that has to be extravagantly attended to by its citizens is tyranny—not exactly a cut-off-your-head king-type of tyranny, but tyranny nonetheless. You have a job (or two), and you have a family, friends, other interests. Why should you have to look after every small detail of your enormous and complex federal government? Political associations hire people to do that work for you that so you can go on about your life knowing that your interests are being strategically advanced with your lawmakers, legislation you are interested in is being tracked, and that you will be told when your input is necessary and left alone when it isn't.

Types of "Special Interest" Groups (Broad Definition)

Trade Association

A political group formed around some profession or commercial market, e.g., the American Welding Society or the American Society of Travel Agents. Trade associations usually lobby government to influence laws or regulations that apply to their business and to protect and promote their markets. Such associations are also often affiliated with PACs and ask their members to donate money for the campaigns of sympathetic candidates.

Public Interest Group

A political group that lobbies on behalf of the poor, or the uneducated, or the uninformed, or on behalf of securing a more equitable democracy for everyone, e.g., Common Cause or the The League of Women Voters.

Nonprofit Association

An Association formed around some specific educational or legislative cause. In most cases nonprofit associations are not taxed on the money that they raise, but they must also adhere to strict guidelines that regulate the type of lobbying that they can do. Nonprofits cannot participate in elections or raise money for candidates. The American Heart Association is an example of a nonprofit association.

Coalition

A group of any of the above associations that temporarily cooperate around a pending piece of legislation or common set of legislative goals. The idea is to pool resources to increase influence in areas where goals are held in common.

Reasons to Join an Association, Group, or Coalition

You Are More Powerful

In a land where every person is created equal, power accrues to those who can join together and pool their influence. While the majority cannot decide to trample on the civil rights of the minority, elections are won and laws are passed on majority vote. If you want to make a difference, you must consider joining with others who share your views even as you must learn to use your own individual voice.

An Association Can Educate You About an Issue

Much of the work that associations do is to educate legislators who do not understand an issue so that they, hopefully, will support rational policy measures. Associations almost always generate educational materials in pursuit of this task, and they can share them with you.

An Association Can Work on Your Issues Around the Clock

As an American citizen, you should have access to all of the actions your government takes and all of the information it produces, but you should not have to keep tabs on your elected officials to the exclusion of your own career, loved ones, and other interests. A political association will do that job for you, maintaining a staff that works five days a week (or more) on your issues and keeps a close eye on government.

An Association Will Mobilize You When the Time Is Right

With a vigilant staff and an active network of interested citizens, an association is able to alert you to key votes when they are taken and to the critical times to communicate with your legislators. With conflicting levels of government and elusive legislative processes at work, an association that cuts through the morass and lets you know when you are needed often provides a welcome service.

An Association Maintains Voting Records

And when it is time to vote, your association should be able to pool all of the votes on all of the issues that it followed in the course of a legislative session and let you know specifically how your member voted on the issues that are important to you. This is an excellent way for you to decide if you want to support the incumbent or if you want to give the new guy a chance.

An Association Works to "Get It Right" in the Media

Associations are often the first place print and broadcast media go to get feedback on proposed legislation or to field possible interview subjects related to pending legislation. Just as associations work to establish and feed vital relationships with lawmakers, they also work to build relationships with the media so coverage of your issues is accurate and sympathetic to your point of view. If your association is doing its job, you don't have to throw your shoe at the television because your side was not included in a news story or because the reporter completely misunderstood critical aspects of the issue at hand.

Skill 1: Conduct background research.

Caring about an issue is not the same as truly understanding it in a legislative context. To truly understand an issue, you need to know something of its history, something of its nature, and what's been done in the past to encourage a solution. If it is a complex problem, you can bet that certain approaches have already been tried. Some have shown promise. Some have wasted money. And it is almost always time to try a new, good idea. All of this information should do more than interest you: it is essential if you want to contribute to the public debate that surrounds an issue. A national association should be able to provide abundant educational materials that help you better understand where you have been, exactly what it is you are fighting for, and what the future may hold.

Skill 2: Find the legislative agenda.

A political association or group does not exist to simply make you feel better. A political association should be externally focused. It should exist to help educate government on a specific issue—to serve as an information resource, as much as a grassroots battering ram to drive home the popular support for its objectives. For that reason, every political association or group is likely to have a list of current legislation that it supports, and a list of current legislation that it opposes. If an association is effective, it will also provide a written strategy on how it proposes to influence these bills.

Skill 3: Join.

The amount of information available on association web sites and their desire to encourage grassroots activism means that a lot of legislative information may be available to you whether or not you are a member of the association. Consider *not* being a cheapskate. Your paid membership in an association helps fund the salaries of the people who research your issues, and design the web site and also helps the association demonstrate its clout on Capitol Hill or in the state capital by being able to justify a broad base of support.

But make sure you join the right association. You might agree with most of the positions on the American Dental Association's web site, but it might not be completely appropriate for you to become a member of that association if you are not a dentist. Like vampires, grassroots organizers are often starved for warm bodies, inviting any and all comers to participate in their action alerts and insisting that their positions are legitimate for all Americans, no matter what their age, income, education, or political affiliation. The differences in organizations that represent working professionals and organizations related to the issues you care about as an unpaid citizen should not be drastic, but those differences are sometimes important, as are the priorities they generate.

Skill 4: Participate in action alerts.

Nowadays, your on-line broker can automatically inform you if your portfolio is going down the toilet; news outlets can send you only the articles you would care to read; why shouldn't you expect your political association to inform you when the wheels of government are barreling down the tracks toward your rights?

The time-tested vehicle for mobilizing the membership of a political association at critical legislative junctures is called "the action alert." An action alert is a brief one- or two-page message that tells members of a political association when it is time to act. Typically an action alert will target a key legislator, or a key committee, and provide all the pertinent contact information you need to send your message, including suggested talking points that you may want to incorporate and a final request that you should make verbatim.

E-mail is particularly adept as an action alert conduit. Letters that used to take a few days to reach members and thousands of dollars in postage can be received almost instantly at little or no cost. This allows associations to respond quickly and cheaply to even fast-moving legislation in Congress or the state capital.

Keep in mind that although many action alerts come with a sample letter for you to copy, you should (briefly) personalize any message you send to your lawmakers with your own anecdotes or expertise, and always be sure to include your address so that the legislative office can verify that you are indeed a constituent. After you personalize your message, make sure that your final request conforms with the action alert exactly as it is written, e.g., "I would like you to oppose H.R. 1210." It is confusing and counterproductive if the members of a specific group make different requests as part of a grassroots campaign.

And don't forget to demand that your association provide a follow-up notice on any action alert in which you participate. As a vocal constituent, you need to know if your actions made a difference or if you need to pitch a new battle. Nothing can dampen the enthusiasm of a grassroots activist like an association that hysterically demands that you send a message and then never lets you know what happened on this issue that threatened the very stability of our universe. Demand that your associations provide this feedback.

Skill 5: Review voting report cards.

When Election Day rolls around, you are going to want to know how your legislator voted on the issues you care about, and it is the job of your

How to Conduct Opposition Research

As long as you are online, you might as well find out what the other side is up to. In a previous age, getting the opposition's strategy or arguments involved all the intrigue of a James Bond thriller—organizations had to be infiltrated, key documents obtained. The Internet has, in one fell swoop, made opposition research an easy exercise that you can do from the comfort of your own home. Don't be an Internet prude who won't give the opposition the satisfaction of even one more hit on their web site. Go there often, study their positions, their strategy. If you can respond directly and eloquently to the specific arguments of your opposition, you can neutralize them far more effectively than if you remain distanced in a cloud of moral superiority. Things to look for:

Arguments Scoffing at or disregarding the opposition's arguments does nothing to dismantle them or to inform your lawmakers about flaws in their reasoning. Any argument that is ignored stands, and any argument that is attacked in an unfair, bombastic fashion also tends to persevere. Arguments must be dismantled in order to be destroyed—that is, you must respectfully and intelligently attack their logic to disarm them.

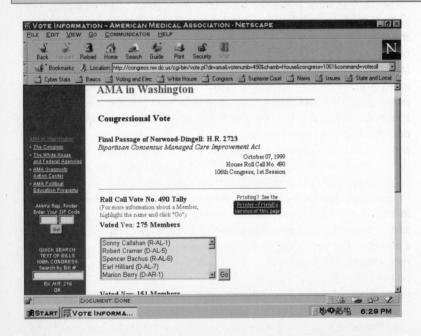

Strategy knowing the legislative agenda of your opposition is as important as knowing the agenda of the groups you support, and they do not always exist in mirrorlike contrast. Sometimes your opposition can surprise you by moving in an unexpected direction. Getting an early copy of suggested bill language from their web site can help you prepare to respond to anything they might dream up.

Mobilization It is also helpful to get on the E-mail action alert lists of your opposition, so that when they mobilize their membership, you can send a rebuttal to the same legislative or media targets, helping to balance the story, and alert both the media and government that there are voters who disagree with the position being advocated by your opposition.

What Not to Do Trying to hack into their web site, or posting outrageous bulletin board messages, or engaging in any other immature or censuring behavior is not doing opposition research; it is acting like a little tyrant. Remember what was said in the introduction—everything has opposition in this country, so don't take their web site as a personal threat. Utilize the information as a sophisticated, confident advocate, and you will not only vindicate yourself, you may end up compelling your lawmakers to follow.

political association to keep tabs on important votes and let you know how the priorities of your legislator matched up with the priorities of your association. This also makes you, the grassroots activist, exponentially more intimidating because it adds *accountability* to your arsenal—you are well aware of the actions that your lawmaker takes after you send him or her a message. A legislator who is especially helpful on your issues may warrant a campaign donation or even your time as a volunteer; a legislator who does not seem to care should find one more person in the community actively working to unseat an incumbent.

Skill 6: Search related sites.

Your association's political web site does not have to be everything to everybody, especially if there is a "sister site" out there that provides additional information or support on your issues. Links are easy to post on a web site and should be used to index every possible juncture in cyberspace that is of use to you as a cybercitizen. Such links help coalesce a political community around a common set of goals, and abundant hyperlinks should be available on your association's web site.

The Truth About On-line Petitions

Threatened are the days when you could be greeted at the grocery store by a scraggly haired youth with a petition to legalize the growing of high-quality hashish for the making of . . . rope. Because now, with less effort, and an even more lax bathing schedule, you can post an on-line petition and get people by the millions to sign their name and circulate the petition for you.

The on-line petition seems like a good idea. So good that a fair number of them have already been circulated on the Internet and made their way back to government or to major American corporations, sometimes with over a hundred thousand electronic signatures. This, it would seem, is an electronic mandate and an amazing, irresistible grassroots tool.

Recently a bunch of high-profile web sites that rely on the petition model have sprung up, proclaiming themselves the missing link between citizens and their government—the balm of all democracy. Examples include VOTE.com, e-thepeople.com, and SpeakOut.com. Unfortunately, their enthusiasm is overstated, and on-line petitions share the limited political efficacy of their plain-paper predecessors.

On-line petitions are too easy and too simplistic to either educate the constituent or to convince your legislators that you understand the issue, care deeply

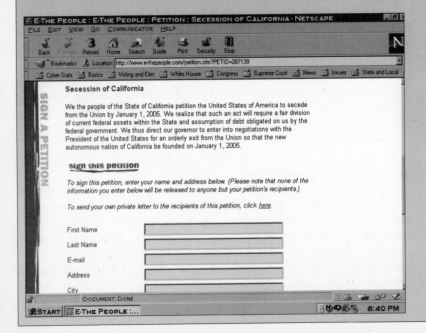

about it, and will hold them accountable on Election Day. They are all almost sadly futile, unless they are attached to some larger mechanism that uses the petition simply to identify supporters in key districts.

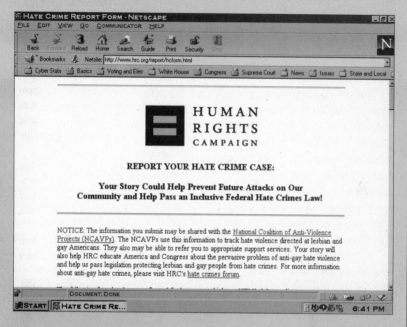

This supposed democratic "connect" threatens to further alienate the electorate when it is revealed that it is simply an illusion of citizenship. Remember that, despite the Internet myths, policy is *not* easy or fast; and any proposed piece of legislation will likely be far more specific than any "yes" or "no" question or statement made on an on-line petition.

Here are some tips to keep in mind when you come across an on-line petition:

Write Your Own Personal, Individual E-mail Message to the Person Who Is Being Targeted by the Petition—Your commitment and understanding cannot be questioned if you use your own words and send your own message to your lawmakers.

Send E-mail to the Individual or the Group That Is Circulating the Petition and Ask for Comprehensive Background Information That Explains Their Position and Their Legislative Strategy Before You Participate—If they cannot adequately explain the issue to you, or if they do not have supporting materials readily available to share with lawmakers, they are probably not savvy enough to effect real change. Even if you support the issue in general, don't lend your name to an effort that is not well thought out and organized or that otherwise proposes an unrealistic solution to an important problem.

Demand a Follow-up Report Before You Sign—When you sign your name to something, it should not matter if it was easy or electronic. You have made a personal declaration and you should expect any group that gets your signature to value your participation. They should commit to keeping you informed about their progress and gladly keep you informed about the consequences of your actions.

Skill 7: Communicate with association staff.

Any association that claims to represent you should facilitate direct communication with staff and welcome input from its members. Different associations may respond to their members in different ways, but you should be able to forge some sort of two-way communication with the people behind the web site and the lobbyists behind the legislative agenda. Remember, this is not so that you can make friends or find dates—and certainly not for you to waste other people's time with petty requests—but you deserve the same access and accountability from those associations that attempt to speak on your behalf as you expect from your lawmakers, and you might question your membership in any association that claims to value grassroots but seems reluctant to interact with them.

In addition to actually participating, your association should be able to provide you with legislative and other information in a prompt, polite, and reliable fashion. For these reasons, detailed contact information should always be provided on a web site for your convenience as an active member.

The Issues: A Guide to Association, Group, and Coalition Web Sites

Animals Rights	Foreign Relations	Religious Interests
Arts, The	Gun Control	Reproductive Rights
Campaign Finance	Health	Seniors/Aging
Reform	Higher Education	Small Business
Children/Youth	Housing/Poverty	Taxes/Budget
Civil Rights	Immigration	Think Tanks
Death Penalty	International Human	Transportation
Disabled	Rights	Veterans
Education	Internet Issues	Trade Associations
Environment	Labor Unions	
Euthanasia	Nonprofits	

Cybercitizen Web Listings

Action for Animals
http://www.enviroweb.org/aan
Action for Animals Network is a diverse group of grassroots activists united by the desire to help animals.

SKILLS

http://www.enviroweb.org/aan/join.html ★ Skill 3: Membership

http://www.enviroweb.org/aan/alerts.html ★ Skill 4: Action Alerts

http://www.enviroweb.org/aan/links.html ★ Skill 6: Related Links

http://www.enviroweb.org/aan/index.html ★ Skill 7: Contact Info/E-mail

American Society for the Prevention of Cruelty to Animals (ASPCA)
http://www.aspca.org/

ASPCA promotes humane principles, strives to prevent cruelty, and alleviates pain, fear, and suffering of animals through information, awareness, and advocacy programs.

SKILLS

http://www.lobbynet.com/ASPCA/ ★ Skill 1: Issue Background

http://www.aspca.org/help/ ★ Skill 3: Membership

http://www.lobbynet.com/ASPCA/ ★ Skill 4: Action Alerts

http://www.aspca.org/links/ ★ Skill 6: Related Links

http://www.aspca.org/help/ ★ Skill 7: Contact Info/E-mail

Animal Legal Defense Fund (ALDF)
www.aldf.org
Founded in 1979, ALDF is an animal rights law organization working nationally to defend animals from abuse and exploitation through a network of over 750 attorneys.

SKILLS

http://www.aldf.org/ ★ Skill 1: Issue Background

http://www.aldf.org/ ★ Skill 2: Legislative Agenda

http://www.aldf.org/ ★ Skill 3: Membership

http://www.aldf.org/ ★ Skill 4: Action Alerts

http://www.aldf.org/ ★ Skill 6: Related Links

http://www.aldf.org/ ★ Skill 7: Contact Info/E-mail

In Defense of Animals (IDA)
http://www.idausa.org
IDA is dedicated to ending the exploitation and abuse of animals by defending their rights, welfare, and habitats.

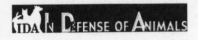

SKILLS

http://www.idausa.org/Resource/resource.html ★ Skill 1: Issue Background
http://www.idausa.org/Campaigns/campaigns.html ★ Skill 2: Legislative Agenda
http://www.idausa.org/Support/support.html ★ Skill 3: Membership
http://www.idausa.org/Alerts/ ★ Skill 4: Action Alerts
http://www.idausa.org/links.html ★ Skill 6: Related Links
http://www.idausa.org/About/contact_info.html ★ Skill 7: Contact Info/E-mail

ARTS

American Arts Alliance
http://www.artswire.org
American Arts Alliance is an organization committed to advocacy on behalf of the arts.

SKILLS

http://www.artswire.org/ ★ Skill 1: Issue Background
http://www.artswire.org/awbrox.html ★ Skill 3: Membership
http://www.artswire.org/webbase/main.cgi ★ Skill 6: Related Links
http://www.artswire.org/awstaff.html ★ Skill 7: Contact Info/E-mail

Americans for the Arts
http://www.artsusa.org
Americans for the Arts works with cultural organizations, arts, business leaders, and individuals to provide leadership, education, and information that will encourage support for the arts and culture in our nation's communities.

SKILLS

http://www.artsusa.org/advocacy/update.html ★ Skill 1: Issue Background
http://www.artsusa.org/advocacy/ ★ Skill 2: Legislative Agenda
http://www.artsusa.org/about/membership.html ★ Skill 3: Membership
http://www.artsusa.org/advocacy/update.html ★ Skill 4: Action Alerts
http://www.artsusa.org/research/ ★ Skill 6: Related Links
http://www.artsusa.org/ ★ Skill 7: Contact Info/E-mail

UNIQUE FEATURES

http://www.artsusa.org/clearinghouse/ ★ "National Arts Policy Clearinghouse" is a searchable database of federal, state, and local policy regarding the arts.

Advocates for Youth
http://www.advocatesforyouth.org
Advocates for Youth exists to fight pregnancy, sexually transmitted diseases, and HIV among adolescents.

SKILLS

http://www.advocatesforyouth.org/FACTSHET.HTM ★ Skill 1: Issue Background

http://www.advocatesforyouth.org/ ★ Skill 2: Legislative Agenda

http://www.advocatesforyouth.org/publicaffairs/ALERTMBR.HTM ★ Skill 3: Membership

http://www.advocatesforyouth.org/publicaffairs/alert.htm ★ Skill 4: Action Alerts

http://www.advocatesforyouth.org/PeerEd/PEERLINK.HTM ★ Skill 6: Related Links

http://www.advocatesforyouth.org/FEEDBACK.HTM ★ Skill 7: Contact Info/E-mail

Child Welfare League of America (CWLA)
http://www.cwla.org
CWLA is an association of more than one thousand public and private nonprofit agencies that assist over 2.5 million abused and neglected children and their families each year.

SKILLS

http://www.cwla.org/cwla.advocacy.html ★ Skill 1: Issue Background

http://www.cwla.org/cwla.advocacy.html ★ Skill 2: Legislative Agenda

http://www.cwla.org/donate.html ★ Skill 3: Membership

http://www.cwla.org/cwla.advocacy.html ★ Skill 4: Action Alerts

http://www.cwla.org/cwla.advocacy.html ★ Skill 7: Contact Info/E-mail

UNIQUE FEATURES

http://www.cwla.org/cwla/publicpolicy/statefactsheets/199astatefactsheets.html
★ "State Fact Sheets" give state-by-state statistics and policies regarding welfare of children.

Children's Defense Fund (CDF)
http://www.childrensdefense.org
CDF provides a voice for the children of America who cannot vote, lobby, or speak for themselves.

SKILLS

http://www.childrensdefense.org/issues.html ★ Skill 1: Issue Background

http://www.childrensdefense.org/issues.html ★ Skill 2: Legislative Agenda

http://www.childrensdefense.org/give.html ★ Skill 3: Membership

http://www.childrensdefense.org/takeaction/ ★ Skill 4: Action Alerts

http://www.childrensdefense.org/links.html ★ Skill 6: Related Links

http://www.childrensdefense.org/contacts.html ★ Skill 7: Contact Info/E-mail

Stand For Children
http://www.stand.org
Stand For Children is a grassroots movement that works for children to
have the opportunity to grow up healthy, educated, and safe.

SKILLS

http://www.stand.org   ★ Skill 1: Issue Background
http://www.capweb.net/stand/contact.morph   ★ Skill 2: Legislative Agenda
http://www.stand.org/membership/index.html   ★ Skill 3: Membership
http://www.capweb.net/stand/contact.morph   ★ Skill 4: Action Alerts
http://www.stand.org/about/contact/index.html   ★ Skill 7: Contact Info/E-mail

CIVIL RIGHTS

American Civil Liberties Union (ACLU)

http://www.aclu.org
ACLU is a national advocate of individual rights. ACLU litigates, legislates, and edu-
cates the public on a broad array of issues affecting individual freedom in the United
States.

SKILLS

http://www.aclu.org/   ★ Skill 1: Issue Background
http://www.aclu.org/index.html   ★ Skill 2: Legislative Agenda
https://secure20.client-mail.com/aclulink/forms/join.shtml   ★ Skill 3: Membership
http://www.aclu.org/action/mailist.html   ★ Skill 4: Action Alerts
http://scorecard.aclu.org/   ★ Skill 5: Voting Report Cards
http://www.aclu.org/feedback.html   ★ Skill 7: Contact Info/E-mail

American Conservative Union (ACU)
http://www.conservative.org
ACU's purpose is to effectively communicate and advance the goals
and principles of conservatism through the support of capitalism,
belief in the doctrine of the original intent of the framers of the
Constitution, confidence in traditional moral values, and
commitment to a strong national defense.

SKILLS

http://www.conservative.org/col.htm   ★ Skill 1: Issue Background
http://www.conservative.org/col.htm   ★ Skill 2: Legislative Agenda
http://commerce.townhall.com/conservative/join-s.html   ★ Skill 3: Membership
http://www.conservative.org/la.htm   ★ Skill 4: Action Alerts
http://www.conservative.org/res.htm   ★ Skill 6: Related Links
http://www.conservative.org/ssbd.htm   ★ Skill 7: Contact Info/E-mail

The American Jewish Committee (AJC)
http://www.ajc.org

AJC works to safeguard the welfare and security of Jews
in the United States, in Israel, and throughout the world,
and to strengthen the basic principles of pluralism as the
best defense against anti-Semitism and other forms of bigotry.

SKILLS

http://www.ajc.org/ ★ Skill 1: Issue Background
http://www.ajc.org/da/index.asp ★ Skill 2: Legislative Agenda
http://www.ajc.org/m/index.asp ★ Skill 3: Membership
http://www.ajc.org/ ★ Skill 4: Action Alerts
http://www.ajc.org/l/index.asp ★ Skill 6: Related Links
http://www.ajc.org/wwa/index.asp ★ Skill 7: Contact Info/E-mail

Anti-Defamation League (ADL)
http://www.adl.org

ADL teaches the values of diversity and fighting bigotry,
anti Semitism, racism, and all forms of hatred. They work
with policy makers, civic leaders, and educators to develop comprehensive approaches for
the prevention of bias.

SKILLS

http://www.adl.org/frames/front_backgrounders.html ★ Skill 1: Issue Background
http://www.adl.org/frames/front_government.html ★ Skill 2: Legislative Agenda
https://secure.adl.org/ ★ Skill 3: Membership
http://www.adl.org/frames/front_legislastive.html ★ Skill 4: Action Alerts
http://www.adl.org/frames/front_legislative.html ★ Skill 5: Voting Report Cards
http://www.adl.org/frames/front_contact.html ★ Skill 7: Contact Info/E-mail

UNIQUE FEATURES

http://www.adl.org/hate-pathol/info/default.htm ★ "HateFilter" can be downloaded to
block access to racist and anti-Semitic web sites.

The Feminist Majority
http://www.feminist.org

The Feminist Majority advocates the political, economic, and social equality of
women.

SKILLS

http://www.feminist.org/research/1_public.html ★ Skill 1: Issue Background
http://www.feminist.org/action/1_action.html ★ Skill 2: Legislative Agenda
https://secure09.client-mail.com/fmflink/forms/join.html ★ Skill 3: Membership

http://www.feminist.orgl/action/1action.html   ★ Skill 4: Action Alerts
http://www.feminist.org/gateway/1_gatway.html   ★ Skill 6: Related Links
http://www.feminist.org/forms/comments.html   ★ Skill 7: Contact Info/E-mail

Human Rights Campaign (HRC)
http://www.hrc.org
HRC fights for personal, professional, and social accept-
ance of gays and lesbians.

SKILLS

http://www.hrc.org/issues/index.html   ★ Skill 1: Issue Background
http://www.hrc.org/issues/index.html   ★ Skill 2: Legislative Agenda
http://www.hrc.org/joinus/index.html   ★ Skill 3: Membership
http://www.hrc.org/   ★ Skill 4: Action Alerts
http://www.hrc.org/camp2000/states.html   ★ Skill 6: Related Links
http://www.hrc.org/hrc/staff/index.html   ★ Skill 7: Contact Info/E-mail

UNIQUE FEATURES

http://www.hrc.org   ★ Hate crime and discrimination questionnaires helps gather real-life
examples for legislative and legal pursuits.

League of United Latin American Citizens (LULAC)
http://www.lulac.org
LULAC advances the economic condition, educational attainment, political
influence, health, and civil rights of Hispanic Americans through community-
based programs.

SKILLS

http://www.lulac.org/Issues.html   ★ Skill 1: Issue Background
http://www.lulac.org/Issues.html   ★ Skill 2: Legislative Agenda
http://www.lulac.org/Members/Meminfo.html   ★ Skill 3: Membership
http://www.lulac.org/Issues/Alerts.html   ★ Skill 4: Action Alerts
http://www.lulac.org/NHLA.html   ★ Skill 5: Voting Report Cards
http://www.lulac.org/Links.html   ★ Skill 6: Related Links
http://www.lulac.org/About/Email.html   ★ Skill 7: Contact Info/E-mail

NAACP (National Association for the Advancement of Colored People)
http://www.naacp.org
NAACP is dedicated to the rights of African Americans and the promotion of nondiscrimination policies.

SKILLS

http://www.naacp.org/join/ ★ Skill 3: Membership
http://www.naacp.org/issues/ ★ Skill 4: Action Alerts
http://www.naacp.org/links/ ★ Skill 6: Related Links
http://www.naacp.org/about/ ★ Skill 7: Contact Info/E-mail

National Congress of American Indians (NCAI)
http://www.ncai.org

NCAI is the oldest and largest national Indian organization advocating unity and cooperation among tribal governments for the security protection of treaty and sovereign rights.

SKILLS

http://www.ncai.org/indianissues/issuesinindiancountry.htm ★ Skill 1: Issue
  Background
http://www.ncai.org/indianissues/issuesinindiancountry.htm ★ Skill 2: Legislative
  Agenda
http://www.ncai.org/NCAIHomePage/membership/membership1.htm ★ Skill 3:
  Membership
http://www.ncai.org/AboutNCAI/ncaistaff.htm ★ Skill 7: Contact Info/E-mail

UNIQUE FEATURES

http://www.ncai.org/NCAICalander/ncainational.calander.htm ★ "Senate Committee
  on Indian Affairs Hearing Schedule" lists all hearings, meetings, and markups by month.

National Council of La Raza (NCLR)
http://www.nclr.org

NCLR is a private, nonprofit, nonpartisan organization fighting to reduce poverty and discrimination and improve the lives of Hispanic Americans.

SKILLS

http://www.nclr.org/policy/ ★ Skill 1: Issue Background
http://www.nclr.org/policy/ ★ Skill 2: Legislative Agenda
http://www.nclr.org/assco/ ★ Skill 3: Membership
http://www.nclr.org/policy/ ★ Skill 4: Action Alerts
http://www.nclr.org/links/ ★ Skill 6: Related Links
http://www.nclr.org/contact.html ★ Skill 7: Contact Info/E-mail

NOW (National Organization for Women)
http://www.now.org

NOW is a national feminist organization committed to fighting against gender discrimination and for the civil rights of all Americans.

SKILLS

http://www.now.org/issues/ ⋆ Skill 1: Issue Background
http://www.now.org/issues/legislat/03-09-00.html ⋆ Skill 2: Legislative Agenda
http://www.now.org/support.html ⋆ Skill 3: Membership
http://www.now.org/actions/ ⋆ Skill 4: Action Alerts
http://www.now.org/resource.html ⋆ Skill 6: Related Links
http://www.now.org/cgi-bin/comments.pl ⋆ Skill 7: Contact Info/E-mail

Parents, Families and Friends of Lesbians and Gays (PFLAG)

http://www.pflag.org
PFLAG promotes the health and well-being of gay, lesbian, bisexual and transgendered persons, their families, and friends to cope with an adverse society, to enlighten an ill-informed public, and to end discrimination.

SKILLS

http://www.pflag.org/store/resource/info.html ⋆ Skill 1: Issue Background
http://www.pflag.org/ ⋆ Skill 2: Legislative Agenda
http://www.pflag.org/join/join.html ⋆ Skill 3: Membership
http://www.pflag.org/ ⋆ Skill 4: Action Alerts
http://www.pflag.org/store/resource/links.html ⋆ Skill 6: Related Links
http://www.pflag.org/ ⋆ Skill 7: Contact Info/E-mail

People for the American Way (PFAW)

http://www.pfaw.org
PFAW works to promote full citizen participation in our democracy and safeguard the principles of our Constitution.

PEOPLE FOR THE AMERICAN WAY

SKILLS

http://www.pfaw.org/issues/ ⋆ Skill 1: Issue Background
http://www.pfaw.org/caphill/ ⋆ Skill 2: Legislative Agenda
https://secure.pfaw.org/join/ ⋆ Skill 3: Membership
http://www.pfaw.org/activist/ ⋆ Skill 4: Action Alerts
http://www.pfaw.org/ ⋆ Skill 6: Related Links
http://www.pfaw.org/ ⋆ Skill 7: Contact Info/E-mail

The Council on American-Islamic Relations (CAIR)

Putting Faith Into Action

CAIR
Council on American-Islamic Relations

http://www.cair-net.org
CAIR is dedicated to improving the image, rights, and welfare of America's diverse Islamic community.

SKILLS

http://www.cair-net.org/   ★ Skill 1: Issue Background
http://www.cair-net.org/   ★ Skill 2: Legislative Agenda
http://www.cair-net.org/   ★ Skill 3: Membership
http://www.cair-net.org/   ★ Skill 4: Action Alerts
http://www.cair-net.org/   ★ Skill 6: Related Links
http://www.cair-net.org/   ★ Skill 7: Contact Info/E-mail

DEATH PENALTY

Amnesty International
Death Penalty Pages
http://www.amnestyusa.org/
abolish

Amnesty International has initiated this special project to abolish the death penalty.

SKILLS

http://www.amnestyusa.org/abolish/dpus.html   ★ Skill 1: Issue Background
http://www.amnestyusa.org/abolish/   ★ Skill 2: Legislative Agenda
http://www.amnestyusa.org/join/   ★ Skill 3: Membership
http://www.amnestyusa.org/abolish/   ★ Skill 4: Action Alerts
http://www.amnestyusa.org/rightsforall/dplinks.html   ★ Skill 6: Related Links
http://www.amnestyusa.org/abolish/   ★ Skill 7: Contact Info/E-mail

National Coalition to Abolish
the Death Penalty (NCADP)
http://www.ncadp.org

National Coalition To
Abolish The Death Penalty

NCADP is a coalition of organizations and individuals committed to eliminating capital punishment.

SKILLS

http://www.ncadp.org/factsandstats.html   ★ Skill 1: Issue Background
http://www.ncadp.org/alerts.html   ★ Skill 2: Legislative Agenda
http://www.ncadp.org/ncadp.html   ★ Skill 3: Membership
http://www.ncadp.org/action.html   ★ Skill 4: Action Alerts
http://www.ncadp.org/links.html   ★ Skill 6: Related Links
http://www.ncadp.org/ncadp.html   ★ Skill 7: Contact Info/E-mail

Bazelon Center for Mental Health Law
http://www.bazelon.org
The "Judge David L. Bazelon Center for Mental Health Law" is a non-profit legal advocacy organization based in Washington, D.C., that advocates for choice and dignity of individuals with mental illness.

SKILLS

http://www.bazelon.org/pubs.html ★ Skill 1: Issue Background
http://www.bazelon.org/alerts.html ★ Skill 2: Legislative Agenda
http://www.bazelon.org/howhelp.html ★ Skill 3: Membership
http://www.bazelon.org/alerts.html ★ Skill 4: Action Alerts
http://www.bazelon.org/what.html ★ Skill 6: Related Links
http://www.bazelon.org/welcome.html ★ Skill 7: Contact Info/E-mail

Consortium for Citizens with Disabilities (CCD)

http://www.c-c-d.org
CCD is a coalition of consumer, advo-cacy, provider, and professional organizations that advocate on behalf of people of all ages with physical and mental disabilities.

SKILLS

http://www.c-c-d.org/legislative_news.htm ★ Skill 1: Issue Background
http://www.c-c-d.org/legislative_news.htm ★ Skill 2: Legislative Agenda
http://www.c-c-d.org/contact.htm ★ Skill 7: Contact Info/E-mail

Tash
http://www.tash.org
TASH is an international association of people with disabilities, their family members, other advocates, and professionals fighting for the inclusion of all people in all aspects of society.

SKILLS

http://www.tash.org/publications/index.htm ★ Skill 1: Issue Background
http://www.tash.org/resolutions/index.htm ★ Skill 2: Legislative Agenda
http://www.tash.org/membership/index.htm ★ Skill 3: Membership
http://www.tash.org/calendar/action_needed.htm ★ Skill 4: Action Alerts
http://www.tash.org/links/index.htm ★ Skill 6: Related Links
http://www.tash.org/contacts/tashstaff.htm ★ Skill 7: Contact Info/E-mail

The ARC of the United States
http://www.thearc.org
The ARC is committed to the welfare of all children and adults with
mental retardation and their families.

SKILLS

http://www.TheArcPub.com/ ★ Skill 1: Issue Background
http://www.thearc.org/governmental-affairs.htm ★ Skill 2: Legislative Agenda
http://www.thearc.org/join.htm ★ Skill 3: Membership
http://www.thearc.org/action-center.htm ★ Skill 4: Action Alerts
http://www.thearc.org/misc/dislnkin.html ★ Skill 6: Related Links
http://www.thearc.org/contact.htm ★ Skill 7: Contact Info/E-mail

United Cerebral Palsy (UCP)
http://www.ucp.org
UCP is committed to change and progress
for persons with cerebral palsy and other disabilities.

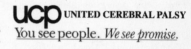

SKILLS

http://www.ucpa.org/html/resources/index.html ★ Skill 1: Issue Background
http://www.ucpa.org/html/advocacy/position_state.html ★ Skill 2: Legislative Agenda
http://www.ucpa.org/html/helping/index.html ★ Skill 3: Membership
http://www.ucpa.org/html/advocacy/index.html ★ Skill 4: Action Alerts
http://www.ucpa.org/html/resources/internet.html ★ Skill 6: Related Links
http://www.ucpa.org/html/index.html ★ Skill 7: Contact Info/E-mail

Disabled American Veterans (DAV)
http://www.dav.org
Formed in 1920 and chartered by Congress in 1932, DAV gives
voice to America's service-connected disabled veterans, their
families, and survivors.

SKILLS

http://www.dav.org/issues/ ★ Skill 1: Issue Background
http://congress.nw.dc.us/dav/ ★ Skill 2: Legislative Agenda
http://www.dav.org/members/ ★ Skill 3: Membership
http://congress.nw.dc.us/dav/ ★ Skill 4: Action Alerts
http://www.dav.org/links/ ★ Skill 6: Related Links
http://dav.serverdata.com/feedback/ ★ Skill 7: Contact Info/E-mail

NEA (National Education Association)
http://www.nea.org
NEA is an association of educators dedicated to advancing the cause of
public education.

SKILLS

http://www.nea.org/teaching/refs.html   ★ Skill 1: Issue Background
http://www.nea.org/lac/papers/briefs.html   ★ Skill 2: Legislative Agenda
http://www.neamb.com/   ★ Skill 3: Membership
http://www.nea.org/lac/   ★ Skill 4: Action Alerts
http://congress.nw.dc.us/nea/scorcard.html   ★ Skill 5: Voting Cards
http://www.nea.org/partners/   ★ Skill 6: Related Links
http://www.nea.org/feedback/   ★ Skill 7: Contact Info/E-mail

PTA (National Parent Teacher Association)
http://www.pta.org
The PTA is a volunteer association that advocates on behalf of children and youth.

SKILLS

http://www.pta.org/ptastore/tools.htm   ★ Skill 1: Issue Background
http://www.pta.org/programs/direct.htm   ★ Skill 2: Legislative Agenda
http://www.pta.org/membership/index.htm   ★ Skill 3: Membership
http://www.pta.org/programs/legini.asp   ★ Skill 4: Action Alerts
http://www.pta.org/programs/advlinks.htm   ★ Skill 6: Related Links
http://www.pta.org/email.htm   ★ Skill 7: Contact Info/E-mail

American Forests
http://www.americanforests.org
American Forests is the nation's oldest citizen conservation
organization working to bridge the gap between science and
policy and to reach a consensus on how best to protect our
nation's forests.

SKILLS

http://www.americanforests.org/garden/news_and_pubs/newspubs_subhome.html
   ★ Skill 1: Issue Background
http://www.americanforests.org/fpc/polfpc.html   ★ Skill 2: Legislative Agenda
http://www.americanforests.org/member/membership.html   ★ Skill 3: Membership
http://www.americanforests.org/   ★ Skill 7: Contact Info/E-mail

Defenders of Wildlife
http://www.defenders.org
Defenders of Wildlife is dedicated to the protection of all native
wild animals and plants in their natural communities.

SKILLS

http://www.defenders.org/publish.html ★ Skill 1: Issue
    Background

http://www.defenders.org/index.html ★ Skill 2: Legislative Agenda

http://www.defenders.org/learnaboutus/benefits.html ★ Skill 3: Membership

http://www.defenders.org/alerts.html ★ Skill 4: Action Alerts

http://www.defenders.org/links.html ★ Skill 6: Related Links

http://www.defenders.org/learnaboutus/memcon.html ★ Skill 7: Contact Info/E-mail

Environmental Defense
http://www.edf.org
Environmental Defense is a not-for-profit environmental advocacy group with four main goals: stabi-
lizing the Earth's climate, safeguarding the world's
oceans, protecting human health, and defending and
restoring biodiversity.

SKILLS

http://www.edf.org/pubs/ ★ Skill 1: Issue Background

http://www.actionnetwork.org/ ★ Skill 2: Legislative Agenda

http://www.edf.org/Join4Free/ ★ Skill 3: Membership

http://www.actionnetwork.org/ ★ Skill 4: Action Alerts

http://www.actionnetwork.org/ ★ Skill 6: Related Links

http://www.edf.org/AboutEDF/contact.html ★ Skill 7: Contact Info/E-mail

UNIQUE FEATURES

http://www.scorecard.org/ ★ "Scorecard" allows users to get up-to-date information
    about pollution in their areas by entering their local zip codes.

Global Climate Coalition (GCC)
http://www.globalclimate.org
GCC is an organization of business trade associations and private
companies established to coordinate business participation in the
scientific and policy debate on the global climate change issue.

SKILLS

http://www.globalclimate.org/Primer.htm ★ Skill 1: Issue
    Background

http://www.globalclimate.org/links.htm ★ Skill 6: Related Links

http://www.globalclimate.org/home.htm ★ Skill 7: Contact Info/E-mail

Greenpeace
http://www.greenpeace.org
Greenpeace is an independent international organization dedicated to the protection of the environment by peaceful means.

SKILLS

http://www.greenpeace.org/information.shtml ★ Skill 1: Issue Background
http://www.greenpeace.org/interact.shtml ★ Skill 2: Legislative Agenda
http://www.greenpeace.org/join.shtml ★ Skill 3: Membership
http://www.greenpeace.org/join.shtml ★ Skill 4: Action Alerts
http://www.greenpeace.org/information.shtml ★ Skill 6: Related Links
http://www.greenpeace.org/information.shtml ★ Skill 7: Contact Info/E-mail

League of Conservation Voters (LCV)
http://www.lcv.org/home.htm
LCV works to elect a bipartisan Congress that regards environmental concerns as a priority.

SKILLS

http://secure3.nmpinc.com/lcvlink/forms/join.htm ★ Skill 3: Membership
http://scorecard.lcv.org/index.cfm ★ Skill 5: Voting Report Cards
http://www.lcv.org/aboutlcv/contactinfo.htm ★ Skill 7: Contact Info/E-mail

UNIQUE FEATURES

http://www.lcvedfund.org/publications/enviroprofiles/ ★ "Environmental Profiles" offers voting profiles of newly elected members of Congress.

National Audubon Society
http://www.audubon.org
The National Audubon Society works to conserve and restore natural ecosystems, focusing on birds and other wildlife for the benefit of humanity and the Earth's biological diversity.

SKILLS

http://www.audubon.org/market/ ★ Skill 1: Issue Background
http://www.audubon.org/campaign/ ★ Skill 2: Legislative Agenda
http://www.audubon.org/sa ★ Skill 3: Membership
http://congress.nw.dc.us/audubon/ ★ Skill 4: Action Alerts
http://www.audubon.org/net/link/index.html ★ Skill 6: Related Links
http://www.audubon.org/ ★ Skill 7: Contact Info/E-mail

UNIQUE FEATURES

http://www.audubon.org/bird/watch/state2/ ★ "State Watchlists" keep voters appraised of state initiatives regarding environmental and conservation issues.

National Wildlife Federation (NWF)
http://www.nwf.org
NWF is an environmental organization focused on five core issue areas: endangered habitat, water quality, land steward-ship, wetlands, and sustainable communities.

SKILLS

http://www.nwf.org/ ★ Skill 1: Issue Background

http://www.nwf.org/issues.html ★ Skill 2: Legislative Agenda

http://www.nwf.org/nwf/membership/index.html ★ Skill 3: Membership

http://www.nwf.org/nwf/action/index.html ★ Skill 4: Action Alerts

http://www.nwf.org/scripts/nwf/feedback.cgi ★ Skill 7: Contact Info/E-mail

The Sierra Club
http://www.sierraclub.org
The Sierra Club is dedicated to the protection of the environment for current and future generations.

SKILLS

http://www.sierraclub.org/books/ ★ Skill 1: Issue Background

http://www.sierraclub.org/cgi-sh/activism.pl ★ Skill 2: Legislative Agenda

https://ww2.sierraclub.org/member/forms/new_member/new.html ★ Skill 3: Membership

http://www.sierraclub.org/cgi-sh/activism.pl ★ Skill 4: Action Alerts

http://www.sierraclub.org/votewatch/ ★ Skill 5: Voting Report Cards

http://www.sierraclub.org/ ★ Skill 7: Contact Info/E-mail

World Wildlife Fund (WWF)
http://www.worldwildlife.org
WWF is an environmental group dedi-cated to protecting the world's wildlife and wildlands.

SKILLS

http://www.worldwildlife.org/defaultsection.cfm?sectionid=71&newspaperid=12&conten tid=261 ★ Skill 1: Issue Background

http://www.worldwildlife.org/defaultsection.cfm?sectionid=71&newspaperid=12&conten
  tid=261 ★ Skill 2: Legislative Agenda
https://secure01.worldwildlife.org/wwfuslink/forms/support.cfm ★ Skill 3: Membership
http://www.worldwildlife.org/actions/actioncenter.cfm ★ Skill 4: Action Alerts
http://www.worldwildlife.org/defaultsection.cfm?sectionid=48&newspaperid=12&conte
  ntid=364 ★ Skill 6: Related Links
http://www.worldwildlife.org/forms/feedback.cfm ★ Skill 7: Contact Info/E-mail

UNIQUE FEATURES

http://www.worldwildlife.org/fun/kids.cfm ★ "Kid's Stuff" has quizzes, games, projects,
  and education information about animals and conservation.

Zero Population Growth (ZPG)
http://www.zpg.org
ZPG is a national nonprofit organization working to slow
population growth and achieve a sustainable balance
between the Earth's people and its resources.

SKILLS

http://www.zpg.org/Reports_Publications/ ★ Skill 1: Issue Background
http://www.zpg.org/Action_Alerts/alert26.html ★ Skill 2: Legislative Agenda
http://www.zpg.org/Get_Involved/becomingmember.html ★ Skill 3: Membership
http://www.zpg.org/Action_Alerts/alert26.html ★ Skill 4: Action Alerts
http://www.zpg.org/Contact_Us/ ★ Skill 7: Contact Info/E-mail

Choice In Dying
http://www.choices.org
Choice In Dying, the inventor of living wills in 1967, is dedicated to fos-
tering communication about end-of-life decisions and provides direc-
tives, counseling, training, and other resources.

SKILL

http://www.choices.org/issues.htm ★ Skill 1: Issue Background
http://www.choices.org/member.htm ★ Skill 3: Membership
http://www.choices.org/links.htm ★ Skill 6: Related Links
http://www.choices.org/backgnd.htm ★ Skill 7: Contact Info/E-mail

Compassion in Dying
http://www.compassionindying.org
Compassion in Dying provides legal advocacy and public education
to improve pain management, patient empowerment, and to expand
end-of-life choices to include aid-in-dying for terminally ill, mentally
competent adults.

SKILLS

http://www.compassionindying.org/legal/legal.html ★ Skill 1: Issue Background

http://www.compassionindying.org/help.html ★ Skill 3: Membership
http://www.compassionindying.org/newsalert.html ★ Skill 4: Action Alerts
http://www.compassionindying.org/Affiliates.html ★ Skill 6: Related Links
http://www.compassionindying.org/contact.html ★ Skill 7: Contact Info/E-mail

The Hemlock Society
http://www.hemlock.org

The Hemlock Society supports euthanasia and believes that people who wish to retain their dignity and choice at the end of life should have the option of a peaceful, gentle, certain, and swift death in the company of their loved ones.

SKILLS

http://www.hemlock.org/background.htm ★ Skill 1: Issue Background
http://www.hemlock.org/changing_laws.htm ★ Skill 2: Legislative Agenda
http://www.hemlock.org/join.htm#member ★ Skill 3: Membership
http://www.hemlock.org/other_resources.htm ★ Skill 6: Related Links
http://www.hemlock.org/index.htm ★ Skill 7: Contact Info/E-mail

FOREIGN RELATIONS

American Israel Public Affairs Committee (AIPAC)
http://www.aipac.org/

AIPAC was established in 1954 by leaders of the American Jewish community who recognized that Israel's needs could not be satisfied by philanthropy alone.

SKILLS

http://www.aipac.org/ ★ Skill 1: Issue Background
http://www.aipac.org/ ★ Skill 2: Legislative Agenda
http://www.aipac.org/ ★ Skill 3: Membership
http://www.aipac.org/ ★ Skill 5: Voting Report Cards
http://www.aipac.org/ ★ Skill 7: Contact Info/E-mail

International Committee of Lawyers for Tibet (ICLT)
http://www.tibeticlt.org

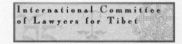

ICLT advocates self-determination for the Tibetan people through legal action and education.

SKILLS

http://www.tibeticlt.org/reports/ ★ Skill 1: Issue Background

http://www.tibeticlt.org/involved/join.html ★ Skill 3: Membership
http://www.tibeticit.org/involved/action/index.html ★ Skill 4: Action Alerts
http://www.tibeticlt.org/about/contact.html ★ Skill 7: Contact Info/E-mail

Public Ciitzen Global Trade Watch
http://www.tradewatch.org
Public Citizen Global Trade Watch fights for international trade and investment policies that promote accountability, consumer health and safety, and environmental protection.

SKILLS

http://www.citizen.org/pctrade/publications/gtwpubs.htm ★ Skill 1: Issue Background
http://www.citizen.org/pctrade/activism/activist.htm ★ Skill 2: Legislative Agenda
https://www.citizen.org/pcjoin.html ★ Skill 3: Membership
http://www.citizen.org/pctrade/activism/activist.htm ★ Skill 4: Action Alerts
http://www.citizen.org/pctrade/vote/votehome.html ★ Skill 5: Voting Report Cards
http://www.citizen.org/pctrade/resources/other.html ★ Skill 6: Related Links
http://www.tradewatch.org/ ★ Skill 7: Contact Info/E-mail

USA ENGAGE
http://www.usaengage.org
USA ENGAGE is an organization concerned with U.S. economic strength as an integral part of our nation's security and worldwide leadership.

SKILLS

http://www.usaengage.org/resources/index.html ★ Skill 1: Issue Background
http://www.usaengage.org/resources/index.html ★ Skill 2: Legislative Agenda
http://www.usaengage.org/background/joinform.html ★ Skill 3: Membership
http://www.usaengage.org/legislative/ ★ Skill 5: Voting Report Cards
http://www.usaengage.org/ ★ Skill 7: Contact Info/E-mail

GUN CONTROL

Citizens Committee for the Right to Keep and Bear Arms
http://www.ccrkba.org
CCRKBA is an advocacy group that fights for the right of law-abiding citizens to bear arms.

SKILLS

http://www.ccrkba.org/legal-issues.html ★ Skill 1: Issue Background
http://www.ccrkba.org/ ★ Skill 2: Legislative Agenda
http://www.ccrkba.org/contribute/citizen_comm_form.html ★ Skill 3: Membership
http://www.ccrkba.org/cap.html ★ Skill 4: Action Alerts
http://www.ccrkba.org/links.html ★ Skill 6: Related Links
http://www.ccrkba.org/ ★ Skill 7: Contact Info/E-mail

Gun Free Kids
http://gunfreekids.policy.net
The Gun Free Kids site is an Internet action
center that exists as a link between gun control advocates and their elected officials.

SKILLS

http://gunfreekids.policy.net/resources/ ★ Skill 2: Legislative Agenda
http://gunfreekids.policy.net/ ★ Skill 3: Membership
http://gunfreekids.policy.net/ ★ Skill 4: Action Alerts
http://gunfreekids.policy.net/directory/ ★ Skill 5: Voting Report Cards
http://gunfreekids.policy.net/resources/ ★ Skill 6: Related Links

Handgun Control
http://www.handguncontrol.org
Handgun Control is a nonpartisan, not-for-profit organization that
lobbies for reasonable gun regulations at local, state, and
national levels.

SKILLS

http://www.handguncontrol.org/information.htm ★ Skill 1: Issue Background
http://www.handguncontrol.org/legislation/index.htm ★ Skill 2: Legislative Agenda
http://www.handguncontrol.org/join.htm ★ Skill 3: Membership
http://www.handguncontrol.org/ ★ Skill 4: Action Alerts
http://www.handguncontrol.org/action.asp ★ Skill 6: Related Links
http://www.handguncontrol.org/ ★ Skill 7: Contact Info/E-mail

UNIQUE FEATURES

http://www.handguncontrol.org/statefed.asp ★ "Federal and State Firearms Laws" allow
users to research various gun control laws state-by-state.

NRA (National Rifle Association Of America)
http://www.nra.org
NRA exists to defend the right of Americans to bear arms and to provide
firearms education.

HEALTH

SKILLS

http://www.nraila.org/   ★ Skill 1: Issue Background
http://www.nraila.org/   ★ Skill 2: Legislative Agenda
http://www.nraila.org/   ★ Skill 3: Membership
http://www.nraila.org/   ★ Skill 4: Action Alerts
http://www.nraila.org/   ★ Skill 5: Voting Report Cards
http://www.nraila.org/   ★ Skill 7: Contact Info/E-mail

Action on Smoking and Health (ASH)
http://www.ash.org

ASH is a national nonprofit legal action and educational organization fighting for the rights of nonsmokers against many problems related to smoking.

SKILLS

http://www.ash.org/   ★ Skill 1: Issue Background
http://ash.org/joinash3.html   ★ Skill 3: Membership
http://ash.org/newslinks.html   ★ Skill 6: Related Links
http://www.ash.org/   ★ Skill 7: Contact Info/E-mail

AIDS Action
http://www.aidsaction.org

AIDS Action is a network of 3,200 national community-based health organizations and the 1 million HIV-positive Americans they help serve.

SKILLS

http://www.aidsaction.org/policy.html   ★ Skill 1: Issue Background
http://congress.nw.dc.us/aac/   ★ Skill 2: Legislative Agenda
http://www.aidsaction.org/members.html   ★ Skill 3: Membership
http://www.aidsaction.org/legislation.html   ★ Skill 4: Action Alerts
http://congress.nw.dc.us/aac/   ★ Skill 5: Voting Report Cards
http://www.aidsaction.org/links.html   ★ Skill 6: Related Links
http://www.aidsaction.org/contact.html   ★ Skill 7: Contact Info/E-mail

Alzheimer's Association
http://www.alz.org

The Alzheimer's Association works to provide leadership to eliminate Alzheimer's disease through the advancement of research while enhancing care and support services for individuals and their families.

SKILLS

http://www.alz.org/involved/advocacy/ ★ Skill 2: Legislative Agenda
http://www.alz.org/involved/ ★ Skill 3: Membership
http://www.alz.org/involved/advocacy/alerts.htm ★ Skill 4: Action Alerts
http://www.alz.org/chapter/ ★ Skill 6: Related Links
http://www.alz.org/contactus/ ★ Skill 7: Contact Info/E-mail

American Cancer Society
http://www.cancer.org
The American Cancer Society is a nationwide community-based voluntary health organization dedicated to eliminating cancer through prevention and diminishing suffering through research, education, and service.

SKILLS

http://www.cancer.org ★ Skill 1: Issue Background
http://www2.cancer.org/advocacy/new_advo/index.cfm ★ Skill 2: Legislative Agenda
http://www2.cancer.org/advocacy/new_advo/main.cfm?sc=fight ★ Skill 3: Membership
http://www2.cancer.org/advocacy/new_advo/index.cfm ★ Skill 4: Action Alerts
http://www2.cancer.org/resources/ ★ Skill 6: Related Links
http://www2.cancer.org/contact/ ★ Skill 7: Contact Info/E-mail

UNIQUE FEATURES

http://www2.cancer.org/advocacy/new_advo/map.cfm ★ "Advocacy Contact Locator" provides links to local and state advocacy groups.

American Diabetes Association
http://www.diabetes.org
The American Diabetes Association is a nonprofit health organization dedicated to providing diabetes research, information, and advocacy.

SKILLS

http://www.diabetes.org/ada/diabetesinfo.asp ★ Skill 1: Issue Background
http://www.diabetes.org/advocacy/default.asp ★ Skill 2: Legislative Agenda
http://www.diabetes.org/ada/cont.asp ★ Skill 3: Membership
http://www.diabetes.org/takeaction/delegate.asp ★ Skill 4: Action Alerts
http://congress.nw.dc.us/ada/ ★ Skill 5: Voting Report Cards
http://www.diabetes.org/internetresources.asp ★ Skill 6: Related Links
http://www.diabetes.org/ada/moreinfo.asp#contact ★ Skill 7: Contact Info/E-mail

American Heart Association
http://americanheart.org

The American Heart Association is dedicated to providing Americans with education and information on fighting heart disease and stroke and to advocating for sound health policy.

SKILLS

http://americanheart.org/Heart_and_Stroke_A_Z_Guide/ ★ Skill 1: Issue Background
http://www.americanheart.org/Support/Advocacy/paprior.htm ★ Skill 2: Legislative Agenda
http://americanheart.org/catalog/Support_catpage32.html ★ Skill 3: Membership
http://congress.nw.dc.us/aha/issues.html ★ Skill 4: Action Alerts
http://americanheart.org/contact.html ★ Skill 7: Contact Info/E-mail

American Lung Association
http://www.lungusa.org

The American Lung Association has been fighting lung disease since 1904 through education, community service, advocacy, and research.

SKILLS

http://www.lungusa.org/research/ ★ Skill 1: Issue Background
http://www.lungusa.org/advocacy/ ★ Skill 2: Legislative Agenda
http://www.lungusa.org/donate/ ★ Skill 3: Membership
http://www.lungusa.org/advocacy/ ★ Skill 4: Action Alerts
http://www.lungusa.org/links/ ★ Skill 6: Related Links
http://www.lungusa.org/contact/ ★ Skill 7: Contact Info/E-mail

American Psychological Association (APA)
http://www.apa.org

APA provides public education and research on psychological issues as well as support and accreditation guidelines for phychologists.

SKILLS

http://research.apa.org/ ★ Skill 1: Issue Background
http://www.apa.org/ppo/topic.html ★ Skill 2: Legislative Agenda
http://members.apa.org/ ★ Skill 3: Membership
http://www.apa.org/ppo/ppofrm.html ★ Skill 4: Action Alerts
http://www.apa.org/about/contact.html ★ Skill 7: Contact Info/E-mail

American Public Health Association (APHA)
http://www.apha.org

APHA represents more than fifty thousand members from over fifty occupations of public health. The association and its members have been influencing policies and setting priorities in public health since 1872.

SKILLS

http://www.apha.org/legislative/factsheets.htm ★ Skill 1: Issue Background
http://www.apha.org/legislative/ ★ Skill 2: Legislative Agenda
http://www.apha.org/membership/ ★ Skill 3: Membership
http://www.apha.org/legislative/actionalerts.htm ★ Skill 4: Action Alerts
http://www.apha.org/public_health/ ★ Skill 6: Related Links
http://www.apha.org/contact/ ★ Skill 7: Contact Info/E-mail

Arthritis Foundation
http://www.arthritis.org
Throughout its fifty-year history, the Arthritis Foundation has become
a leading sponsor in arthritis research.

SKILLS

http://www.arthritis.org/resource/ ★ Skill 1: Issue Background
http://www.arthritis.org/jvd/ ★ Skill 3: Membership
http://www.arthritis.org/advocate/your_voice_counts.asp ★ Skill 4: Action Alerts
http://www.arthritis.org/resource/other_resources.asp ★ Skill 6: Related Links
http://www.arthritis.org/ ★ Skill 7: Contact Info/E-mail

Brain Injury Association (BIA)
http://www.biausa.org
BIA strives to create a better future through
brain injury prevention, research, education,
and advocacy.

SKILLS

http://www.biausa.org/costsand.htm ★ Skill 1: Issue Background
http://www.biausa.org/policy.htm ★ Skill 2: Legislative Agenda
http://www.biausa.org/Funding.htm ★ Skill 3: Membership
http://www.biausa.org/policy.htm ★ Skill 4: Action Alerts
http://www.biausa.org/Links.htm ★ Skill 6: Related Links
http://www.biausa.org/postoffi.htm ★ Skill 7: Contact Info/E-mail

Center for Patient Advocacy
http://www.patientadvocacy.org/main/index.html
The Center for Patient Advocacy strives for timely patient access to
the highest quality healthcare in the world.

SKILLS

http://www.patientadvocacy.org/main/index.html
    ★ Skill 1: Issue Background
http://www.patientadvocacy.org/main/index.html ★ Skill 2:
    Legislative Agenda

http://www.patientadvocacy.org/main/index.html ★ Skill 3: Membership
http://www.patientadvocacy.org/main/index.html ★ Skill 4: Action Alerts
http://www.patientadvocacy.org/main/index.html ★ Skill 6: Related Links
http://www.patientadvocacy.org/main/index.html ★ Skill 7: Contact Info/E-mail

Cystic Fibrosis Foundation
http://www.cff.org

The Cystic Fibrosis Foundation strives to assure the
development of the means to cure and control cystic
fibrosis and to improve the quality of life for those with the disease.

SKILLS

http://www.cff.org/publications.htm ★ Skill 1: Issue Background
http://www.cff.org/publicpolicy.htm ★ Skill 2: Legislative Agenda
http://www.cff.org/donate.htm ★ Skill 3: Membership
http://www.cff.org/publicpolicy.htm ★ Skill 4: Action Alerts
http://www.cff.org/additional.htm ★ Skill 6: Related Links
http://www.cff.org/contact.htm ★ Skill 7: Contact Info/E-mail

Epilepsy Foundation
http://efa.org/index.html

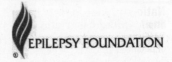

Through research, education, advocacy, and service, the Epilepsy Foundation advocates on behalf
of people affected by seizures.

SKILLS

http://209.70.29.4/efastore/index.cfm?&DID=6 ★ Skill 1: Issue Background
http://www.efa.org/advocacy/phealth/phealth.html ★ Skill 2: Legislative Agenda
http://www.epilepsyfoundation.org/tohelp/member.htm ★ Skill 3: Membership
http://congress.nw.dc.us/cgi-bin/joinmaillist.pl?dir=efa ★ Skill 4: Action Alerts
http://congress.nw.dc.us/efa/ ★ Skill 5: Voting Report Cards
http://www.epilepsyfoundation.org/education/links.html ★ Skill 6: Related Links
http://www.epilepsyfoundation.org/index.html ★ Skill 7: Contact Info/E-mail

Families USA
http://www.familiesusa.org

Families USA is a national, nonprofit, nonpartisan organization dedicated to the achievement of high-quality,
affordable health and long term care for all Americans.

SKILLS

http://www.familiesusa.org.pubsite.htm ★ Skill 1: Issue Background
http://www.familiesusa.org/ ★ Skill 2: Legislative Agenda

http://www.familiesusa.org/fainvo.htm ⋆ Skill 3: Membership
http://congress.nw.dc.us/familiesusa/ ⋆ Skill 4: Action Alerts
http://congress.nw.dc.us/familiesusa/ ⋆ Skill 5: Voting Report Cards
http://www.familiesusa.org/links.htm ⋆ Skill 6: Related Links
http://www.familiesusa.org/ ⋆ Skill 7: Contact Info/E-mail

Long Term Care Campaign
http://www.ltcampaign.org

The Long Term Care Campaign is a coalition of national organizations dedicated to enacting comprehensive legislation to protect American families against the devastating costs of long-term care.

SKILLS

http://www.ltccampaign.org/allabout/whatisltc.htm ⋆ Skill 1: Issue Background
http://www.ltccampaign.org/alerts/alerts.htm ⋆ Skill 2: Legislative Agenda
http://www.ltccampaign.org/alerts/alerts.htm ⋆ Skill 4: Action Alerts
http://www.ltccampaign.org/who/memborg.htm ⋆ Skill 6: Related Links
http://www.ltccampaign.org/talk/feedback.htm ⋆ Skill 7: Contact Info/E-mail

National Alliance for the Mentally Ill (NAMI)
http://www.nami.org

NAMI provides support, advocacy, and research on behalf of people with severe mental illnesses.

SKILLS

http://www.apollonian.com/book/catalog_get.asp ⋆ Skill 1: Issue Background
http://www.nami.org/policy.htm ⋆ Skill 2: Legislative Agenda
https://www.apollonian.com/namissl/member.asp ⋆ Skill 3: Membership
http://www.nami.org/policy.htm ⋆ Skill 4: Action Alerts
http://www.apollonian.com/namilocals/linkmgr/linkmgr.asp ⋆ Skill 6: Related Links
http://www.nami.org/poc.htm ⋆ Skill 7: Contact Info/E-mail

National Association of People With AIDS (NAPWA)
http://www.napwa.org

NAPWA advocates on behalf of all people living with HIV and AIDS in order to end the pandemic caused by HIV/AIDS.

SKILLS

http://www.napwa.org/publications.htm ⋆ Skill 1: Issue Background
http://www.napwa.org/pubpol.htm ⋆ Skill 2: Legislative Agenda
http://www.napwa.org/join.htm ⋆ Skill 3: Membership

http://www.napwa.org/advonet.htm   ★ Skill 4: Action Alerts
http://www.napwa.org/resource.htm   ★ Skill 6: Related Links
http://www.napwa.org/ourstaff.htm   ★ Skill 7: Contact Info/E-mail

National CPR (Coalition for Patient Rights)
http://www.nationalcpr.org

The National CPR is a nonprofit organization comprised of medical professionals and concerned citizens dedicated to protecting confidentiality to health care through advocacy and public education.

SKILLS

http://congress.nw.dc.us/cpr/   ★ Skill 2: Legislative Agenda
http://www.nationalcpr.org/joincpr.html   ★ Skill 3: Membership
http://www.nationalcpr.org   ★ Skill 4: Action Alerts
http://www.nationalcpr.org/   ★ Skill 5: Voting Report Cards
http://www.nationalcpr.org/lookitup.html   ★ Skill 6: Related Links
http://www.nationalcpr.org/index.html   ★ Skill 7: Contact Info/E-mail

National Mental Health Association
http://www.nmha.org

The National Mental Health Association strives to spread tolerance and awareness, improve mental health services, prevent mental illness, and promote mental health.

SKILLS

http://www.nmha.org/position/index.cfm   ★ Skill 1: Issue Background
http://www.nmha.org/federal/index.cfm   ★ Skill 2: Legislative Agenda
http://www.nmha.org/fund/index.cfm   ★ Skill 3: Membership
http://www.nmha.org/newsroom/system/lal.main.cfm   ★ Skill 4: Action Alerts
http://www.nmha.org/jumplist/index.cfm   ★ Skill 6: Related Links
http://www.nmha.org/   ★ Skill 7: Contact Info/E-mail

HIGHER EDUCATION

Coalition for Student Loan Reform (CSLR)
http://www.cslr.org

CSLR is a nationwide group of state and nonprofit organizations that administer and fund the federal guaranteed student loan program.

SKILLS

http://www.cslr.org/studinfo.htm   ★ Skill 1: Issue Background
http://www.cslr.org/leghot.htm   ★ Skill 2: Legislative Agenda
http://www.cslr.org/register.htm   ★ Skill 3: Membership

http://www.cslr.org/leghot.htm ★ Skill 4: Action Alerts
http://www.cslr.org ★ Skill 7: Contact Info/E mail

National Association of Graduate Professional Students (NAGPS)

http://www.nagps.org
NAGPS information and advice to people who are concerned about student aid and proposed cuts in aid and education.

SKILLS

http://www.nagps.org/Student_Aid/facts_n_figures.html ★ Skill 1: Issue Background
http://www.nagps.org/Student_Aid/updates.html ★ Skill 2: Legislative Agenda
http://www.nagps.org/Student_Aid/save.html ★ Skill 4: Action Alerts
http://www.nagps.org/Student_Aid/student-aid.html ★ Skill 7: Contact Info/E-mail

UNIQUE FEATURES

http://www.nagps.org/Student_Aid/talking-points.html ★ "Talking Points" provides an outline of issues to discuss when meeting with elected officials.

National Direct Student Loan Coalition (NDSLC)

http://www.siue.edu/directloan
NDSLC is a coalition of the universities and colleges that participate in the Federal Direct Student Loan Program.

SKILLS

http://www.siue.edu/directloan/intro.htm ★ Skill 1: Issue Background
http://www.siue.edu/directloan/index.html ★ Skill 2: Legislative Agenda
http://www.siue.edu/directloan/index.html ★ Skill 6: Related Links
http://www.siue.edu/directloan/index.html ★ Skill 7: Contact Info/E-mail

UNIQUE FEATURES

http://www.siue.edu/directloan/index.html ★ "Useful Links" to members of Congress sorted into relevant committees.

The United States Student Association (USSA)

http://www.essential.org/ussa/ussa.html
USSA is a national student organization committed to increasing access to higher education.

SKILLS

http://www.essential.org/ussa/foundati/foundati.html ★ Skill 2: Legislative Agenda
http://www.essential.org/ussa/org/join.html ★ Skill 3: Membership
http://www.essential.org/ussa/leginfo/info.html ★ Skill 4: Action Alerts

http://www.essential.org/ussa/links.html ★ Skill 6: Related Links
http://www.essential.org/ussa.html ★ Skill 7: Contact Info/E-mail

HOUSING/POVERTY

National Fair Housing Advocate (NFHA)
http://www.fairhousing.com

NFHA is on-line resource providing timely information regarding the issues of housing discrimination.

SKILLS

http://www.fairhousing.com/101/index.htm ★ Skill 1: Issue Background
http://www.fairhousing.com/action_alerts/index.htm ★ Skill 2: Legislative Agenda
http://www.fairhousing.com/action_alerts/index.htm ★ Skill 4: Action Alerts
http://www.fairhousing.com/resources/finder/index.htm ★ Skill 6: Related Links
http://www.fairhousing.com/contact_us.htm ★ Skill 7: Contact Info/E-mail

National Law Center for Homelessness and Poverty (NLHP)
http://www.nlchp.org

National Law Center
On Homelessness And Poverty

NLHP advocates to protect the rights of homeless people and to implement solutions to end homelessness in America.

SKILLS:

http://www.nlchp.org/general.htm ★ Skill 1: Issue Background
http://www.nlchp.org/legislat.htm ★ Skill 2: Legislative Agenda
http://www.nlchp.org/legislat.htm ★ Skill 4: Action Alerts
http://www.nlchp.org/links.htm ★ Skill 6: Related Links
http://www.nlchp.org/contact.htm ★ Skill 7: Contact Info/E-mail

National Low Income Housing Coalition (NLIHC)
http://www.nlihc.org

NATIONAL LOW INCOME
HOUSING COALITION/LIHIS

NLIHC is committed to educating, organizing, and advocating to ensure decent, affordable housing within healthy neighborhoods for every American.

SKILLS

http://www.nlihc.org/pubs/index.htm ★ Skill 1: Issue Background
http://www.nlihc.org/news/legupdate.htm ★ Skill 2: Legislative Agenda
http://www.nlihc.org/membinfo.htm ★ Skill 3: Membership
http://www.nlihc.org/news/index.htm ★ Skill 4: Action Alerts
http://www.nlihc.org/linkshsg.htm ★ Skill 6: Related Links
http://www.nlihc.org/people.htm ★ Skill 7: Contact Info/E-mail

Center for Community Change (CCC)

http://www.communitychange.org

The Center for Community Change is committed to reducing poverty in the United States and rebuilding low-income communities.

SKILLS

http://www.communitychange.org/index.html	★ Skill 1: Issue Background
http://www.communitychange.org/index.html	★ Skill 2: Legislative Agenda
http://www.communitychange.org/index.html	★ Skill 3: Membership
http://www.communitychange.org/index.html	★ Skill 4: Action Alerts
http://www.communitychange.org/index.html	★ Skill 6: Related Links
http://www.communitychange.org/index.html	★ Skill 7: Contact Info/E-mail

IMMIGRATION

The Association of Americans for Spouse Reunification (AASR)

http://www.aasr.org

AASR is a grassroots organization dedicated to changing current government policies that prevent husbands and wives from being together in the United States.

SKILLS

http://www.aasr.org/about/summary.html	★ Skill 1: Issue Background
http://www.aasr.org/congress/legislation.html	★ Skill 2: Legislative Agenda
http://www.aasr.org/membership/index.html	★ Skill 3: Membership
http://www.aasr.org/congress/index.html	★ Skill 4: Action Alerts
http://www.aasr.org/about/index.html	★ Skill 7: Contact Info/E-mail

Micasa-Sucasa

http://ilw.com/micasa/home.htm

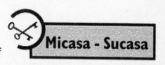

Micasa-Sucasa is an immigrants-rights group dedicated to the reform, correction, and modification of punitive immigration laws.

SKILLS

http://ilw.com/micasa/bb.htm	★ Skill 1: Issue Background
http://ilw.com/micasa/lm.htm	★ Skill 2: Legislative Agenda
http://ilw.com/micasa/lm.htm	★ Skill 4: Action Alerts
http://ilw.com/micasa/links.htm	★ Skill 6: Related Links
http://ilw.com/micasa/home.htm	★ Skill 7: Contact Info/E-mail

National Network for Immigrant and Refugee Rights (NNIRR)
http://www.nnirr.org/nnirr/frame.html
NNIRR is composed of local coalitions and immigrant, refugee, community, religious, civil rights, labor organizations, and activists that share information on important immigrant and refugee issues.

SKILLS

http://www.nnirr.org/nnirr/fact_sheets.html ★ Skill 1: Issue Background

http://www.nnirr.org/nnirr/current_campains.html ★ Skill 2: Legislative Agenda

http://www.nnirr.org/nnirr/membership.html ★ Skill 3: Membership

http://www.nnirr.org/nnirr/links.html ★ Skill 6: Related Links

http://www.nnirr.org/nnirr/contact_us.html ★ Skill 7: Contact Info/E-mail

INTERNATIONAL HUMAN RIGHTS

Amnesty International USA
http://www.amnestyusa.org
Amnesty International is a Nobel Prize–winning grassroots activists organization founded in 1961 with over one million members worldwide dedicated to protecting the human rights of all people.

SKILLS

http://www.amnestyusa.org/group/pubs/index.html ★ Skill 1: Issue Background

http://www.amnestyusa.org/campaigns/index.html ★ Skill 2: Legislative Agenda

http://www.amnestyusa.org/join/index.html ★ Skill 3: Membership

http://www.amnestyusa.org/campaigns/index.html ★ Skill 4: Action Alerts

http://www.amnestyusa.org/contact/index.html ★ Skill 7: Contact Info/E-mail

Derechos Human Rights
http://www.derechos.org
Derechos Human Rights is an Internet-based human rights organization that works for the promotion and respect of human rights and privacy all over the world.

SKILLS

http://www.derechos.org/ ★ Skill 1: Issue Background

http://www.derechos.org/human-rights/actions/ ★ Skill 4: Action Alerts

http:sh/www.derechos.net/links/ ★ Skill 6: Related Links

http://www.derechos.net/about/contact.html ★ Skill 7: Contact Info/E-mail

Human Rights Watch (HRW)

http://www.hrw.org

HRW is dedicated to protecting the human rights of people around the world from discrimination and inhumane conduct in wartime.

SKILLS

http://www.hrw.org/ ★ Skill 1: Issue Background
http://www.hrw.org/campaigns/campaigns.html ★ Skill 2: Legislative Agenda
http://store.yahoo.com/hrwpubs/membership.html ★ Skill 3: Membership
http://www.hrw.org/campaigns/campaigns.html ★ Skill 4: Action Alerts
http://www.hrw.org/links.html ★ Skill 6: Related Links
http://www.hrw.org/contact.html ★ Skill 7: Contact Info/E-mail

INTERNET ISSUES

The Center for Democracy and Technology (CDT)

http://www.cdt.org

CDT works to promote democratic values and constitutional liberties in the digital age through practical solutions that enhance free expression and privacy.

SKILLS

http://www.cdt.org/ ★ Skill 1: Issue Background
http://www.cdt.org/legislation/ ★ Skill 2: Legislative Agenda
http://www.cdt.org/join/ ★ Skill 3: Membership
http://www.cdt.org/join/ ★ Skill 4: Action Alerts
http://www.cdt.org/links/ ★ Skill 6: Related Links
http://www.cdt.org/ ★ Skill 7: Contact Info/E mail

Digital Future Coalition (DFC)

http://www.dfc.org

Recognizing the legitimate security concerns of proprietors such as motion picture companies and publishers and the access needs of libraries, scholars, and the general public, the DFC advocates a fair and balanced approach to implementing the World Intellectual Property Organization treaties.

SKILLS

http://www.dfc.org/issues/issues.html ★ Skill 1: Issue Background
http://www.dfc.org/index.html ★ Skill 2: Legislative Agenda
http://www.dfc.org/about/members/members.html ★ Skill 3: Membership
http://www.dfc.org/congress/congress.html ★ Skill 4: Action Alerts
http://www.dfc.org/links/links.html ★ Skill 6: Related Links
http://www.dfc.org/contact/contact.html ★ Skill 7: Contact Info/E-mail

Electronic Frontier Foundation (EFF)
http://www.eff.org
EFF works to protect fundamental civil liberties, including privacy and freedom of expression in the arena of computers and the Internet.

SKILLS

http://www.eff.org/   ★ Skill 1: Issue Background
http://www.eff.org/join/join_eff.html   ★ Skill 3: Membership
http://www.eff.org/blueribbon.html   ★ Skill 4: Action Alerts
http://www.eff.org.EFFdocs/about_eff.html   ★ Skill 7: Contact Info/E-mail

LABOR UNIONS

AFL CIO
http://www.aflcio.org/home.htm
One of the largest unions in the world, AFL-CIO's mission is to bring social and economic justice to U.S. workers by enabling them to have a voice on the job, in government, in a changing global economy, and in their communities.

SKILLS

http://www.aflcio.org/   ★ Skill 1: Issue Background
http://www.aflcio.org/front/wfa.htm   ★ Skill 2: Legislative Agenda
http://www.aflcio.org/front/joinunions.htm   ★ Skill 3: Membership
http://www.aflcio.org/front/wfa.htm   ★ Skill 4: Action Alerts
http://www.aflcio.org/vrecord/index.htm   ★ Skill 5: Voting Report Cards
http://www.aflcio.org/front/unionand.htm   ★ Skill 6: Related Links
http://www.aflcio.org/front/contact.htm   ★ Skill 7: Contact Info/E-mail

American Federation of State, County and Municipal Employees (AFSCME)
http://www.afscme.org
AFSCME is a labor union of state and local government employees.

SKILLS

http://www.afscme.org/publications/index.html   ★ Skill 1: Issue Background
http://www.afscme.org/action/index.html#la   ★ Skill 2: Legislative Agenda
http://www.afscme.org/join/index.html   ★ Skill 3: Membership
http://congress.nw.dc.us/cgi-bin/joinmaillist.pl?dir=afscme   ★ Skill 4: Action Alerts
http://www.afscme.org/action/afscmevg.htm   ★ Skill 5: Voting Report Cards
http://www.afscme.org/otherlink/index.html   ★ Skill 6: Related Links
http://www.afscme.org/about/contact.htm   ★ Skill 7: Contact Info/E-mail

The International Brotherhood of Teamsters
http://www.teamster.org
The Teamsters is a labor union of the shipping and trucking industries.

SKILLS

http://www.teamster.org/   ★ Skill 1: Issue Background
http://www.teamster.org/   ★ Skill 2: Legislative Agenda
http://www.teamster.org/   ★ Skill 3: Membership
http://www.teamster.org/   ★ Skill 4: Action Alerts
http://www.teamster.org/   ★ Skill 6: Related Links
http://www.teamster.org/   ★ Skill 7: Contact Info/E-mail

UAW
http://www.uaw.org
UAW is the international union of auto workers.

SKILLS

http://www.uaw.org   ★ Skill 1: Issue Background
http://www.uaw.org   ★ Skill 2: Legislative Agenda
http://uaw.org/solidarity/welcome98/index.html   ★ Skill 3: Membership
http://www.uaw.org   ★ Skill 4: Action Alerts
http://www.uaw.org/publications/happening.html   ★ Skill 5: Voting Report Cards
http://db.uaw.org/linx/toc.cfm   ★ Skill 6: Related Links
http://www.uaw.org/email.html   ★ Skill 7: Contact Info/E-mail

NONPROFITS

Alliance for Justice (AFJ)
http://www.afj.org
AFJ is a national association of environmental, civil rights, mental health, women's, children's, and consumer advocacy organizations.

SKILLS

http://www.afj.org/pubs.html   ★ Skill 1: Issue Background
http://www.afj.org/napalert.html   ★ Skill 2: Legislative Agenda
http://www.afj.org/mem/memb.html   ★ Skill 3: Membership
http://www.afj.org/napalert.html   ★ Skill 4: Action Alerts
http://www.afj.org/resources.html   ★ Skill 6: Related Links
http://www.afj.org/   ★ Skill 7: Contact Info/E mail

Independent Sector (IS)
http://www.independentsector.org
IS is a national leadership forum working to encourage philanthropy, volunteering, not-for-profit initiative, and citizen action to better serve people and communities.

SKILLS

http://www.independentsector.org/cgi-bin/cart.cgi ★ Skill 1: Issue Background

http://www.independentsector.org/programs/gr/govrelat.html ★ Skill 2: Legislative Agenda

http://www.independentsector.org/members.html ★ Skill 3: Membership

http://www.independentsector.org/programs/gr/govrelat.html#grnew
★ Skill 4: Action Alerts

http://www.independentsector.org/about.html ★ Skill 7: Contact Info/E-mail

OMB Watch

http://www.ombwatch.org

OMB Watch was formed to lift the veil of secrecy shrouding the White House Office of Management and Budget (OMB), which oversees regulation, the budget, information collection and dissemination, proposed legislation, testimony by agencies, and much more.

SKILLS

http://www.ombwatch.org/ ★ Skill 1: Issue Background

http://www.ombwatch.org/html/npi.html ★ Skill 2: Legislative Agenda

http://www.ombwatch.org/www/ombw/html/join.html ★ Skill 3: Membership

http://www.capweb.net/omb/ ★ Skill 4: Action Alerts

http://www.ombwatch.org/html/forum.html ★ Skill 6: Related Links

http://www.ombwatch.org/ ★ Skill 7: Contact Info/E-mail

NUTRITION

Center for Science in the Public Interest (CSPI)

http://www.cspinet.org

CSPI is a nonprofit education and advocacy organization that focuses on improving the safety and nutritional quality of our food supply and on reducing the carnage caused by alcoholic beverages.

SKILLS

http://www.cspinet.org/reports/index.html ★ Skill 1: Issue Background

http://www.capweb.net/cspi/ ★ Skill 2: Legislative Agenda

http://www.cspinet.org/ga/index.html ★ Skill 4: Action Alerts

http://www.cspinet.org/other/other.html ★ Skill 6: Related Links

http://www.cspinet.org/ ★ Skill 7: Contact Info/E-mail

Advocacy Institute
http://www.advocacy.org

The Advocacy Institute is an international organization working to strengthen leadership and movements for political, social, and economic justice, with a significant effort in tobacco control.

SKILLS

http://www.advocacy.org/pub.htm ★ Skill 1: Issue Background
http://www.advocacy.org/donate.htm ★ Skill 3: Membership
http://www.advocacy.org/scarclinks.htm ★ Skill 6: Related Links
http://www.advocacy.org/ ★ Skill 7: Contact Info/E-mail

Common Cause
http://commoncause.org

Common Cause is a nonprofit, nonpartisan citizen's lobbying organization promoting open, honest, and accountable government and is supported by the dues and contributions of over 250,000 members who wish to

counter the influence of big money special interests. Their web site provides information on state campaign finance issues as well as federal issues.

SKILLS

http://www.commoncause.org/publications/news.htm ★ Skill 1: Issue Background
http://commoncause.org/issue_agenda/issues.htm ★ Skill 2: Legislative Agenda
https://secure4.nmpinc.com/ccauselink/forms/join.htm ★ Skill 3: Membership
http://www.commoncause.org/causenet/ ★ Skill 4: Action Alerts
http://www.commoncause.org/congress/ ★ Skill 5: Voting Report Cards
http://commoncause.org/special/pisites.htm ★ Skill 6: Related Links
http://commoncause.org/forms/feedback.htm ★ Skill 7: Contact Info/E-mail

UNIQUE FEATURES

http://commoncause.org/laundromat ★ "Soft Money Laundromat" tabulates soft money donations to political parties by donor and industry.

http://www.commoncause.org/causenet/ ★ "CauseNet" provides regular action alerts and updates on campaign finance reform issues.

http://www.commoncause.org/congress/ ★ "Know Your Congress" feature provides a Common Cause Profile that gives you contact information, campaign finance information, and a voting record on campaign finance issues all in one.

National Safety Council (NSC)
http://www.nsc.org
The mission of NSC is to educate and influence society to adopt safety, health, and environmental policies, practices, and procedures that prevent and mitigate human suffering and economic losses arising from preventable causes.

SKILLS

http://www.nsc.org/pubstop.htm ★ Skill 1: Issue Background
http://www.nsc.org/ ★ Skill 2: Legislative Agenda
http://www.nsc.org/memtop.htm ★ Skill 3: Membership
http://ww.nsc.org/library.htm ★ Skill 6: Related Links
http://www.nsc.org/ ★ Skill 7: Contact Info/E-mail

Public Citizen
http://www.citizen.org
Public Citizen is the consumer's eyes and ears in Washington, fighting for safer drugs and medical devices, cleaner and safer energy sources, a cleaner environment, fair trade, and a more open and democratic government.

SKILLS

http://www.citizen.org/newweb/publicat.htm ★ Skill 1: Issue Background
http://www.citizen.org/takeaction.htm ★ Skill 2: Legislative Agenda
http://www.citizen.org/pcjoin.html ★ Skill 3: Membership
http://www.citizen.org/takeaction.htm ★ Skill 4: Action Alerts
http://www.citizen.org/email_us.htm ★ Skill 7: Contact Info/E-mail

RELIGIOUS INTERESTS

American Atheists
http://www.atheists.org
American Atheists fights for the civil liberties of atheists and complete separation of government and religion.

SKILLS

http://www.atheists.org/visitors.center/index.html ★ Skill 1: Issue Background
http://www.atheists.org/affiliation/ ★ Skill 6: Related Links
http://www.atheists.org/contact.us.html ★ Skill 7: Contact Info/E-mail

Americans United for Separation of Church and State (AU)
http://www.au.org
Since 1947, AU has worked to protect the constitutional principle of church-state separation. Their organization welcomes Americans of many faiths and political viewpoints.

SKILLS

http://www.au.org/bookst~1.htm   ★ Skill 1: Issue Background
http://www.au.org/legislat.htm   ★ Skill 2: Legislative Agenda
http://www.au.org/membinfo.htm   ★ Skill 3: Membership
http://www.au.org/activist.htm   ★ Skill 4: Action Alerts
http://www.org/chapnews.htm   ★ Skill 6: Related Links
http://www.au.org/   ★ Skill 7: Contact Info/E mail

Christian Coalition
http://www.cc.org
The Christian Coalition was founded in 1989 by Pat Robertson to give Christians a voice in government.

SKILLS

http://www.cc.org/news/issues.html   ★ Skill 1: Issue Background
http://christian-coalition.org/cgi bin/issue.pl?dir=cc&command=bills
   ★ Skill 2: Legislative Agenda
http://www.cc.org/join.html   ★ Skill 3: Membership
http://christian-coalition.org/cgi bin/issue.pl?dir=cc&command=la   ★ Skill 4: Action Alerts
http://christian-coalition.org/cgi-bin/issue.pl?dir=cc   ★ Skill 5: Voting Report Cards
http://www.cc.org/links.html   ★ Skill 6: Related Links
http://www.cc.org/contact.html   ★ Skill 7: Contact Info/E-mail

Religious Freedom Coalition (RFC)
http://www.rfcnet.org
RFC is dedicated to the restoration of religious freedom in the United States as envisioned by the authors of the Constitution.

SKILLS

http://www.rfcnet.org/archives/Legislation/   ★ Skill 2: Legislative Agenda
http://www.rfcnet.org/archives/Legislation/   ★ Skill 4: Action Alerts
http://www.rfcnet.org/links.htm   ★ Skill 6: Related Links

ACLU Reproductive Rights Freedom Network
http://www.aclu.org/issues/reproduct/hmrr.html

Since its inception, the ACLU has recognized personal privacy and reproductive rights as inimically tied with civil liberties. Since the 1960s the ACLU Reproductive Rights Project has acted as legal advocates for the right to contraception, the right to abortion, and the right to bear a child.

SKILLS

http://www.aclu.org/issues/reproduct/hmrr.html ★ Skill 1: Issue Background
http://www.aclu.org/issues/reproduct/hmrr.html ★ Skill 2: Legislative Agenda
http://secure20.client-mail.com/aclulink/forms/join.shtml ★ Skill 3: Membership
http://www.aclu.org/action/mailist.html ★ Skill 4: Action Alerts
http://www.aclu.org/issues/reproduct/irrr.html ★ Skill 6: Related Links
http://www.aclu.org/issues/reproduct/irrr.html ★ Skill 7: Contact Info/E-mail

american life league
http://www.all.org

American life league strives to build a society that protects human life from fertilization to natural death, without compromise, without exception, without apology.

SKILLS

http://www.all.org/pubs/index.htm ★ Skill 1: Issue Background
http://www.all.org/issues/index.htm ★ Skill 2: Legislative Agenda
http://www.all.org/activism/index.htm ★ Skill 3: Membership
http://www.all.org/activism/index.htm ★ Skill 4: Action Alerts
http://www.all.org/links.htm ★ Skill 6: Related Links
http://www.all.org/signup.htm ★ Skill 7: Contact Info/E-mail

Association of Reproductive Health Professionals (ARHP)
http://www.arhp.org/arhpframe.html

ARHP is an interdisciplinary association composed of professionals who provide reproductive health services and education, research, and advocacy.

SKILLS

http://www.arhp.org/books1.htm ★ Skill 1: Issue Background
http://www.arhp.org/advocacy.htm ★ Skill 2: Legislative Agenda
http://www.arhp.org/memform.html ★ Skill 3: Membership

http://www.arhp.org/advocacy.htm ★ Skill 4: Action Alerts
http://www.arhp.org/resources2.htm ★ Skill 6: Related Links
http://www.arhp.org/arhpframe.html ★ Skill 7: Contact Info/E-mail

Center for Reproductive Law & Policy (CRLP)

THE CENTER FOR REPRODUCTIVE LAW AND POLICY

http://www.crlp.org
CRLP is a nonprofit legal and policy advocacy organization dedicated to promoting women's reproductive rights.

SKILLS

http://www.crlp.org/publications.html ★ Skill 1: Issue Background
http://www.crlp.org/congress_usasub.html ★ Skill 2: Legislative Agenda
http://www.crlp.org/supportcrlp.html ★ Skill 3: Membership
http://www.crlp.org/contact.html ★ Skill 7: Contact Info/E-mail

National Abortion Federation (NAF)

http://www.prochoice.org
NAF is the professional association of abortion providers in the United States and Canada.

SKILLS

http://www.prochoice.org/facts/index.htm ★ Skill 1: Issue Background
http://www.prochoice.org/issues/index.htm ★ Skill 2: Legislative Agenda
http://www.prochoice.org/aboutnaf/members.htm ★ Skill 3: Membership
http://www.prochoice.org/issues/alerts.htm ★ Skill 4: Action Alerts
http://www.prochoice.org/resource.htm ★ Skill 6: Related Links
http://www.prochoice.org/aboutnaf/feedback.htm ★ Skill 7: Contact Info/E-mail

National Abortion Rights Action League (NARAL)

http://www.naral.org
NARAL is an advocate of reproductive freedom and dignity for women choosing abortion.

SKILLS

http://www.naral.org/home.html ★ Skill 1: Issue Background
http://www.naral.org/federal/federal.html ★ Skill 2: Legislative Agenda
http://www.naral.org/choice/involved/index.html ★ Skill 3: Membership
http://www.naral.org/choice/involved/index.html ★ Skill 4: Action Alerts
http://www.naral.org/federal/congov.html ★ Voting Report Cards
http://www.naral.org/forms/feed.html ★ Skill 7: Contact Info/E-mail

UNIQUE FEATURES

http://www.naral.org/actnow/media.html ★ "Contact the Media" provides hyperlinks to media outlets.

http://www.naral.org/actnow/letind.html ★ "Letters to the Editor" provides sample letters on reproductive and sexual health issues.

http://www.naral.org/choice/forms/census/index.html ★ "Take the Census" allows you to register your opinions on reproductive and sexual health and education issues.

National Right to Life
http://www.nrlc.org
National Right to Life is an organization that opposes the institution of abortion in this country.

SKILLS

http://www.nrlc.org/ ★ Skill 1: Issue Background
http://www.nrlc.org/Federal/Index.html ★ Skill 2: Legislative Agenda
http://www.nrlc.org/donations.htm ★ Skill 3: Membership
http://www.nrlc.org/contact.html ★ Skill 7: Contact Info/E-mail

Planned Parenthood Federation of America
http://www.plannedparenthood.org
Pro-choice Planned Parenthood believes every individual has a fundamental right to decide when or whether to have a child and that every child should be wanted and loved.

SKILLS

http://www.plannedparenthood.org/research/index.html ★ Skill 1: Issue Background
http://www.plannedparenthood.org/action/index.html ★ Skill 2: Legislative Agenda
https://ssl.ctsg.com/ppfa/donateform_new.asp ★ Skill 3: Membership
http://www.plannedparenthood.org/choices/lac/whatsup.asp ★ Skill 4: Action Alerts
http://www.plannedparenthood.org/about/thisispp/contact.html ★ Skill 7: Contact Info/E-mail

SENIORS/AGING

The AARP Foundation (American Association of Retired Persons)
http:www.aarp.org
AARP is the nation's leading organization for people age fifty and older. It provides information, education, advocacy, and community services through a network of local chapters and experienced volunteers.

SKILLS

http://www.aarp.org/press/issue.html ★ Skill 1: Issue Background
http://www.aarp.org/legipoly.html ★ Skill 2: Legislative Agenda

http://www.aarp.org/join/ ★ Skill 3: Membership
http://congress.nw.dc.us/aarp/ ★ Skill 5: Voting Report Cards
http://www.aarp.org/feedback/contact.html ★ Skill 7: Contact Info/E-mail

National Committee to Preserve Social Security and Medicare (NCPSSM)

http://www.ncpssm.org
NCPSSM was founded to advocate for social security and medicare and for all Americans who seek a healthy, productive, and secure retirement.

SKILLS

http://www.ncpssm.org/issues/index.html ★ Skill 1: Issue Background
http://www.ncpssm.org/issues/index.html ★ Skill 2: Legislative Agenda
http://www.ncpssm.org/join/index.html ★ Skill 3: Membership
http://www.ncpssm.org/issues/index.html ★ Skill 4: Action Alerts
http://www.ncpssm.org/news/index.html ★ Skill 6: Related Links
http://www.ncpssm.org/ ★ Skill 7: Contact Info/E-mail

National Council on the Aging (NCOA)

http://www.ncoa.org
NCOA is dedicated to promoting the dignity, self-determination, well being, and continuing contributions of older persons through leadership, service, education, and advocacy.

SKILLS

http://www.ncoa.org/issues/issues.htm ★ Skill 1: Issue Background
http://www.ncoa.org/advocacy/advocacy.htm ★ Skill 2: Legislative Agenda
http://www.ncoa.org/about/join_ncoa.htm ★ Skill 3: Membership
http://www.ncoa.org/advocacy/advocacy.htm ★ Skill 4: Action Alerts
http://www.ncoa.org/advocacy/advocacy.htm ★ Skill 6: Related Links
http://www.ncoa.org/about/contact_us.htm ★ Skill 7: Contact Info/E-mail

SMALL BUSINESS & REGULATION

National Federation of Independent Business (NFIB)

http://www.nfibonline.org
NFIB is a community of six hundred thousand small business owners who employ more than seven million people in industries ranging from high tech manufacturers and family farmers to neighborhood retailers and service companies.

SKILLS

http://www.nfibonline.com/media/index.asp   ★ Skill 1: Issue Background
http://www.nfibonline.com/about/index.asp?ContNF=smbiz_agenda/index.asp
   ★ Skill 2: Legislative Agenda
http://www.nfibonline.com/register/index.asp   ★ Skill 3: Membership
http://www.nfibonline.com/policy/index.asp   ★ Skill 4: Action Alerts
http://www.nfibonline.com/policy/index.asp   ★ Skill 5: Voting Report Cards
http://www.nfibonline.com/policy/index.asp   ★ Skill 6: Related Links
http://www.nifbonline.com/policy/index.asp   ★ Skill 7: Contact Info/E-mail

U.S. Chamber of Commerce
http://www.uschamber.org
The U.S. Chamber of Commerce represents
nearly 3 million companies, 3,000 state
and local chambers, 850 business associations, and 87 American Chambers of Commerce
abroad.

U.S. CHAMBER OF COMMERCE

SKILLS

http://www.uschamber.org/policy/index.html   ★ Skill 1: Issue Background
http://www.chamberbiz.com/govaffairs/govaffairs.cfm   ★ Skill 2: Legislative Agenda
http://www.uschamber.com/member/index.html   ★ Skill 3: Membership
http://www.uschamber.policy.net/   ★ Skill 4: Action Alerts
http://uschamber.policy.net/congdir/   ★ Skill 5: Voting Report Cards
http://www.uschamber.com/about/feedback.htm   ★ Skill 6: Related Links
http://www.uschamber.com/about/feedback.htm   ★ Skill 7: Contact Info/E-mail

TAXES/BUDGET

Americans for Fair Taxation
http://www.fairtax.org
Americans for Fair Taxation is a nonpartisan citizens organization seeking to replace
all federal income taxes with a single-rate
retail sales tax for personal consumption above the poverty level.

AMERICANS FOR FAIR TAXATION
WWW.FAIRTAX.ORG

SKILLS

http://www.fairtax.org/what/   ★ Skill 1: Issue Background
http://www.fairtax.org/legis/   ★ Skill 2: Legislative Agenda
http://www.fairtax.org/volcentr/join.html   ★ Skill 3: Membership
http://www.fairtax.org/legis/   ★ Skill 4: Action Alerts
http://www.fairtax.org/policy/   ★ Skill 6: Related Links
http://www.fairtax.org/about/contact.html   ★ Skill 7: Contact Info/E-mail

Americans for Tax Reform (ATR)
http://www.atr.org

ATR opposes all tax increases as a matter of principle. They support a system in which taxes are sim-
pler, fairer, flatter, more visible, and lower than
they are today.

SKILLS

http://www.atr.org/policybriefs/index1.htm ★ Skill 1: Issue Background
http://www.atr.org/main.htm ★ Skill 2: Legislative Agenda
http://www.atr.org/join/index1.htm ★ Skill 3: Membership
http://www.atr.org/TaxAlert/index1.htm ★ Skill 4: Action Alerts
http://www.atr.org/Links/index1.htm ★ Skill 6: Related Links
http://www.atr.org/main.htm ★ Skill 7: Contact Info/E-mail

UNIQUE FEATURES

http://www.atr.org/taxpledge/index.htm ★ ATR sponsors the Taxpayer Protection Pledge
and lists federal-and state elected representatives who have signed the pledge.

Citizens Against Government Waste (CAGW)
http://www.cagw.org.

CAGW is a private, nonpartisan, nonprofit organization dedicated to
educating Americans about the waste, mismanagement, and inefficiency in the federal government.

SKILLS

http://www.cagw.org/publications/index.htm ★ Skill 1: Issue
Background
http://www.cagw.org/policy/index.htm ★ Skill 2: Legislative Agenda
http://www.cagw.org/getinvolved/gi.join.htm ★ Skill 3: Membership
http://www.cagw.org/index.htm ★ Skill 4: Action Alerts
http://www.cagw.org/links/index.htm ★ Skill 6: Related Links
http://www.cagw.org/about/index.htm ★ Skill 7: Contact Info/E-mail

Citizens for a Sound Economy (CSE)
http://www.cse.org

CSE advocates market-based solutions to public problems,
believing that a strong and vibrant free-market economic system offers the best hope for creating opportunity and improving the quality for life of every American

SKILLS

http://www.cse.org/informed/ ★ Skill 1: Issue Background
http://www.cse.org/action/ ★ Skill 2: Legislative Agenda

http://www.cse.org/know/member.html ★ Skill 3: Membership
http://www.cse.org/daily/ ★ Skill 4: Action Alerts
http://www.cse.org/action/outside.html ★ Skill 6: Related Links
http://www.cse.org/know/staff.html ★ Skill 7: Contact Info/E-mail

Citizens for an Alternative Tax System (CATS)
http://www.cats.org

CATS exists to abolish the federal income tax completely and replace it with a national retail sales tax and rebates to ensure no additional tax burden on the poor or elderly.

SKILLS

http://www.cats.org/articles/index.html ★ Skill 1: Issue Background
http://www.cats.org/index.html ★ Skill 2: Legislative Agenda
http://www.cats.org/member.html ★ Skill 3: Membership
http://www.cats.org/index.html ★ Skill 4: Action Alerts
http://www.cats.org/contact1.html ★ Skill 7: Contact Info/E-mail

Citizens for Tax Justice (CTJ)
http://www.ctj.org

CTJ is a nonpartisan, nonprofit research and advocacy organization dedicated to fair taxation at the federal, state, and local levels.

SKILLS

http://www.ctj.org/html/publist.htm ★ Skill 1: Issue Background
http://www.ctj.org/html/publist.html#congress ★ Skill 2: Legislative Agenda
http://www.ctj.org/html/member.htm ★ Skill 3: Membership
http://www.ctj.org/ ★ Skill 4: Action Alerts
http://www.ctj.org/html/links.htm ★ Skill 6: Related Links
http://www.ctj.org/html/contact.htm ★ Skill 7: Contact Info/E-mail

National Taxpayers Union (NTU)
http://www.ntu.org

▼ NATIONAL TAXPAYERS UNION *and*
NATIONAL TAXPAYERS UNION FOUNDATION

NTU lobbies both Congress and state legislatures on taxpayer issues and teaches its members how to become effective, united citizen advocates.

SKILLS

http://www.ntu.org/pubs/pubs.htm ★ Skill 1: Issue Background
http://www.ntu.org/issues/issues1.htm ★ Skill 2: Legislative Agenda
http://www.ntu.org/join/join1.htm ★ Skill 3: Membership

http://www.ntu.org/issues/issues1.htm ⋆ Skill 4: Action Alerts
http://www.ntu.org/bill-votetally/welcome.html ⋆ Skill 5: Voting Report Cards
http://www.ntu.org/tools.htm ⋆ Skill 6: Related Links
http://www.ntu.org/contact.html ⋆ Skill 7: Contact Info/E-mail

Center on Budget and Policy Priorities (CBPP)
http://www.cbpp.org

CBPP concentrates on fiscal policy issues and issues affecting low-and moderate-income families and individuals.

SKILLS

http://www.chpp.org ⋆ Skill 1: Issue Background

National Center for Policy Analysis (NCPA)
http://www.ncpa.org

NCPA is a nonprofit public policy research institute conducting and collecting analysis, debate, and in-depth research from around the world.

SKILLS

http://www.ncpa.org ⋆ Skill 1: Issue Background

RAND
http://www.rand.org

RAND's mission is to improve policy and decision making through original research and policy analysis.

SKILLS

http://www.rand.org. ⋆ Skill 1: Issue Background

The Brookings Institution
http://www.brookings.org

THE BROOKINGS INSTITUTION
Washington, D.C.

The Brookings Institution functions as an independent analyst and critic and is committed to publishing its findings for the information of the public.

SKILLS

http://www.brookings.org ⋆ Skill 1: Issue Background

The Cato Institute
http://www.cato.org
Founded in 1977, the Cato Institute is a nonpartisan public policy research foundation headquartered in Washington, D.C.

SKILLS

http://www.cato.org ★ Skill 1: Issue Background

The Heritage Foundation
http://www.heritage.org

The Heritage Foundation is a research and educational institute whose mission is to formulate and promote conservative public policies based on the principles of free enterprise, limited government, individual freedom, traditional American values, and a strong national defense.

SKILLS

http://www.heritage.org ★ Skill 1: Issue Background

Hudson Institute
http://www.hudson.org
Hudson Institute is a public policy research organization that forecasts trends and develops solutions for governments, business, and the public.

SKILLS

http://www.hudson.org ★ Skill 1: Issue Background

Reason Public Policy Institute (RPPI)
http://www.reason.org
RPPI is a national research and educational organization that explores and promotes public policies based on rationality and freedom.

SKILLS

http://www.reason.org ★ Skill 1: Issue Background

The Urban Institute
http://www.urban.org
The Urban Institute investigates social and economic problems confronting the nation and analyzes efforts to solve these problems.

SKILLS

http://www.urban.org ★ Skill 1: Issue Background

TRADE ASSOCIATIONS

Association of American Publishers (AAP)
http://www.publishers.org
The trade association of book publishers.

SKILLS

http://www.publishers.org/home/congrpt/index.htm ★ Skill 2: Policy Information

American Academy of Family Physicians (AAFP)
http://www.aafp.org
Trade association of physicians specializing in family practice.

SKILLS

http://www.aafp.org/gov/ ★ Skill 2: Policy Information

The American Academy of Neurology (AAN)
http://www.aan.com.
Trade association of neurologists.

American Academy of Ophthalmology (AAO)
http://www.aao.org
Trade association of ophthalmologists.

SKILLS

http://www.aao.org/member/products/wash_rep/wash_rep.html ★ Skill 2: Policy Information

American Academy of Orthopedic Surgeons (AAOS)
http://www.aaos.org
Trade association of orthopedic surgeons.

SKILLS

http://www.aaos.org/wordhtml/health.htm ★ Skill 2: Policy Information

American Arbitration Association
http://www.adr.org
Trade association of arbitrators.

SKILLS

http://www.adr.org/   ★ Skill 2: Policy Information

American Association of Critical-Care Nurses (AACN)
http://www.aacn.org
Trade association of critical-care nurses

SKILLS

http://www.aacn.org/aacn/pubpolcy.nsf/vwdoc/mainpublicpolicy?opendocument
  ★ Skill 2: Policy Information

American Association of Museums (AAM)
http://www.aam-us.org
Trade association of museums.

SKILLS

http://www.aam-us.org/gov.htm   ★ Skill 2: Policy Information

The American Bankers Association (ABA)
http://www.aba.com
Trade association representing bankers.

SKILLS

http://www.aba.com/aba/ABANews&Issues_IssMenu.asp   ★ Skill 2: Policy Information

American Bar Association (ABA)
http://www.abanet.org
Trade association of lawyers.

AMERICAN BAR ASSOCIATION

SKILLS

http://www.abanet.org/legadv/home.html   ★ Skill 2: Policy Information

American Chemical Society (ACS)
http://www.acs.org
Trade association of the chemical industry.

American Chemical Society
ChemCenter

SKILLS

http://www.acs.org/government/ ★ Skill 2: Policy Information

American Chiropractic Association (ACA)
http://amerchiro.org
Trade association of chiropractors.

SKILLS

http://amerchiro.org/government/index.html ★ Skill 2: Policy Information

American College of Surgeons (ACS)
http://www.facs.org
Trade association of surgeons.

SKILLS

http://www.facs.org/about_college/acsdept/socio_dept/
    semenu.html ★ Skill 2: Policy Information

American Dental Association (ADA)
http://www.ada.org
Trade association of dentists.

SKILLS

http://www.ada.org/govt/index.html ★ Skill 2: Policy Information

American Hospital Association (AHA)
http://www.aha.org
Trade association of hospitals.

SKILLS

http://www.aha.org/ar/advocate.html ★ Skill 2: Policy Information

American Hotel & Motel Association (AH&MA)
http://www.ahma.com
Trade association of hotels and motels.

SKILLS

http://www.ahma.com/government/ga_ndx.htm ★ Skill 2: Policy Information

The American Institute of Architects (AIA)
http://www.aiaonline.com
Trade association of architects.

SKILLS

http://www.e-architect.com/ ★ Skill 2: Policy Information

American Iron and Steel Institute (AISI)
http://www.steel.org
Trade association of iron and steel industries.

SKILLS

http://www.steel.org/policy/ ⋆ Skill 2: Policy Information

American Library Association(ALA)
http://www.ala.org
Trade association of libraries.

ALA

SKILLS

http://www.ala.org/advocacy/ ⋆ Skill 2: Policy Information

American Mathematical Society (AMS)
http://www.ams.org
Trade association of mathematicians.

AMS
AMERICAN MATHEMATICAL SOCIETY

SKILLS

http://www.ams.org/government/ ⋆ Skill 2: Policy Information

American Nurses Association (ANA)
http://www.ana.org
Trade association of nursing.

**ANA
JOIN TODAY!**

SKILLS

http://www.ana.org/gova/index.htm. ⋆ Skill 2: Policy Information

American Psychological Association (APA)

APA's MISSION

http://www.apa.org
Trade association of the psychological profession.

SKILLS

http://www.apa.org/ppo/ ⋆ Skill 2: Policy Information

American Society of Association Executives (ASAE)

asae

http://www.asaenet.org
Trade association of associations.

SKILLS

http://www.asaenet.org/policy/ ★ Skill 2: Policy Information

American Society of Civil Engineers (ASCE)
http://www.asce.org
Trade association of civil engineers.

American Society of Civil Engineers

SKILLS

http://www.asce.org/govnpub/gov_pub.html ★ Skill 2: Policy Information

ASCAP (American Society of Composers, Authors, and Publishers)
http://www.ascap.com
Trade association of creative writers and publishers.

SKILLS

http://www.ascap.com/legislative/legislative.html ★ Skill 2: Policy Information

The American Society of Mechanical Engineers (ASME)
http://www.asme.org
Trade association of mechanical engineers.

ASME International

SKILLS

http://www.asme.org/gric/ ★ Skill 2: Policy Information

American Society of Newspaper Editors (ASNE)
http://www.asne.org
Trade association of newspaper editors.

SKILLS

http://asne.org/ideas/ideas.htm ★ Skill 2: Policy Information

American Zoo and Aquarium Association (AZA)
http://www.aza.org
Trade association of zoos and aquariums.

SKILLS

http://www.aza.org/dept/govaff/ ★ Skill 2: Policy Information

Assisted Living Federation of America (ALFA)
http://www.alfa.org
Trade association of assisted living facilities.

SKILLS

http://www.alfa.org ★ Skill 2: Policy Information

Association of America's Public Television Stations (APTS)
http://www.apts.org

APTS's mission is to support the continued growth of a dynamic and financially sound noncommercial television services for the American public. Its members are the nation's public television stations.

SKILLS

http://www.apts.org/advocacy/index.cfm ★ Skill 2: Policy Information

Association of American Railroads (AAR)
http://www.aar.org
Trade association of the rail industry.

SKILLS

http://www.aar.org/aarhome.nsf?OpenDatabase ★ Skill 2: Policy Information

National Association of Broadcasters (NAB)
http://www.nab.org
Trade association of broadcasters.

SKILLS

http://www.nab.org ★ Skill 2: Policy Information

National Association of Home Builders (NAHB)
http://www.nab.org
Trade association of home builders.

SKILLS

http://www.nahb.org/hot_topics/default.htm ★ Skill 2: Policy Information

National Association of Manufacturers (NAM)
http://www.nam.org
Trade association of manufacturers.

SKILLS

http://www.nam.org/ ★ Skill 2: Policy Information

National Association of Social Workers (NASW)
http://www.naswdc.org
Trade association of social workers.

SKILLS

http://www.naswdc.org/ADVOCACY.HTM ★ Skill 2: Policy Information

National Corn Growers Association (NCGA)
http://www.ncga.com
Trade association of corn farmers.

SKILLS

http://www.ncga.com/04growers/main/index.html ★ Skill 2: Policy Information

National Farmers Union (NFU)
http://www.nfu.org
Trade association of farmers.

SKILLS

http://www.nfu.org/Issues/issues.cfm ★ Skill 2: Policy Information

National Fire Protection Association (NFPA)
http://www.nfpa.org
Trade association of firefighters.

National Mining Association (NMA)
http://www.nma.org
Trade association of the mining industry.

SKILLS

http://www.nma.org/ ★ Skill 2: Policy Information

National Newspaper Association (NNA)
http://www.nna.org
Trade association of newspapers.

SKILLS

http://www.nna.org/Leg%2oBriefings/issues.html ★ Skill 2: Policy
Information

National Restaurant Association
http://www.restaurant.org
Trade association of the restaurant industry.

SKILLS

http://www.restaurant.org/govt/govt.htm ★ Skill 2:
Policy Information

National Rural Electric Cooperative Association (NRECA)
http://www.nreca.org
Trade association of power companies.

SKILLS

http://www.nreca.org/leg_reg/ ★ Skill 2: Policy Information

National Society of Professional Engineers (NSPE)
http://www.nspe.org
Trade association of engineers.

SKILLS

http://www.nspe.org/govrel/gr-home.asp ★ Skill 2: Policy Information

The National Telephone Cooperative Association (NTCA)
http://www.ntca.org
Trade association of rural telephone companies.

SKILLS

http://www.ntca.org/leg_reg/index.html ★ Skill 2: Policy Information

Newspaper Association of America (NAA)
http://www.naa.org
Trade association of newspapers.

SKILLS

http://www.naa.org/ppolicy/index.html ★ Skill 2: Policy Information

Printing Industries of America, Inc. (PIA)
http://www.printing.org
Trade association of printers.

SKILLS

http://www.printing.org/Government.htm ★ Skill 2: Policy Information

Recording Industry Association of America, Inc. (RIAA)
http://www.riaa.org
Trade association of the music industry.

SKILLS

http://www.riaa.com/musicleg/ml_fed.htm ★ Skill 2: Policy Information

Society of American Florists (SAF)
http://www.safnow.org
Trade association of florists.

SKILLS

http://www.safnow.org/capitolhillwatch.html ★ Skill 2: Policy Information

Society of Automotive Engineers (SAE)
http://www.sae.org
Trade association of automotive engineers.

SKILLS

http://www.sae.org/congress/index.htm ★ Skill 2: Policy Information

The Society of the Plastics Industry (SPI)
http://www.plasticsindustry.org
Trade association of the plastics industry.

SKILLS

http://www.plasticsindustry.org/public/index.htm ★ Skill 2: Policy Information

Telecommunications Industry Association (TIA)
http://www.tiaonline.org
Trade association of the telecommunications industry.

SKILLS

http://www.tiaonline.org/government/ ⋆ Skill 2: Policy Information

Travel Industry Association of America (TIA)
http://www.tia.org
Trade association of the travel industry.

SKILLS

http://www.tia.org/govt/default.asp ⋆ Skill 2: Policy Information

United Fresh Fruit & Vegetable Association
http://www.uffva.org
Trade association of the produce industry.

SKILLS

http://www.uffva.org/goverment/index.htm ⋆ Skill 2: Policy Information

Urban Land Institute (ULI)
http://www.uli.org
Trade association of developers and real estate agents concerned with responsible planning and growth.

SKILLS

http://www.uli.org/indexJS.htm ⋆ Skill 2: Policy Information

U.S. Apple Association (U.S. Apple)
http://www.usapple.org
Trade association of apple growers.

SKILLS

http://www.usapple.org/ ⋆ Skill 2: Policy Information

UNIQUE FEATURES

http://www.usapple.org/ ⋆ "Sample Letters to Congress" provides sample letters on related issues.

Video Software Dealers Association (VSDA)
http://www.vsda.org
Trade association of the video software agency.

SKILLS

http://www.vsda.org ★ Skill 2: Policy Information

Yellow Pages publishers Association (YPPA)
http://www.yppa.org
Trade association of Yellow Pages publishers.

SKILLS

http://www.yppa.org ★ Skill 2: Policy Information

TRANSPORTATION

Advocates for Highway and Auto Safety
http://www.saferoads.org
Advocates for Highway and Auto Safety is comprised of consumer, health, and safety groups, insurance companies, and agents working together to make America's roads safer.

SKILLS

http://www.saferoads.org/ ★ Skill 1: Issue Background
http://www.saferoads.org/policy/fedleg.html ★ Skill 2: Legislative Agenda
http://www.saferoads.org/ ★ Skill 6: Related Links
http://www.saferoads.org/general/address.html ★ Skill 7: Contact Info/E-mail

Mothers Against Drunk Driving (MADD)
http://www.madd.org/dm/window.fm
MADD is a nonprofit grassroots organization whose focus is to look for effective solutions to drunk driving and underage drinking problems while supporting those who have already experienced the pain of these senseless crimes.

SKILLS

http://www.madd.org/PUB_POL/positions.shtml ★ Skill 1: Issue Background
http://www.madd.org/PUB_POL/20x2000.shtml ★ Skill 2: Legislative Agenda
http://www.madd.org/chapters/ ★ Skill 3: Membership
http://congress.nw.dc.us/madd/ ★ Skill 4: Action Alerts
http://jtodirect.madd.org/plugin.jtml?siteID=MADD&P=1 ★ Skill 6: Related Links
http://www.madd.org/ ★ Skill 7: Contact Info/E-mail

Transportation Action Network (TAN)
http://www.transact.org
TAN is dedicated to the development of transportation options that conserve energy, protect environmental and aesthetic quality, strengthen the economy, promote social equity, and make communities more livable.

SKILLS

http://www.transact.org/repandres.asp ★ Skill 1: Issue Background

VETERANS

Veterans of Foreign Wars (VFW)
http://www.vfw.org
VFW is dedicated to honoring the dead by helping the living survivors of foreign wars.

SKILLS

http://206.246.115.210/PA/public.shtml ★ Skill 2: Legislative
   Agenda
http://www.vfw.org/member/appl.shtml ★ Skill 3: Membership
http//206.246.115.210/AC/action.html ★ Skill 4: Action Alerts
http://www.vfw.org/homenon.shtml ★ Skill 7: Contact Info/E-mail

It is by taking share in legislation that the
American learns to know the law; it is by
governing that he becomes educated about the
formalities of government. The great work of
society is daily performed before his eyes, and
so to say, under his hands.

—ALEXIS DE TOCQUEVILLE

Chapter Nine

Your Own
Private Idaho

★

Introduction

So why not just scream out in cyberspace? Quite aside from the wealth of information and connection with government that the Internet provides, the World Wide Web allows anyone, with the aid of text and graphics, to yell out in the great information void without the approval of an editor from *The New York Times* or a resolution in Congress.

It seems only logical that the Internet, having made traditional forms of citizen activism easier and quicker, might give rise to whole new models of citizenship. So why not, considering the time required to gain a working understanding of our government or the editorial constraints of our major newspapers, just post the complete, uncensored transcript of your feelings with the hope that thousands, or even millions, of eyes will come across your thoughts and click away in sympathy, maybe even send you an E-mail saying you are not alone, that others feel the same way you do, and that if the president, or that clumsy, heaving bulwark of Congress, cannot fathom your thoughts, then it is *their* problem?

And besides, screaming is fun! It gets the blood flowing, the adrenaline shooting through your veins spurred on by the thrill of verbal aggression—that feeling that might makes right—a harkening back to our primal roots where, in the absence of a large and heavy rock, the sheer volume of the voice could decide all matters of truth and quickly and irrevocably establish a clear act of policy.

And while we are at it, let us not forget the power of writing—a far more sophisticated method of communication that relies on reason as much as volume to explain or enlighten or convince or inspire—a marvelous act of discovery where thoughts coalesce, ideas are refined, and one sees that one does indeed possess a voice worthy of joining the seething mass of ideas out there that form the cultural fabric of our nation.

Screaming is good. Writing is good. Putting yourself "out there" is good. So good, in fact, that they may be excuses in and of themselves. Free speech. Hear! Hear!

And now that we have conceded the psychological, creative, and symbolic importance of screaming into cyberspace, let's get back to reality. Despite all the hype, the Internet is not likely to fundamentally change the way our government works in this country. Our government will continue to respond to three things more than anything else—money, people, and geography—not web sites, outrageous allegations, or anguished diatribes. There are no plans to make Congress a group of six hundred "at-large" members who represent virtual communities.

And yet the Internet's potential as a tool in the hands of policy entrepreneurs who grow impatient with uninspired or incompetent legislators and plodding, unproductive associations is just beginning to be realized. As a method of assembling an interested, geographically dispersed network of people across the country, the Internet will again be unprecedented.

So if you want to scream, scream. If you really want to push the buttons of government—to effect change, to bring people together, to mobilize individuals for a common goal—consider some of the following skills when you design and maintain your unique outpost of humanity in cyberspace.

Idea 1: Get Folks Together—Start Something Big

Using a web site to attract like-minded individuals is the most powerful organizing action that you can take online. Alone you represent one vote, equal to everyone else. Join with one other person, and you have doubled your power. If you bind a hundred or a thousand like-minded individuals together, you instantly command a coalition that if mobilized has to be reckoned with.

Individuals have begun to use the power of the Internet and their own web sites to actually start organizations. As new issues emerge, perhaps the most logical action to take will be to put up a web site and see if you can raise any money to address the issue. Remember that deciding to found a new group online not only requires lots of dedication, it may also involve official documentation (if you want to form a nonprofit, for example).

Idea 2: Challenge the Established Organizations

The Founding Fathers might be surprised at how large and how entrenched the special interests are that have put down roots in Washington. Not only are elected officials constantly bombarded by these organized and ever-present groups, but you, the would-be activist, are dependent on them to do the work that you care about.

The narrow focus of individual groups makes it unlikely that you will ever have more than a few political associations to choose from that focus on any one specific issue—no matter how good or bad they are at doing their job. Like so many things, lackluster performance is the rule rather than the exception. And an association that is not providing you with action alerts, voting records, and a legislative agenda might need a wake-up call from the would-be member who provides an on-line alternative to the work that they are *not* doing.

Idea 3: Mount a "Flash Campaign"

You may not want to start a full-fledged organization, but you might want to lend your organizing talents to one narrow, specific battle. Although circulating an on-line petition may have dubious effects on lawmakers; in the hands of a savvy lobbyist, it can be used to identify supporters in key districts. A key vote in a committee with an unsympathetic chairperson might benefit from a short-term, on-line campaign that generates a flood of E-mail, phone calls, and faxes directed at the problematic lawmaker. In other words, you may want to conduct a small, discrete, on-line campaign—often referred to as a "flash campaign"—that addresses a single vote, or a small but important detail of public policy on some issue. In these cases, you can use a web site to identify supporters, mobilize them around a single, specific action, and then continue on in your busy life.

The Cybercitizen Awards 2000: Information, Issues, and Elections

Here are four individuals who have used the nascent power of digital ether to impact our democracy and to effectively encourage others to do so as well. The Cybercitizen Awards are not given for stunning design or killer applications. The award is neither liberal nor conservative but recognizes significant achievements anywhere along the political spectrum (although some of our initial recipients are truly nonpartisan). The award is given to those who have used the Internet as a grassroots tool to mobilize others beyond their own specific experiences and concerns, and have thereby created a model whereby the power of this new medium to the American democratic process can be realized, implemented, and duplicated.

Our initial Cybercitizen Award recipients have provided information, shaped policy issues, or had an impact on elections in this country by using the Internet. A common characteristic of these cybercitizens is that none of them had any real idea that they were doing anything "big" when they started. However, all of our recipients, despite their humble intentions, ended up contributing something significant to the frontier of digital democracy.

The Award Recipients

Juan Cabanela, Zip To It! web site
Joan Blades and Wes Boyd, Move on web site
Ilona Nickels, Capitol Question web site
Zach Exley, gwbush web site

Juan Cabanela: Mad scientist

Maybe the reason students are often at the forefront of change in America is because they have the time to chase down anything that thwarts their actions. Such was the case when Juan Cabanela wanted to write a letter to his congressmember opposing funding for the space station *Freedom*.

Juan knew enough about the space station to know that he opposed it. He did not, however, have much idea who his member of Congress was, much less how to contact him or her. What started as an urge to contact the federal government about the space program became a frustrating search for the simple address and phone number of his member of Congress.

Once Juan finally tracked down the contact information, he decided to be a pal to his fellow Americans and post the information as freeware in those pre–World Wide Web days. Eventually this address list was turned into html, became database driven, and is now Zip To It!, an interface that connects you to the Contacting the Congress web site and provides all the basic information you could want about your federal representatives once you enter your zip code. Despite a host of commercial "zip code" alternatives on the Internet, Zip To It! remains one of the best places to find out who represents you, how to contact them, what they look like, and the key committees they serve on.

Since embarking on his initial congressional odyssey, Juan has got-

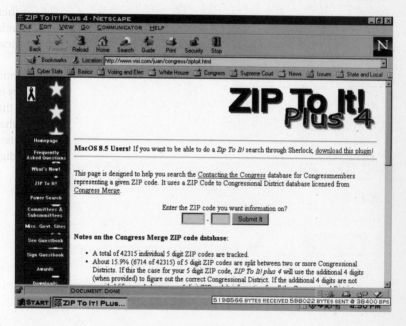

ten his doctorate and started teaching, but he maintains the web site as a fun and rewarding diversion and still regularly receives E-mails from grateful Americans who appreciate his site as a welcome public service. "I feel like at least I'm doing something."

Both the space station *Freedom* and Juan Cabanela still maintain their relationship with the federal government. Closer to Earth, and without any reliance on public tax dollars, Cabanela's web site leads thousands of Americans into the vastly unexplored frontier of their own government. When a controversial issue is before Congress, Zip To It! can receive upward of ten thousand hits per day from Americans who want to contact their members of Congress about anything that piques their interest.

Joan Blades and Wes Boyd: Ignore us at your peril

Leave it to a democracy to give everyday Americans the idea that they should not be ignored without dire consequences. Such was the feeling that Joan Blades and Wes Boyd, married, computer-savvy Californians, got during the impeachment proceedings of President Clinton. Born of frustration and their sense that an overwhelming number of Americans supported censuring the president and putting the Monica Lewinsky scandal behind them, Blades and Boyd decided to use the Internet as a tool to unify and express their opinion, succinctly contained in their original name: Censure and Move On.

What started out as a simple on-line petition sent among family and friends snowballed into an on-line document with five hundred thousand original signatures, and over $13 million in subsequent pledges. Censure and Move On became an Internet phenomenon and a powerful political tool, largely because it transcended its Internet confines by attracting the attention of the news media and successfully gathering millions of dollars

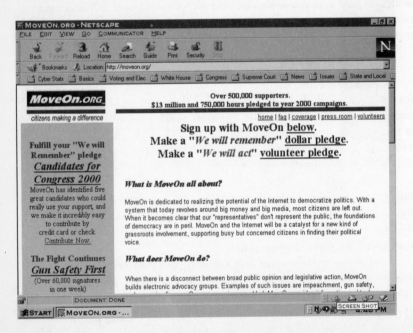

to dispense to the campaigns of congressional candidates running against proimpeachment incumbents. The Move On pledge: "I will work to elect candidates who courageously address key national issues, who reject the politics of division and personal destruction, and who respect the voice of ordinary citizens."

Asked about the original success of their petition, Blades says that "people felt very helpless" during the impeachment proceedings. "People did not know how to participate, and they wanted to." The resulting on-line effort has taken Blades and Boyd from angry Americans to political players at warp speed.

What separates Move On from most on-line petitions was that the petition ended up being just the first of many grassroots options offered to those who came across the Move On web site. The original petition has been combined with both fund-raising and press relations to create a sophisticated policy tool. "The Internet is a wonderful way to bring people back into the system and to feel that they've been effective," Blades says.

Asked about the dangers of populism and subjecting complex issues to majoritarian sentiments, Blades explains that the issues Move On tackles are the ones that Americans have developed sophisticated opinions on rather than knee-jerk reactions. "Every American was an expert on impeachment."

Ilona Nickels: Complexity made simple

Although Capitol Questions was born on the C-SPAN web site and is not the basement brainchild of an individual American striving to get their voice heard, it is, at once, an idea so simple, but so helpful, and executed so thoughtfully, that it deserves recognition. It is the sort of interactive resource that the Internet promised to afford Americans, even if it doesn't blink a lot or make groovy sounds.

With over twenty years working with the Library of Congress and numerous details with congressmembers as a parliamentary advisor, Ilona Nickels came to C-SPAN (which broadcasts gavel-to-gavel coverage of Congress) as a resident scholar to assist the staff and viewers with technical questions related to Congress.

What started as a column in the internal newsletter to clarify congressional concepts for C-SPAN employees was eventually put online and opened up to the public so that anyone with a question about Congress, its history, its procedures, the players, the scandals, the victories

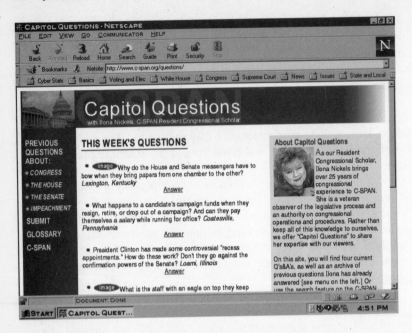

can "Ask Ilona" and get a thoughtful answer, even if it isn't always a simple one.

Her answers are not didactic or condescending. There is an enthusiasm behind the words of an American who not only finds her government interesting and complex but possible to understand, tempered by an insider's appreciation of being succinct.

Americans, she says, tend to have some understanding of their federal government, but there almost are always gaps in the knowledge, gaps that we tend to fill with the "least favorable" assumptions. Nickels sees the American policy process as being made up of intertwined procedural, policy, and political strands. And the traditional news media almost always focus on the political aspects in Congress while ignoring the other two.

"There is not an institution in town that will let you tell the whole story about the American government," Nickels says, and that includes members of Congress themselves. Capitol Questions provides everyday Americans an accessible resource that tackles the cagey American policy process as it is executed in Congress.

Zach Exley: Thorn, provocateur, comedian

No sooner was the Internet heralded as a cost-effective campaign tool that could bypass the nasty mudslinging of paid political advertising with a more civil, information-based alternative, then satire sites started springing up at a startling and welcome rate.

Zach Exley was not the first person to use the Internet to launch a parody site of a political candidate, but thanks to the campaign of George W. Bush, he is probably the most visible, and having the most fun—that is, if you have the stomach to take being called a "garbage man" in stride and threatened with expensive lawsuits by superpowerful beltway lawyers.

"At first I was scared," Exley says. Any expensive lawsuit would have necessitated this bedroom bandit to "just take down the web site and stop."

But like most Americans, the one thing that can forge an iron-clad resolve to scream like a banshee is any attempt to be silenced. Exley, irked at the threats and name-calling, is now determined to have fun at Bush's expense. He is even attempting to raise money to take his satire off the Internet and produce paid campaign ads—even though he is not affiliated with any competing campaign.

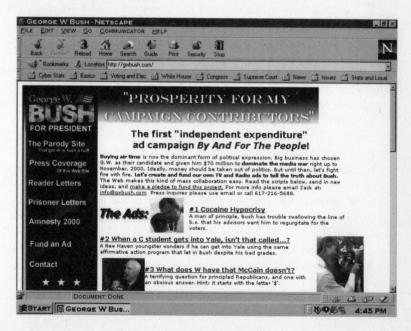

Chatting Online

How do you know you are having a debate rather than just passing the time? Like screaming, chatting online is fun, but not to be confused with saving the world. The first thing you should check is any expectation that you are going to ferret out the ignorant or the ill-informed and, armed with nothing but dazzling repartee, convince them to agree with you, take up the banner, and march. You have more of a chance of falling in love and marrying the person you are chatting with than compelling them to look at the world the same way you do, so if your goals for chatting online are other than holy matrimony, keep the following realistic possibilities in mind:

If You Are Chatting with Someone Who Agrees with Your Position, You Can:

Share stories and ideas. There is no reason that your experiences should only be shared with legislators. Knowing that other people share the same values or have had similar experiences generates a solidarity often lacking in the physically isolating confines of cyberspace. Such support can help sustain you and keep you fighting for your issues.

Share information about other sites and groups. Someone who feels the same way about the issues you do can be a font of information about web sites on the Internet that you have not yet discovered, including effective political groups

---

Meanwhile, the FEC attempts to categorize and regulate this new medium. (Exley likens himself to the press and believes parody web sites provide information with humor and should be exempt from financial or reporting restrictions.)

And for all of this, he has to thank George W. Bush, high-profile Republican candidate for president, who caught wind of Exley's "gwbush" site and talked about it, over and over again, not only illustrating for all Americans the free speech implications of perhaps unpopular web sites on the Internet, but bringing the web site into the news time and time again—a textbook case for all future candidates of how *not* to handle a parody web site.

But Exley's endeavor is not all fun and games. At the heart of the web site is Exley's deeply felt conviction that George W. Bush is a hypocrite, especially in the area of drug policy, where his "youthful indiscretions" were asked to be dismissed, even as he implemented some of the most stringent drug laws in the country as governor of Texas.

you may want to join. Alternatively, if you chat with someone who really cares about your issue but is not hooked up to an association that sends you good action alerts, you may want to encourage him or her to join.

If you are Chatting with Someone Who Disagrees with You, You Can:

Practice being civil. People love flaming online, but instead of calling the person you are chatting with ten kinds of idiot, try respectfully and professionally having an exchange of ideas. This will teach you to maintain your poise in the face of the opposition. There is no reason for you to fly off in an all-consuming rage or dissolve into self-pity just because people feel differently than you do on an issue. And a little composure will take much of the fun out of chat for jerks who are online just to see who they can rile up.

Gather up the opposition's arguments and learn how to rebut them. An argument used online is likely to also be heard in the corridors of power. Chatting with the opposition is a great way to do opposition research—to hear and rebut the very arguments the other side uses.

Judge for yourself how well you are able to counter their arguments. You might also try to understand the kinds of people who oppose your issue: their demographics, their background, and the nature of their concerns. Developing a deep understanding of the opposition from an in-depth and fearless exchange can contribute to your growth as a cybercitizen.

Traditional news media are fickle, and once an issue is covered, they tend to move on to other issues; but public education and decision making happens at a much slower and more reflective rate than the front page of *The New York Times*. For that reason, Exley's site, and others like it, allow "Americans to draw the connections that are there" but that may take time to coalesce.

And that focus relies on, among other things, humor. Belying the seriousness of the issues he makes fun of, Exley sees political satire as a forgotten art form that is being reborn on the Internet, and an excellent vehicle for creativity and political education.

Sure, parody sites can be irresponsible. Issues around integrity of information are especially important when one creates, or consumes, a political parody site. There will be people who are ruthless, nasty, and, worse yet, not funny; but candidates need not lose their sense of humor. Those satirists who do it effectively, honestly, and hysterically provide Americans an alternative way to learn about politics and follow the issues.

Cybercitizen Web Listings

Capitol Questions with Ilona Nickels
http://www.c-span.org/questions
Resident scholar Ilona Nickels provides an interactive Q & A that is simple, accessible and interesting. Viewers are invited to E-mail questions

about congressional proceedings; Ilona provides research, responses, and pictures to
answer questions. There was no better guide to the machinations of Congress during President Clinton's impeachment hearings.

SKILLS

http://www.c-span.org/questions/   ★ Skill 1: Private Idaho

UNIQUE FEATURES

http://www.c-span.org/questions/congress.asp   ★ Archives organized by topic may
already provide a thorough answer to your question.

gwbush
http://www.gwbush.com
Presidential candidate George W. Bush was not
amused by this political spoof site, the rebirth of political satire in America, a sign of things to come, and a
textbook case of how not to handle first amendment
issues as a candidate.

SKILLS

http://www.gwbush.com/   ★ Skill 1: Private Idaho

UNIQUE FEATURES

★ Hear George Bush attack free speech on the Internet in a fit of picque.

MoveOn
http://moveon.org
From exasperation to communication . . . hus-
band and-wife team Joan Blades and Wes Boyd

began Move On.org as an on-line petition to urge Congress to end the impeachment hearings against President Clinton. It has since become a grassroots fund-raising powerhouse.
Combining their web site with media relations, new issues, and mobilization, they have
created a multifaceted web campaign to be reckoned with.

Zip To It! Plus 4

http://www.visi.com/juan/congress/ziptoit.html
One of the first and still one of the best, zip code districting programs on the World Wide Web, Zip To It! was started by a frustrated citizen who couldn't find the address of his Congress member.

SKILLS

http://www.visi.com/juan/congress/ziptoit.html ★ Skill 1: Private Idaho

UNIQUE FEATURES

http://www.visi.com/juan/congress/search.html ★ "Power Search" allows you to find representatives by state, party, and also provides lists of committee members (http://www.visi.com/juan/congress/committees.html).

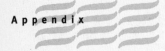

Appendix

Internet Basics

★

Getting Connected

To get on the Internet, you need to do two things after you buy the biggest, fastest computer you can afford:

Step 1: Dial Your Internet Service Provider (ISP)

This is the company that puts the call from your computer's modem through to the Internet. Examples of ISPs include America Online, Microsoft Network, EarthLink, MindSpring, and literally hundreds of others. Dialing an ISP usually involves directing your computer to make a phone call and then entering a User ID (name) and a password. At work, your office might be connected to the Internet twenty-four hours a day and you might never have to "dial in." As technology increases, the speed and the amount of information that you can download from the Internet will increase. Already, large band-width Options are available through some cable companies or other service providers that allow twenty-four hour home access that will not require you to dial an ISP.

Step 2: Launch Your Web Browser

This is the program on your computer that acts as the interface between your computer and the information coming off the Internet—

it formats stuff for your screen, lets you type and send messages, etc. The most common examples of browsers are America Online (which is both an ISP and browser in one), Netscape Navigator, and Microsoft Explorer. Once you are connected to an ISP, you usually just have to "open" your browser the same way you open any program on your computer.

Five Skills to Navigate the World Wide Web

Skill 1: Search.

There is as much garbage along the information superhighway as there is along any other busy road in the country. Your challenge is to find the information you need without spending all afternoon looking for it. Search engines are the "little trains that could" of the Internet. They ask you for keywords and then tell you what is out there. There are three different kinds of search engines you can use when you are searching for information on the Internet:

Internet search engines (Yahoo, Excite, Alta Vista, etc.). These are the search engines you usually hear about. Your browser probably has a symbol that connects you to one of these with a simple click of the mouse button. These search engines scan the entire World Wide Web for information related to any keywords you designate. One drawback of the explosive growth of the Internet is that Internet search engines now regularly return hundreds or even thousands of possibilities from a few keywords.

Search in window. Your browser also has the ability to search the entire document that is currently on your screen for a key word or phrase. This can sometimes save you from having to read through a lengthy document to find what you need or help you quickly scan through information that does not fit on the screen.

Web site search engines (on web sites). These applications are embedded in web sites themselves and allow you to search that web site's content for key information. For example, entering the title of a book you are looking for on Amazon.com utilizes their web site search engine.

Boolean Search Commands

There are several basic logic functions that you can employ when using a search engine. These are known as *Boolean commands,* and they can help you narrow your search and make it more specific. The more specific your search is, the less likely you are to be overwhelmed by hundreds of matches that you have no real interest in.

- ★ Use AND to search for the presence of *all* keywords *only,* e.g., "President AND Heart AND Research."
- ★ Use Or to search for *any* of the keywords appearing separately *or* together, e.g., "Heart Attack OR Heart Disease."
- ★● Use NOT to search for *the absence* of the keywords, e.g., "Heart NOT Valentine."

Another hint: Use "quotation marks" to search for a string of words together in a specific order, e.g., "American Heart Association."

Skill 2: Surf.

The euphemism "surfing" is supposed to make your computer sound as fun as a day at the beach. It isn't really. Surfing the Internet involves clicking along to see if you find anything interesting among all the hyperlinks that take you from web site to web site like an electronic Tarzan. It is a legitimate way to get a sense of what is available, or to locate useful information that you did not realize existed. But be warned, surfing can swallow whole hours of your time—much like a day at the beach indeed.

Essential Plug-ins

The Internet seems determined to emulate that now-ancient technology called television, and web sites are increasingly incorporating sound and video. Although the doomsayers among us worry that the World Wide Web may soon become a vast multichannel infomercial, sometimes sound and animation can enhance the information we receive. For these reasons, *plug-ins* are essential additions to your browser. Plug ins are little programs that expand the capabilities of your browser but are not automatically included with your browser software (usually because they are manufactured by different companies).

Plug-ins are usually free but must be downloaded from the web site of the company that manufactured them. Because they are programs and not simply documents, after they are downloaded, they must be *installed*, usually by clicking on the icon of the downloaded program once it is on your hard drive. The good news is that once installed, most plug-ins will automatically launch themselves when appropriate—when a file on the Internet makes use of that particular plug-in.

Name of Plug-in	What It Does	Where to Find It
Adobe Acrobat	Allows you to view and print files saved in *PDF* (portable document format). Acrobat allows you to print perfectly formatted forms and reports and is essential for downloading government reports off the Web.	www.adobe.com/ supportservice/ custsupport/ download.html
RealPlayer	Allows streaming video and sound to be played on your computer or saved on your computer. Among other things, RealPlayer allows you to watch television stations like CNN and listen to radio stations online without consuming all of your hard drive memory and crashing your system.	www.real.com/ products/index.html
QuickTime	An alternative multimedia plug-in developed by Apple Computer and preferred by some multimedia applications. QuickTime also allows for streaming sound and video capabilities.	www.apple.com/ quicktime/index.html

Skill 3: Type URLs.

Every page on the Internet has an address called a *URL* (universal resource locator). Typing a URL in your browser will take you to a specific web page much like dialing a phone number will connect you with a specific person or business. All URLs begin with "http://" which stands for "hypertext transfer protocol." Items on the World Wide Web have URLs that begin with "www." In addition, most URLs end with a series of three letters that usually provide an indication of the type of site they are:

- ★ **.gov government-related site**
- ★ **.com commercial site, posted by a for-profit business**
- ★ **.org organizational site, e.g., nonprofit**
- ★ **.edu school or academic web site**

Skill 4: Use hyperlinks.

Just point and shoot. Many things on the Internet are linked to related items of interest and you can simply click on the text to explore. A rule of thumb is that anything underlined or that turns the arrow cursor on your screen to a pointing finger is probably a hyperlink. In addition, many web sites provide lists of hyperlinks as an informal index to web sites of related information or services.

Skill 5: Bookmark your pages.

Once you have found something useful, or interesting, or entertaining on the Internet, you never, ever want to have to search for it again. Use the *bookmark,* or the "favorites" feature, on your browser to automatically save the URLs of the web sites you want to visit often. The next time you want to go to that destination, you can use a *drop-down menu* on your browser to go right there.

Five Things You Can Do with a Web Page

1. Read it. Make sure you give the page time to finish loading before you scroll through it. Be aware that your phone line and computer are trying to transfer text and graphics and even sound. This is complicated, and more often than any of us would like, it does not work right the first time. If a page stops loading, press the *reload button* on your browser, or retype the URL.

2. Analyze it. Not all of the information on the Internet is verified or edited or necessarily true. It is important for you to take time to determine the validity of the information you find online. Try to get your information from reputable sites that rely on hard statistics and avoid gossipy, hearsay information or outrageous claims.

3. Print it. Just select "print" from your browser menu. Your browser should be able to find your printer and give you a nice hard copy version of what you see on your screen. Again, be sure the page has completely loaded into your browser or it may not all print out.

4. Cut and paste it. This is probably the easiest way to "steal" things off of the World Wide Web. If you find some good text that you want to save or cite—highlight it, and use the *cut* command under the *edit* menu. Then you can open a word processor or other application and, again under the edit menu, select the *paste* command. The words should easily transfer, although they will not always retain the original formatting of the on-line document.

5. Download it. Sometimes, the document you are interested in online is too big to read all at once or even to print out. You may want to save the document as a file on your own computer. In both of these situations, you must *download* information from the Internet. Under the *file* menu, select the *save* command. Pay attention to where on your computer you save files and under what name or you may not be able to find them again. Also be wary of downloading any files that are extremely large or that have mysterious origins. You do not want to contaminate your hard drive with a *virus*.

Glossary

action alert *(call to action)* A letter or E-mail urging constituents to communicate with elected officials at a critical legislative juncture.

agenda *(legislative agenda)* The complete list of legislation that a political group supports, monitors, or opposes during a legislative session.

amendment A formal change to legislation.

amicus curiae brief *(friends of the court brief)* A supplementary document submitted for court consideration that provides relevant information not presented by either of the involved parties.

association *(political group, interest group, coalition)* A group of citizens who work together toward a common vision or goal.

attachments Additional files included with an E-mail message.

backgrounder *(background, issue briefing)* An educational briefing or summary on a legislative issue.

ballot initiative *(initiative)* A proposed law that appears on the election ballot and is implemented by popular vote.

bill See *legislation*

bill analysis The process of determining the substantive, procedural, and political implications of a proposed piece of legislation.

bookmark *(favorites)* A browser capability that allows you to record the URL of a web site you may wish to return to.

Boolean commands Basic logic commands that can be used with most search engines, e.g., AND, OR, and NOT.

briefs Summaries and other substantiating documents that pertain to a specific legal case.

broadcast media *(electronic media)* Television, radio, and other media that are electronically transmitted.

browser *(Netscape Navigator, Microsoft Explorer)* Software that formats text and files from the Internet for your computer.

bulletin board On-line function that allows people to read and post opinions on a specific topic.

bureaucracy The collection of federal executive departments, independent agencies, and state government organizations, their staff, and authority that implement and manage the vast majority of government related business.

calendar The official schedule of legislative consideration and action in federal, state, or local government.

candidate Someone who is running for public office.

chat On-line discussion in real time.

click *(click on, go to, select, double click)* The action of depressing your mouse button.

closed primary A primary election where only registered party members are permitted to vote.

co-sponsor An elected official who adds his or her name to a piece of legislation as an ardent supporter.

committee (1) A small group of elected officials formed to consider related pieces of legislation; (2) a candidate's official election organization; (3) a group formed to collect and distribute money to candidates for public office.

concurring opinion Decision given when justices agree with the Opinion of the Court but for different reasons.

Congress *(legislature)* The legislative branch of the U.S. government, consisting of the U.S. Senate and the U.S. House of Representatives.

constituent *(voter, citizen)* A person represented by an elected official.

contact information The address, phone number, E-mail, and any other pertinent information that can be used to contact an elected official, individual, or organization.

contribution *(donation)* Usually a cash donation to the campaign of a specific candidate or PAC.

copy *(cc)* A duplicate file or message.

cut and paste Computer function that allows you to select text and copy it to another window, application, or file.

cybercitizen An American who intelligently uses the Internet to stay informed about important legislative issues, engage in dialogue with elected officials, and support promising candidates for public office.

deadline The time when a media story must be filed to make it into the next issue or broadcast.

delegate *(elector)* An official representative of a political party or group.

democracy Government of, by, and for the people that it serves, characterized by popular elections and public access to information.

direct democracy *(instant democracy)* The ability to quality ballot initiatives for Election Day.

dissenting opinion Decision and reasoning of the justices who do not agree with the Opinion of the Court.

district The geographic boundaries that determine the constituents for a given legislative representative.

districting The process of determining who one's elected officials are based on their home address.

docket The official list of cases being considered by a U.S. court.

download To transfer a copy of a file from the Internet to your computer.

E-mail *(message)* Messages sent via the Internet.

editorial Essay on a current issue, usually found in a newspaper.

Election Day A day when registered citizens can cast their vote for candidates for public office.

electoral process *(elections)* The process by which a person is elected to public office in a democracy.

executive Of or relating to the president, governor, or mayor, their powers, and their responsibilities.

executive acts Official actions that may be taken by the president of the United States.

federal Of or relating to the US presidency, Congress, Supreme Court, and the national bureaucracy.

flaming Being rude or derogatory online.

flash campaign A grassroots campaign conducted on the Internet to secure an immediate, specific legislative outcome.

grassroots The use of individual constituents to communicate a legislative position to their elected officials or to secure a victory in an election.

homepage *(home)* The first screen you see at a web site, usually an on-line table of contents for the site.

html *(hypertext markup language)* Common language used to design and post web sites.

http *(hypertext transport protocol)* The uniform file management code used by the World Wide Web.

hyperlink *(link)* A connection between two web sites usually indicated by a button, underlined text, or pointing mouse.

install To add a program to your hard drive in a way that allows it to be utilized.

Internet *(cyberspace, virtual_, being online, cyber_)* The global communications network that connects computers and allows them to share information.

Internet service provider *(dial-up, DSL, high-speed connection)* The service that connects your computer to the Internet.

issue advocacy *(issue ads)* Election advertising that educates or supports a position on a specific issue without directly advocating the support or defeat of a candidate.

issues The various topics that government addresses or manages and that constituents might be interested in.

judicial Of or relating to the U.S. courts of law.

judicial review The ability of the judicial branch to declare a law unconstitutional and effectively void.

jurisdiction *(authority)* The issue areas that a legislative body has authority over.

key players *(targets)* Lawmakers, political groups, or individuals that wield significant power related to an issue through expertise, influence, media savvy, or formal position.

law *(code, statutes)* The binding set of rules that govern a people.

legislation *(bill)* A proposed law.

legislative Of or relating to the lawmaking bodies on the national, state, or local levels of government, including Congress.

legislative process *(how a bill becomes a law)* The process by which laws are created in a democracy.

legislator *(elected official, policymaker, lawmaker, decisionmaker)* A person elected to public office.

legislature *(Congress)* State or federal rule making body.

letter to the editor Brief response from a reader printed by a newspaper or magazine.

listserve *(push mail, List Bot, distribution list)* A program that distributes E-mail to a predetermined list of recipients.

lobbying *(advocacy)* Attempting to influence the legislative process for a specific goal.

mobilization *(alert)* A grassroots call to action.

moderator On-Line chat room facilitator that keeps the exchange from meandering or becoming nasty.

multimedia Web components and files that make use of animation, sound, and/or video elements in addition to text.

nonprofit organization A group usually formed for an educational or service-delivery purpose that obtains a special tax designation.

open primary A primary election where all eligible voters are permitted to participate.

opinion A decision rendered in a court of law.

opinion of the court *(decision)* The majority opinion of the U.S. Supreme Court, legally binding.

opposition The collection of individuals, groups, and ideas that oppose your position on an issue.

opposition research The process of identifying your opposition, gathering, and analyzing their statements and strategy.

petition *(on-line petition)* Basic grassroots tool that relies on collecting signatures to demonstrate support for a specific policy position.

plug-ins Computer programs used to expand the capabilities of an Internet browser usually with multimedia files.

poison pill clause A single provision so onerous that it makes an entire piece of legislation unthinkable.

policy *(public policy, provisions)* The substance of proposed or existing laws and regulations.

Political Action Committee (PAC) Group formed to direct money to a field of candidates who share common views or goals.

polling place *(polls, voting booth)* Official place where a citizen may cast his or her vote on Election Day.

position An official stance or proposal on an electoral or legislative issue.

primary An election held before the general election to determine the field of candidates by party.

print media Newspapers and magazines and other media that are printed.

privacy Issues related to the collection and dissemination of personal information on the Internet.

recess A scheduled break in the legislative or judicial calendar.

record *(voting record, report card, history)* The official votes cast by an elected official while in office.

registrar of voters The official keeper of voting records and information.

registration A legal requirement in most states before a citizen is allowed to vote.

regulation Rules enacted to apply existing law to specific circumstances.

report card *(record, votes)* The voting record of a legislator in a specific issue area.

resolution A bill that expresses the sentiments of one or both chambers in Congress without the binding force of law.

search To identify web sites and other information of interest by using specific terms or values.

search engine A program that searches the content of a web page, web site, or the Internet for a keyword or other identifying piece of information.

session The length of time that a legislature conducts all related business between elections.

sitting The time when a court is in session.

soft money Unlimited donations that may be made to political parties for organizational activities not directly related to supporting a candidate for public office.

sound Byte *(Quote)* A brief statement used by the press to document or report a story.

Spam Unwanted, lengthy, or inappropriate E-mail.

special interest group *(group, public interest group, trade association)* Political group that lobbies around a specific issue or goal.

stakeholders *(interested parties, players)* An individual or group who takes a position on some matter of public policy, usually because they believe they will be directly affected by it.

supersite A web site largely consisting of links that organize a vast array of existing web sites on a given topic.

surfing Traveling the Internet via hyperlinks.

term The length of time that an elected official serves in office.

totalitarian regime *(autocracy)* The theoretical opposite of democracy. A system of government characterized by the rule of one person or one ideology without the accommodation of debate, dissent, or popularly elected rulers.

tracking Determining where in the legislative process a bill currently resides.

traditional mail *(snail mail, regular mail)* Letter sent through the post office.

transcripts The text record of an official government proceeding, news media piece, or court case.

URL *(universal resource locator)* A web site address on the Internet; usually begins with "http://".

virus A computer program designed to interfere with normal functioning of your computer.

voter A citizen of voting age who is registered to vote.

web page *(page)* A single screen on the Internet.

web site *(site)* Collection of text, graphics, and other files connected with a single URL.

World Wide Web *(information superhighway)* The part of the Internet that allows citizens, organizations, and businesses to post web pages and share information.

Index

AARP Foundation (American
   Association of Retired Persons),
   218–19
ABCNews.com, 121
abortion, 216–19
action alerts, 173
Action for Animals, 179
Action on Smoking and Health (ASH),
   198
administration, the, 58–61
Adobe Acrobat, 253
Advocacy Institute, 213
Advocates for Highway and Auto
   Safety, 235
Advocates for Youth, 181
AFL CIO, 210
aging, 218–19
AIDS Action, 198
Al Gore, 49, 58
Alabama, 139–40
Alaska, 140
Alliance for Better Campaigns, 41
Alliance for Justice (AFJ), 211
Alzheimers Association, 198–99
America Online (AOL), 51
American Academy of Family
   Physicians (AAFP), 225

American Academy of Neurology
   (AAN), 225
American Academy of Ophthalmology
   (AAO), 225
American Academy of Orthopedic
   Surgeons (AAOS), 225
American Arbitration Association, 226
American Arts Alliance, 180
American Association of Critical-Care
   Nurses, 226
American Association of Museums
   (AAM), 226
American Association of Retired
   Persons (AARP), 218–19
American Atheists, 214
American Bankers Association (ABA),
   226
American Bar Association (ABA), 226
American Cancer Society, 199
American Chemical Society (ACS),
   226–27
American Chiropractic Association
   (ACA), 227
American Civil Liberties Union (ACLU),
   182
   ACLU Reproductive Rights Project,
      216

American College of Surgeons (ACS), 227

American Conservative Union (ACU), 182

American Dental Association (ADA), 227

American Diabetes Association, 199

American Federation of State, County and Municipal Employees (AFSCME), 210

American Forests, 190

American Heart Association, 200

American Hospital Association (AHA), 227

American Hotel and Motel Association (AH&MA), 227

American Institute of Architects (AIA), 227

American Iron and Steel Institute (AISI), 228

American Israel Public Affairs Committee (AIPAC), 195

American Jewish Committee (AJC), 183

AMERICAN JOURNALISM REVIEW NewsLink, 128

American Library Association (ALA), 228

american life league, 216

American Lung Association, 200

American Mathematical Society (AMS), 228

American Nurses Association (ANA), 228

American Politics Journal, 122–23

American Psychological Association (APA), 200, 228

American Public Health Association (APHA), 200–201

American Society for the Prevention of Cruelty to Animals (ASPCA), 179

American Society of Association Executives (ASAE), 228–29

American Society of Civil Engineers (ASCE), 229

American Society of Composers Authors, and Publishers (ASCAP), 229

American Society of Mechanical Engineers (ASME), 229

American Society of Newspaper Editors (ASNE), 229

American Zoo and Aquarium Association (AZA), 229

Americans for Fair Taxation, 220

Americans for Tax Reform (ATR), 221

Americans for the Arts, 180

Americans United for the Separation of Church and State, 215

Amnesty International USA, 208
program to abolish the death penalty, 187

Animal Legal Defense Fund (ALDF), 179

animal rights, 179–80

Annotated Constitution from Government Printing Office, 17

Anti-Defamation League of B'nai B'rith (ADL), 183

ARC of the United States, 189

Arizona, 140–41

Arkansas, 141

Arthritis Foundation, 201

arts, 180

Ask Ilona, 243–44

Assisted Living Federation of America (ALFA), 230

Association of America's Public Television Stations (APTS), 230

Association of American Publishers (AAP), 225

Association of American Railroads (AAR), 230

Association of Americans for Spouse Reunification, 207

Association of Reproductive Health Professionals (ARHP), 216–17

associations (issues, associations, groups, and coalitions), 168–69
communicating with staff, 178
nonprofit associations, 170
reasons to join, 170–71, 172
trade associations, 169–170

Avalon Project, 18

background research, 34
ballot information, 28
ballot initiatives, 36
  questions to ask, 37–38
Bazelon Center for Mental Health Law,
  188
bill analysis, 83–84
bill digest, 82
Bill of Rights, 13–14
bill tracking, 85
bills, downloading, 81–82
bills, federal, 81–83, 83–85, 85–86
bills, state, 136
Blades, Joan, 242–43
  See also Move On
bookmarks, 254
Boolean Commands, 252
Boyd, Wes, 242–43
  See also Move On
Brain Injury Association (BIA), 201
broadcast media
  broadcast and print media,
    difference between, 113–14
  Internet and, 111–12
  web sites, 80
  what to search for, 114
Brookings Institution, 223
  Campaign Finance Pages, 41–42
browser, 250–51
budget and taxes, 220–23
  federal, 66–67
  state, 136
Bush, George W., 49
  See also, gwbush

C-SPAN, 96, 243–44
  Election 2000 Site, 45
Cabanela, Juan, 240–42
  See also Zip to It! Plus 4
California, 141–43
campaign contributions, 32–33
  legal guidelines, 33
campaign finance, 41–45
Campaign Finance Reform, 24–26
campaigns, communicating via E-mail,
  31–32

candidate worksheet, 40
candidates, presidential, 49–50
Capitol Questions, 243–44
  web site, 248
CapWeb, 97
CATO Institute, 224
Center for Community Change, 207
Center for Democracy and Technology
  (CDT), 209
Center for Patient Advocacy, 201–2
Center for Public Integrity, 42
Center for Reproductive Law and Policy
  (CRLP), 217
Center for Responsive Politics (CRP),
  42, 80
Center for Science in the Public Interest
  (CSPI), 212
Center on Budget and Policy Priorities
  (CBPP), 223
Central Intelligence Agency (CIA), 71
Child Welfare League of America
  (CWLA), 181
Children's Defense Fund (CDF), 181
children/youth, 181–82
Choice in Dying, 194
Christian Coalition, 215
Citizens Against Government Waste
  (CAGW), 221
Citizens Committee for the Right to
  Keep and Bear Arms, 196–97
Citizens for a Sound Economy (CSE),
  221–22
Citizens for an Alternative Tax System
  (CATS), 222
Citizens for Tax Justice (CTJ), 222
civil rights, 182–87
Clinton, Bill, 58
CNN Interactive, 121
Coalition for Student Loan Reform
  (CSLR), 204–5
coalitions (issues, associations, groups,
  and coalitions), 168–69, 170
  reasons to join, 170–71, 172
Colbert, Jean Baptiste, 130
Colorado, 143
Committee assignments, 80

Common Cause, 43, 213
Compassion in Dying, 194–95
Congress, 74–75, 75–77, 81
    expectations concerning, 77–78
Congress.org, 101
Congressional Budget Office (CBO), 97
Congressional Record, 82–83
Congressional Representatives,
    information on, 79–80
Connecticut, 143–44
Consortium for Citizens with
    Disabilities (CCD), 188
Constitution Facts.com, 17
constitution, state, 137–38
Constitution, The, 13, 17
Council on American-Islamic Relations
    (CAIR), 186–87
CRAYON, 124
cut and paste, 255
Cybercitizen
    Awards, 240
    web site, 273
Cystic Fibrosis Foundation, 202

De Tocqueville, Alexander, 15–16, 168,
    237
death penalty, 187
Declaration of Independence, The, 12
Defenders of Wildlife, 191
Delaware, 144
Democracy in America, 18
Democracy in America (De
    Tocqueville), 15–16
Democracy Network, 51–52
    media listings, 128
Democratic National Committee
    (DNC), 46
demographics, 23–24
Department of Agriculture, 70
Department of Commerce, 70
Department of Defense, 70
Department of Education, 70
Department of Energy, 70
Department of Health and Human
    Services, 70
Department of Housing and Urban
    Development, 70

Development Department of Interior,
    70
Department of Justice, 70
Department of Labor, 70
Department of State, 71
Department of Transportation, 71
Department of Treasury, 71
Department of Veterans Affairs, 71
Derechos Human Rights, 208
Destination Democracy, 43
Digital Future Coalition (DFC), 209
disabled, 188–89
Disabled American Veterans (DAV),
    189
District of Columbia (Washington,
    D.C.), 144
districting, 78
documents, presidential, 60–61
DRUDGE REPORT, 123

E The People, 99–100, 139
E&P (Editor & Publisher) Online Media
    Directory, 128
E-mail
    copies (cc), 91
    flaming, 90
    on-line subscriptions, 68, 69
    spam, 90–91
    tips, 90–92
    value of, 88
    vs. letters, 93–94
E-mailing
    congress, 86–83
    constructive venting, 93
    political campaigns, 31–32
    the president, 62, 67
    state and local officials, 137
Economist, The, 125
education, 190
Elecnet, 52
Election Connection, 52
election returns, tracking, 38–39
elections, 45–46
Electoral College, 38
Electronic Frontier Foundation (EFF),
    210
Eliot, George, 20

Emancipation Proclamation, The,
 14–15
environment, 190–94
Environmental Defense Fund (EDF),
 191
Environmental Protection Agency, 71
Epilepsy Foundation, 202
euthanasia, 194–95
Executive Acts, 61
executive departments, 70
Exley, Zach, 245–47

Families USA, 202–3
favorites, 254
FECInfo (Federal Election
 Commission), 43–44
Federal Communications Commission,
 71
federal departments, 67–69
Federal Election Commission, 30, 41, 71
 FECInfo, 43–44
Federal Emergency Management
 Agency, 71
federal legislative process, 86
Federal Register (NARA), 68–69
Federal Trade Commission, 71
Federalist Papers, The, 12–13
Feminist Majority, 183–84
FindLaw, 18, 109
FindLaw Constitutional Law Center, 18
FindLaw Supreme Court Center, 107–8
flaming, 90, 247
flash campaign, 239
Florida, 145
foreign relations, 195–96
4Politics, 51
FoxNews.com, 121–22
FREEDOM CHANNEL, 52–53

Gallup Organization, 48–49
General Accounting Office (GAO),
 97–98
George Magazine, 124
George W. Bush, 49
 See also, gwbush
Georgia, 145–46
Gingrich, Newt, 82

Global Climate Coalition (GCC), 191
Gore, Al, 49, 58
Government Printing Office, Annotated
 Constitution from, 17
governors, 135
GoVote.com, 53
Grassroots.com, 98
 Political Columnists Links, 129
 State Districting, 138–39
Great Internet Debate 2000, 49
Greenpeace, 192
groups (issues, associations, groups,
 and coalitions), 168–69
 public interest groups, 170
 reasons to join, 170–71, 172
 types of special interest groups,
 169–70
gun control, 196–98
Gun Free Kids, 197
gwbush (web site), 245–47, 248

Hamilton, Alexander, 10, 13
Handgun Control, Inc., 197
Hawaii, 146
health, 198–204
Hemlock Society, 195
Heritage Foundation, 224
higher education, 204–6
Hill Campaign 2000, 46
Hill on the Web, 124
History Channel Speech Archive, 72
History Place, the, 19
History Place Sounds of the Presidents,
 72–73
House of Representatives, US, 74–75,
 75–77, 81
 expectations concerning, 77–78
housing, 206–7
Hudson Institute, 224
Human Rights Campaign (HRC), 184
human rights, international, 208–9
Human Rights Watch (HRW), 209
hyperlinks, 254

Idaho, 146–47
independent agencies, 71
Illinois, 147

immigration, 207–8
In Defense of Animals (IDA), 180
Independent Sector (IS), 211–12
Indiana, 147–48
International Brotherhood of Electrical
    Workers (IBEW),
International Brotherhood of
    Teamsters, 211
International Committee of Lawyers for
    Tibet (ICLT), 195–96
Internet issues, 209–10
Internet service provider (ISP), 250
Iowa, 148
issue advocacy, 25
    issues, associations, groups, and
        coalitions, 168–69
issue positions, 34–35
issues (issues, associations, groups, and
        coalitions), 168–69
    background research, 171–72
    types of special interest groups,
        169–70
Issues 2000, 50

Jay, John, 13
Jefferson, Thomas, 3, 13, 250

Kansas, 148–49
Kentucky, 149

labor unions, 210–11
Latino Vote 2000, 50
law, federal, 109
law, state, 138
leadership, 76–77
League of Conservation Voters (LCV),
    192
League of United Latin American
    Citizens (LULAC), 184
League of Women Voters, 53
legislation, state, 135
legislative agenda
    associations and, 172
    federal, 81–83, 83–85, 85–86
legislative process, federal, 86
letters to the editor, 115
    writing, 116–17

Libertarian Party, 47
Library of Congress, 16
Library of Congress Executive Branch
    Pages, 73
Library of Congress Judicial Branch
    Pages, 109
Library of Congress Legislative Branch
    Pages, 101
Library of Congress State and Local
    Government Pages, 139
Lincoln, Abraham, 15
links, 254
Long Term Care Campaign, 203
Louisiana, 150

Madison, James, 13
Maine, 150
Marshalov, Boris, 74
Maryland, 150–51
Massachusetts, 151–52
Mayflower Compact, The, 12
Mean, Margaret, 1
media, 110–11
    broadcast and print media,
        difference between, 113–14
    Internet and, 111–12
    web sites, 80
    what to search for, 114
membership, 170–71, 172
Micasa-Sucasa, 207–8
Michigan, 152
Mill, John Stuart, 10
Minnesota, 152–53
Mississippi, 153
Missouri, 153–54
Montana, 154
Mothers Against Drunk Driving
    (MADD), 235
Motor Voter Act, 26–27
Move On, 242–43
    MoveOn web site, 248–49
MSNBC, 122

Nation, 125–26
National Abortion Federation (NAF),
National Abortion Rights Action League
    (NARAL), 217–18

National Aeronautics and Space Administration, 71

National Alliance for the Mentally Ill (NAMI), 203

National Archives and Records Administration (NARA), 1, 16–17, 71

Federal Register (NARA), 68–69

National Association for the Advancement of Colored People (NAACP), 184–85

National Association of Broadcasters (NAB), 230

National Association of Graduate and Professional Students (NAGPS), 205

National Association of Home Builders (NAHB), 230

National Association of Manufacturers (NAM), 230–31

National Association of People With AIDS (NAPWA), 203–4

National Association of Social Workers (NASW), 231

National Audubon Society, 192–93

National Center for Policy Analysis (NCPA), 223

National CPR (Coalition for Patient Rights), 204

National Coalition to Abolish the Death Penalty (NCADP), 187

National Committee to Preserve Social Security and and Medicare (NCPSSM), 219

National Congress of American Indians (NCAI), 185

National Corn Growers Association (NCGI), 231

National Council of La Raza (NCLR), 185

National Council on the Aging (NCOA), 219

National Direct Student Loan Coalition (NDSLC), 205

National Education Association (NEA), 190

National Endowment for the Arts, 71

National Fair Housing Advocate (NFHA), 206

National Farmers Union (NFU), 231

National Federation of Independent Business (NFIB), 219–20

National Fire Protection Association (NFPA), 231

National Law Center for Homelessness and Poverty (NLHP), 206

National Low-Income Housing Coalition (NLIHC), 206

National Mental Health Association, 204

National Mining Association (NMA), 231

National Network for Immigrant and Refugee Rights (NNIRR), 208

National Newspaper Association (NNA), 232

National Organization of Women (NOW), 185–86

National Parent Teacher Association (PTA), 190

National Public Radio Online, 122

National Restaurant Association (NRA), 232

National Review Online, 125

National Rifle Association (NRA), 197–98

National Right to Life, 218

National Rural Electric Cooperative Association (NRECA), 232

National Safety Council (NSC), 214

National Society of Professional Engineers (NSPE), 232

National Taxpayers Union Federation (NTU), 222–23

National Telephone Cooperative Association (NTCA), 232

National Wildlife Federation (NWF), 193

Nebraska, 154

Nevada, 155

New Hampshire, 155

New Jersey, 155–56

New Mexico, 156–57

New Republic.com, 126

New York, 157
New York Times, 126
News and Newspapers Online, 129
news editor/assignment desk,
    contacting, 118–19
    knowing if event is newsworthy, 120
    reasons for, 119
News Max, 128
news media, 110–11
    broadcast and print media,
        difference between, 113–14
    Internet and, 111–12
    web sites, 80
    what to search for, 114
Newspaper Association of America
    (NAA), 233
Newsweek.com, 125
Nickels, Ilona, 243–44
    See also Capitol Questions
Nizer, Louis, 102
nonprofit associations, 170, 211–12
North Carolina, 158
North Dakota, 158–59
NRA (National Rifle Association),
    197–98
nutrition, 212

Occupational Safety and Health
    Administration (OSHA), 70
Office of Management and Budget
    (OMB), 73, 66–67
    OMB Watch, 212
Ohio, 159
Oklahoma, 159–60
O'Neill, Tip, 111
online
    chatting, 246, 247
    petitions, 176–78
on-line subscriptions, 68, 69
opinion/editorial, 115
    writing, 117–18
opposition research, conduction,
    174–75
Oregon, 160
Oyez Project at Northwestern
    University, 108

Parents and Friends of Lesbians and
    Gays (PFLAG), 186
Peace Corps, 71
Pennsylvania, 160–61
People for the American Way (PFAW),
    186
Perot, Ross, 47
Planned Parenthood Federation of
    America, 218
plug-ins, 252–53
Policy.com, 98
Political Action Committees (PAC),
    30–31
    contributing to, 32–33
political campaigns
    communicating via E-mail, 31–32
    publically funding, 25
    subsidized advertizing, 24–26
political candidates worksheet, 40
Political Humor on About.com, 45
political parties, 35–36
    web sites, 46–48
Political Resources On-Line, 54
Politics1, 54
Politics.com, 50
polling, 48–49
Pope, John Russell, 1
poverty, 206–7
presidency, 58–61
presidential candidates, 49–50
presidential documents, 60–61
Presidential Records Act, 63
primaries, 27
print media
    broadcast and print media,
        difference between, 113–14
    Internet and, 111–12
    web sites, 80
    what to search for, 114
Printing Industries of America, Inc.
    (PIA), 233
privacy, 62–63
Project Vote Smart, 54–55, 80, 81, 101
    state and local information, 139
PTA (National Parent Teacher
    Association), 190

Public Campaign, 44
Public Citizen, 44, 214
Public Citizen Campaign Finance
    Reform Page, 44–45
Public Citizen Global Trade Watch, 196
public interest groups, 170, 213–14
Puerto Rico, 161

QuickTime, 253

RAND, 223
RealPlayer, 65, 253
Reason Public Policy Institute (RPPI),
    224
Recording Industry Association of
    America, Inc. (RIAA), 233
Reform Party, 47
Religious Freedom Coalition (RFC),
    215
religious interests, 214–15
reproductive rights, 216–19
Republican National Committee
    (RNC), 48
Rhode Island, 161
Rock the Vote, 55
ROLL CALL Online, 124
ROLL CALL Politics Page, 45

Salon.com, 123
searching, 251
Securities and Exchange Commission,
    71
SelectSmart.com, 48
Senate, US, 74–75, 75–77, 81
    expectations concerning, 77–78
seniors, 218–19
Sierra Club, 193
Slate, 123
small business & regulation, 219–20
Small Business Administration, 71
Social Security Administration, 71
Society of American Florists (SAF), 233
Society of Automotive Engineers (SAE),
    233
Society of the Plastics Industry, Inc.
    (SPI), 233–34

soft money, 25
South Carolina, 161–62
South Dakota, 162
spam (E-mail), 90–91
SpeakOut.com, 99
special interest groups,
    types of, 169–70
Staff Stand for Children, 182
state and local government, 130–31
    election dates and locations, finding,
        134
    districts, identifying, 133–34
    governors, 135
    reasons for accessing, 131–33
state legislature
    learning about, 135
state statutes, laws, and codes
    downloading, 138
subscriptions, 68, 69
Supersites, 29–33
Supreme Court *Amicus* Briefs, 106
Supreme Court Collection at Cornell
    University, 108
Supreme Court Decisions, 104–5
Supreme Court of the United States,
    102–7
    path to, 104
    web listing, 107
Supreme Court Oral Arguments, 105–7
surfing, 252

TASH, 188
taxes and budget, 220–23
Telecommunications Industry
    Association (TIA), 234
Tennessee, 162–63
Texas, 163–64
TheHistoryNet, 19
think tanks, 223–24
THOMAS, 81, 82, 85, 94–95
TIME.com, 126–27
TotalNEWS, 129
trade associations, 225–35
Transportation, 235–36
Transportation Action Network (TAN),
    236

Travel Industry Association of America (TIA), 234

United Auto Workers (UAW), 211
United Cerebral Palsy (UCP), 189
United Fresh Fruit and Vegetable Association, 234
United States Student Association (USSA), 205–6
Urban Institute, 224
Urban Land Institute (ULI), 234
URL (universal resource locator), typing, 253–54
U.S. Apple Association (US Apple), 234
U.S. Chamber of Commerce, 220
U.S. Code via GPO Access, 109
U.S. Code via University of California's GPO Gate, 109
U.S. Government Printing Office (GPO), 99
U.S. House of Representatives, 80, 95
U.S. House of Representatives Office of the Law Revision, 109
U.S. Judiciary, 107
U.S. Postal Service, 71, 78
U.S. Senate, 80, 95–96
USA Democracy, 100
USA Engage, 196
USA Today, 127
USA Today Supreme Court Index, 107
User ID, 250
USSC+, 108–9
Utah, 164

venting, constructive, 93
Ventura, Jesse, 35
Vermont, 164–65
veterans, 236
Veterans of Foreign Wars (VFW), 236
Video Software Dealers Association (VSDA), 235
Virginia, 165

volunteering for political campaigns, 33–34
VOTE.com, 100
Votenet, 51
voter registration, 26–27
Voter.com, 56
voting, 20–21
Voting Online, 22–23
voting records, federal
    obtaining and reviewing, 31, 89, 93, 101
voting records, state
    obtaining and reviewing, 136–37
voting report cards, 31, 80
    reviewing, 173, 174
VoxCap, 99
VoxCap Campaign 2000 Subchannel, 55–56

Wall Street Journal Interactive Edition, 126
Washington (state), 165–66
Washington, D.C., 144
WashingtonPost.com, 127
Web, White, & Blue, 56
web browser, 250–51
web page, what to do with, 254–55
weekly radio address, 64–65
West Virginia, 166
White House, The, 72
White House web site, 58
    privacy policy, 62–65
Wisconsin, 166–67
World Wildlife Fund (WWF), 193–94
Wyoming, 167

Yellow Pages Publishers Association (YPPA), 235

Zero Population Growth, Inc. (ZPG), 194
zip codes, finding, 78
Zip to It! Plus 4, 80, 96, 240–42, 249

Log on to the *Cybercitizen* web site for more information and updates

http:www.cyber-citizen.org

At the *Cybercitizen* web site, you will find:

* ★ **On-line candidate worksheets**
* ★ **How to obtain customized copies of this guide for your association or organization**
* ★ **Bulk purchase discounts**
* ★ **Notification of new editions when they are published**
* ★ **"Cybercitizen Award" nomination forms**
* ★ **Web site listing request form and update information**
* ★ **Comments and suggestions**